Marxian Political Economy

Also by Bob Milward

ECONOMIC POLICY (*co-author*)
APPLIED ECONOMICS (*co-editor*)

Marxian Political Economy

Theory, History and Contemporary Relevance

Bob Milward
Senior Lecturer in Economics
University of Central Lancashire

First published in Great Britain 2000 by
MACMILLAN PRESS LTD
Houndmills, Basingstoke, Hampshire RG21 6XS and London
Companies and representatives throughout the world

A catalogue record for this book is available from the British Library.

ISBN 0–333–74960–X

First published in the United States of America 2000 by
ST. MARTIN'S PRESS, INC.,
Scholarly and Reference Division,
175 Fifth Avenue, New York, N.Y. 10010

ISBN 0–312–23417–1

Library of Congress Cataloging-in-Publication Data
Milward, Bob.
Marxian political economy : theory, history, and contemporary relevance / Bob
Milward.
p.   cm.
Includes bibliographical references and index.
ISBN 0–312–23417–1 (cloth)
1. Marxian economics. I. Title.

HB97.5 .M5525   2000
335.4'12—dc21

00–023490

This book is printed on paper suitable for recycling and made from fully managed and sustained
forest sources.

10   9   8   7   6   5   4   3   2
09   08   07   06   05   04   03   02   01

Printed and bound in Great Britain by
Antony Rowe Ltd, Chippenham, Wiltshire

To my wife, Gill

Contents

List of Figures

List of Tables

Key to Symbols

M	money
L	labour power
C	commodity capital
K	capital necessary for the production of a commodity
c	constant capital
v	variable capital
s	surplus value
λ	total labour value
r	rate of profit
ϵ	rate of exploitation
c′	used capital
π	profit
ψ	cost price
w	output
k	organic composition of capital
P	price of production
R	total profit
g	rate of economic activity

Acknowledgements

I am indebted to several colleagues who have commented upon earlier drafts of this book, particularly Brian Atkinson, Paul McKeown and Peter Baker. I have also benefited from discussions with students over a number of years that have helped to clarify several areas of confusion in my own mind. The result is a book that is certainly open to criticism from all sides and one that hopes to stimulate such criticism. Only through criticism and debate can enlightenment ensue. Notwithstanding the assistance that I have been given, all mistakes and errors remain mine alone.

I wish to thank the following for permission to use copyright material: *New Left Review* for Karl Marx, *Capital*, Volume 1, translated by Ben Fowkes, Harmondsworth, Penguin, 1976; Karl Marx, *Capital*, Volume 2, translated by David Fernbach, London, 1978; Karl Marx, *Capital*, Volume 3, translated by David Fernbach, London, 1981. Routledge for tables 10.2 and 10.3 from A. G. Kenwood and A. L. Lougheed, *The Growth of the International Economy*, 1992. Cambridge University Press for table 11.1 from W. R. Garside, *British Unemployment 1919–1939: A Study in Public Policy*, 1990. Pearson Education Limited for table 6.1 from M. C. Howard and J. E. King, *The Political Economy of Marx*, Harlow, Longman, 1985. Lawrence & Wishart for Karl Marx, *Theories of Surplus Value*, Volume III, 1972. Progress Publishing for Karl Marx, *The Eighteenth Brumaire of Louis Bonaparte*, 1977. Oxford University Press for table 10.1 from R. Kozul-Wright and R. Rowthorn, 'Spoilt for choice? Multinational corporations and the geography of international production', *Oxford Review of Economic Policy*, 1998, and for table 13.1 from H. Glennerster and J. Hills (eds), *The State of Welfare: The Economics of Social Spending*, 1998, and for table 11.2 from R. C. O. Matthews et al., *British Economic Growth 1856–1973*, 1982. If any copyright holders have been inadvertently overlooked the necessary arrangements will be undertaken at the earliest opportunity.

Finally, my gratitude to the commissioning editors at Macmillan for their assistance and guidance and to Anne Rafique for her patience and professionalism in the task of editing the manuscript.

BOB MILWARD

1
Introduction

A book that examines the economics, philosophy and social relevance of Marx's writings at the turn of the twenty-first century requires a certain degree of explanation as to why it remains of importance to our understanding of the contemporary world. After all, one may suggest that capitalism has triumphed over communism, the Soviet Bloc has disintegrated and what is left is dependent upon the finance of the western world. China has begun the process of fully embracing the free market and moving away from the state-led socialist vision of the revolution. Elsewhere, Cuba appears to have serious economic problems, Vietnam has a highly outward oriented trade strategy combined with market exchange and the former Yugoslavia has degenerated into civil war, social dislocation and the atrocities more associated with Nazi Germany. What we knew as State Socialism is no more, and with its demise has come a revisionism of the value of Marx as an important theorist and philosopher, giving way to the idea that capitalism, far from being on the brink of collapse, is in fact the only system that can deliver the efficient and effective allocation of resources within a framework of increasing prosperity and 'democracy'. Why, then, is it necessary to look again at the writings of Marx and to suggest that he is as relevant today as he was in the second half of the nineteenth century? The answer lies on several planes of theoretical and pragmatic argument, involving a reappraisal of the perceived wisdom of those who would dismiss Marx as simply an essentially interesting, but ultimately ineffectual, critique of capitalism. This capitalism that has supposedly triumphed, produces unemployment, poverty, inequality, free markets in drugs and sexual services, all in the most advanced of the capitalist nations. On a wider sphere, it accepts the inequality between nations, the situation where the majority of the world's population lives in absolute poverty while the tiny minority waste scarce resources on conspicuous consumption.[1] Capitalism continues to generate ever more frequent and long-lasting recessions as markets crash, bankruptcies increase and whole economies are plunged into crisis. This on an increasing geographical scale as capitalism becomes more global in its aspect, such that events in the Far East have an impact in Latin America, North America and Europe, not only in financial markets, but in terms of employment and income levels. To argue, therefore, that because state socialism has collapsed there exists no alternative to capitalism would be tantamount to consigning the human race to a society of inequality in the cause of incentives, unemployment to ensure continued profitability, poverty to maintain the social hierarchy and systemic instability because it happens to be endemic to the capitalist system.

In addition, what we may term 'bourgeois' economic theory finds itself unable to explain, with any degree of clarity, the continuing crises that characterize contemporary capitalism. The economics profession itself is split into rival schools of thought among whom the more prominent are the New Keynesians, the neo-Ricardians, the neo-Austrians, the supply-siders and the chaos theorists, some of whom also contain those who are devoted to the discovery of the explanation as to why capitalism is synonymous with periodic crises through computation of mathematical formulae, the econometricians. None are able to explain persistence of the crises, and rather attempt to advance their ideas and malign their antagonists through the pages of journals devoted to their particular brand of economic pragmatism (cf. Harman, 1996; Ormerod, 1994). The marginalist school of Marshall, Jevons, Menger and Walras, which still represents the framework of analysis for the neoclassicals, abandoned the objective measure of value as represented by Smith and Ricardo, while maintaining the free-market approach of the 'invisible hand' and comparative advantage. Essentially the state of play in bourgeois economics remains the same as at the marginalist revolution, with Say's Law that 'supply creates its own demand', the general equilibrium analysis of the Walrasian auctioneer and the subjective 'measure' of individual utility to arrive at a price for individual commodities in a free market. The basis of the analysis is that the economic system that they portrayed was the best, the optimum system of the allocation of scarce resources that was possible, such that it could be described as a system of 'economic democracy', where all had votes, in the form of money, with which to choose between competing commodities.[2] The result of this process would be a society in which all resources were allocated in the most efficient manner possible and all individuals maximized their utility. Deviation from this ideal was accepted, particularly by Marshall, but any intervention that was required, especially by the state, must conform to the 'laws' as set out in the neoclassical view. The major problems with the theory concern the lack of reality involved in the necessary assumptions involved in attaining the optimum in the model and the lack of dynamic, that is the inability to model time in the analysis. The result is an 'orthodox' model of a capitalist economy that requires assumptions that do not tally with the facts and a static analysis of a highly dynamic system of production and exchange. In the hands of Keynes, this neoclassical theory was tempered as he challenged Say's Law and the supremacy of the demand and supply curves in setting price, particularly with regard to the setting of wages, but the central theme of the optimality properties of the free market remained essentially intact, although recognizing that in certain areas of policy, particularly unemployment, this optimality could not be achieved by the market alone. However, essentially Keynes's *General Theory* remained within the neoclassical tradition, and the collapse of the postwar Keynesian consensus in economic policy naturally led to a return to prewar prescriptions based on the same neoclassical 'orthodoxy'. This then, has led to a situation where the leading economic theory is unable to produce a prescriptive set of policies which could overcome the social problems that are created by the economic system that it advocates. Some have attempted to pursue the so-called 'third way', which suggests that a return to the 'golden age' of the 1950s, using Keynesian interventionist techniques, allied to the free market, is a possibility, but without any real understanding of the laws of motion of the capitalist system (cf. Giddens, 1998, and Hutton, 1996). Hence, we have those who advocate a continuation of the unfettered capitalist market and those who seek to reform capitalism, retaining the free market but intervening to negate its antisocial outcomes. It becomes apparent that neither approach has succeeded in the past and, indeed, there is little to suggest that either could succeed in the future.

The aim of this book, therefore, is to show why the writings of Marx, and of many who have followed, are still of enormous significance to the student of economics, politics, sociology and philosophy. With an understanding of Marxian Political Economy, one has available a system of thought that can be employed to evaluate all aspects of society, to contextualize historical circumstances and to challenge the orthodoxy of neoclassical economics. Marx represents a tradition of social scientists that recognized the need to encompass more that just a narrow focus upon what we now recognize as separate disciplines within social science, and therefore his work represents a synthesis of economics, sociology, philosophy, politics and history. His work owes a debt to Hegel in the realm of philosophy, to Smith and Ricardo in economics and to Feuerbach, Proudhon and Fourier in political science, and therefore it is understandable that for philosophers Marx is a philosopher first and foremost, for sociologists Marx is a essentially a sociologist and for economists Marx represents what one can truly describe as a political economist. Yet none of those who contributed to Marx's understanding would have agreed with his analysis; he was neither Hegelian, nor a classical economist, yet he can be classified as being within both traditions, and his intellectual contribution is arrived at through a critique of the theory of his time and a rationalization of the development of capitalism. Hence his arguments represent an amalgam of all the social sciences, such that his theory can be claimed legitimately by philosophers, sociologists and economists. The argument here is that Marx represents all of these, but at its core, the philosophy, the sociology and the political science of Marx is dependent upon the economics, that the economic analysis is central to the theory. What this synthesis of disciplines did produce was a totally different paradigm, a distinct way in which we can view the world from all of our divergent conceptions as social scientists. Hence, this book gives the opportunity to students of all of these disciplines and others to gain a greater understanding of the writings of Marx and to be able to use this understanding in the process of logical and coherent argument in terms of the many problems faced by contemporary society.

The book is divided into two separate but intimately related parts. Part I examines the method and theory of Marx within its historical context discussing the difficulties that arise and the debates that have ensued as a result of confusions arising from the ambiguities contained in Marx's writings[3] and also from hostile reactions to the implications for 'orthodox' theory from his original work. Part II contemplates the history and contemporary relevance of the framework set out in Part I, with an emphasis on the way in which Marxian political economy can give a greater insight into the problems that face an advanced capitalist economy at the turn of the twenty-first century.

Chapter 2 investigates the method that Marx employed and shows how this represents a unique, but ultimately logical, manner of proceeding to analyse the inner logic of capitalism. For many the totally different approach of Marx can be somewhat bewildering but, this distinctive approach can be viewed as an alternative to those methodologies that are used in economic analysis based on the natural sciences. The Hegelian origins of the method include the use of dialectics which gives an emphasis to the dynamics of capitalism in the analysis, but his critique of Hegel's political philosophy also led Marx to discover the importance of economics and the motive force of history. From this he is able to construct an analysis that is dynamic, founded in economics and incorporating class conflict, but one which requires a full understanding of the system as a whole before a comprehension of the contradictions that exist can be gained. It is argued here, therefore, that Marx's method is distinctive, challenging to the so-called mainstream approaches and therefore it is much criticized by the more 'orthodox' methodologies. However, comprehension of Marx's method is essential if confusion and erroneous criticisms are to be avoided in the subsequent discussions of Marx's political economy. In particular, the dialectical method and the primacy of the economic structure are the central constructs upon which the framework of analysis is based.

In Chapter 3, we examine the theory of value that for Marx is rooted firmly in the surplus tradition of the classical political economy of the eighteenth and nineteenth centuries. However, value relationships are specific to capitalist relations of production, and hence value constitutes a social relationship because only in capitalism do products take the form of commodities produced almost exclusively for exchange. Much debate has ensued, firstly as to the validity of the labour theory of value, and secondly as to whether the labour theory of value is necessary to arrive at the conclusions as to the origins of capitalist profit. However, it is argued that it is an essential element in the analysis of the capitalist economy, not because the thesis will fall without it, but rather that the use of the labour theory of value gives an insight into the production of a surplus and the distribution of that surplus in a capitalist economy. Hence, the depth of analysis would be less substantial in the absence of the labour theory of value. This leads to the discussion, in Chapter 4, of the manner in which Marx's critique of the classical economists precedes the formulation of his economics as an outcome of the need to address what he saw as the fundamental errors in the classical law of value. This includes the distinction between labour and labour power, the theory of capital, the theory of wages, the theory of competition and the so-called 'transformation problem'. He is then able to highlight the logical inconsistencies of the classical economists and to correct the fundamental errors, constructing a comprehensive theory that is specific to capitalism.

Chapter 5 is devoted to the discussion of probably the most controversial and much debated aspect of Marx's work, the transformation problem. It is argued here that the debates can be classified into two separate groups: those who suggest that the transformation of values into prices constitutes a fundamental flaw in Marx's analysis, and those who argue that Marx has been misunderstood and misinterpreted on this issue. Therefore the chapter attempts to follow Marx's procedure quite closely by examining what he actually wrote in Chapter IX of *Capital*, Volume III, before discussing the critiques and supposed 'solutions' that have been produced to show why a 'complicating detour' has been undertaken by those who propose that it represents a fundamental flaw in the Marxian schema. Chapter 6 then returns to the central features of the Marxian discussion of the capitalist system, by examining the dynamic nature of the capitalist relations of production, beginning with the concept of the stages of development and the role of primitive accumulation, in terms of the historical experience of enclosures and the much more recent debate of the role of proto-industrialization in the development of capitalism and its relevance to Marxian political economy. International trade is then considered as a factor in primitive accumulation by examining the role of multi-angular trade, with its pivotal component being the slave trade. Having explained by what means the capitalists come to hold the means of production, the chapter then considers Marx's models of simple and extended reproduction, that is a model of a stationary state capitalist economy and a model of a growing capitalist economy. It is emphasized that Marx is not in this section attempting to investigate the growth process but wishes to illustrate the manner in which the circulation process allows the realization of profit which has been created in production, and also that the dynamic nature of the capitalist mode of production is a product of history and the changing relations of production. This dynamic nature is further discussed in Chapter 7 in terms of the capitalist imperative to accumulate, and the necessity of the competitive process to lead to innovation and the introduction of labour-saving techniques into production. The role of the capitalist is shown to be the sociological imperative to accumulate, which itself is an inherent factor in the capitalist mode of production, in opposition to those theories of capitalist accumulation which concentrate on the probity of the capitalist who abstains from conspicuous consumption.

This is followed by an explanation as to how the level of accumulation is determined and the interrelationship that exists between accumulation and innovation, and how this leads to the phase of monopoly capitalism and the key factor of unemployment. Chapter 8 is concerned with the tendency for the rate of profit to fall over time and the emergence of a realization crisis that is the product of the laws of motion of a capitalist economy. It shows how it is the competitive nature of the capitalist mode of production that leads to the tendency for the rate of profit to fall, even though this is against the individual will of the capitalist, and, indeed, the capitalist imperative of attempting to maximize the rate of profit actually leads to the opposite occurring. The mechanism of the existence of the tendency is examined in terms of the organic composition of capital by involving the concepts of the technical composition of capital and the value composition of capital, such that increasing productivity can occur, shown in a rising technical composition of capital, while at the same time, the value composition of capital will be falling. This is seen by some as a problem of the analysis, but Marx is able to show how, given the definition of the organic composition of capital, the value ratio between constant capital and variable capital can arise from either changes in the value of inputs or technological change in production. The other underlying cause of crisis in the capitalist mode of production is the emergence of the realization problem, which although not a notion exclusive to the Marxian tradition, is treated in a unique manner as being specific to the capitalist system. This forms the basis of the explanation of cyclical fluctuations in capitalism, which appear as exogenous shocks to the system and endogenous factors that are inherent in the capitalist mode of production, with the greater emphasis being placed on the latter. In particular, the deficiency in purchasing power which reduces the ability of the capitalists to realize the surplus value created in production, and the difficulties that arise in the production of surplus value over the course of capitalist development.

The first section ends with an examination of two important economists of this century, who both approached the subject from a Marxian perspective but came to different conclusions and, therefore, have quite different implications for Marxian political economy: Michal Kalecki and Piero Sraffa. Kalecki was concerned with the basic functioning of capitalism and the contradictions contained within the system that produced excess capacity, business cycles, the tendency towards stagnation and unemployment. His approach centres on the relations of production and the implications for a policy of attaining, and then maintaining, full employment in a capitalist economy and the manner in which the capitalists will react to a government strategy based upon such a policy. He distinguishes between two phases of the business cycle, arguing that a recessionary phase can be overcome but that a structural crisis cannot within the capitalist mode of production. Investment, for Kalecki, is the key factor because, although investment spending represents an addition to effective demand, it is also a source of the crisis as it represents an addition to capital stock, leading to excess capacity. This dynamic process leads to cyclical fluctuations and he is able to show that average employment over the course of the cycle will be below the peak of full employment, suggesting that the reserve army of labour and excess capital are typical features of a capitalist economy. Piero Sraffa, on the other hand, endeavours to show how the transformation problem is simply one of a 'complicating detour' by deriving prices directly from knowledge of the conditions of production and the distribution of income. Thus, Marx's journey from labour values to prices and surplus values to profits is shown to be redundant and leads to an undermining of the Fundamental Marxian Theorem that positive profits imply, and are implied by, positive surplus value. This poses problems for the Marxian construct, but we see that there are problems in terms of the Sraffian analysis being set in an equilibrium framework which dilutes the criticisms of Marx.

Part II begins with an examination of the stage of capitalist development referred to as monopoly capitalism, the process of concentration and centralization of capital. The theories of monopoly capitalism are explained before we investigate the history of the move towards increasing concentration and centralization in the form of mergers and takeovers. The chapter then enters the debate on globalization, illustrating that while this is not a new phenomenon, we have entered a new phase in the development of monopoly capitalism. In this area, two views have emerged, first that the nation state has come to be marginalized due to the efficient allocation of resources by the multinational companies on a global scale, and second that in the search for market leadership, capitalist firms extend their competition to the international arena, requiring national governments to adapt their role in the interests of capital to forge international collaborations. Chapter 11 looks at the key factor of unemployment, or the reserve army of labour, in its historical and contemporary perspectives, given the Marxian approach, and shows how such an explanation appears to concur with the facts in a much more plausible manner than other partial models, such as the Non-Accelerating Inflation Rate of

Unemployment (NAIRU) and the hysteresis model of unemployment. Chapter 11 is concerned with public sector aspects of the development of capitalism, explaining the increase in the size and scope of the role of the state over time, and shows how the state is influenced by the requirements of the capitalist class and therefore attempts to provide the necessary environment within which capitalism can flourish. Although Marx had little to say about the role of the state, the Marxian approach is explained, as is the paradox that arises as a result of the conflict between what is in the interests of the capitalist class as a whole and the perceptions of the individual capitalists. Various views are outlined in terms of the role of the public sector whereby the neoclassicals argue for as little intervention as possible and the social democrats suggest that it is the state's role to overcome the unregulated nature of capitalism and to create a consensus of views in society. Neither are shown to be applicable, given the relations of production that pertain in the capitalist mode of production. The chapter ends with a discussion of the public sector in the era of globalization and argues that those who espouse a 'third way' have an over-optimistic view of the regulatory powers of individual states. The crisis of the welfare state, as elucidated in Chapter 13 suggests that the fact that it exists means that, as capitalism approaches successive crises, it must find a solution to the paradox that is entailed in this institution: that is, as capitalism requires unemployment for it to continue to function, the welfare state becomes ever more inappropriate to the economic environment of capitalist production. Two options are available to overcome this problem: first to raise more revenue through taxation from those in employment to maintain a minimum income for those unable to work, or second to dismantle the welfare state and allow its functions to be provided by the private sector. In the first case, this would call forth a realization crisis, and possibly a motivational crisis, and in the latter case, it would demand a drastic reduction in working-class expectations and a moral re-education as to why individual responsibility for welfare provision is superior, morally, to collective provision. It is shown that history has produced this situation because the welfare state arose out of the need to engage in a settlement with labour to win the Second World War and then to provide postwar reconstruction. However, the legacy remained, in the form of the welfare state, despite the change in the economic environment post 1973.

Finally, there is a conclusion which brings together the strands of the book and suggests that although much has been written and debated concerning Marx's critique of capitalism, it still represents the most fruitful and rational framework within which to analyse contemporary capitalism and with which to view the history of capitalist development. There is much more research to be done, particularly in the areas of monopoly capitalism and the rise of the global market as well as the position of the underdeveloped economies in the face of global exploitation. However, it is argued that at the start of the twenty-first century the framework of Marxian political economy remains as relevant as ever to students of contemporary society, politics and the economy. Indeed, it represents a much more logical and rational approach than the neoliberals who would pursue the neoclassical tradition or the social democrats who espouse the virtues of the so-called 'third way'.

It is in many ways a highly personal examination of the state of the world, in terms of its economic structure, its political organization and its philosophical perspectives, and the implications that this has for us all, but it is not a prescription for an alternative society; rather it follows Marx in being a critique of the present system and a framework in which to suggest that certain outcomes are inevitable given the logic of the analysis, but it cannot therefore be predictive, in the sense that capitalism will collapse on a certain day at a certain time, and out of its ashes will rise a specific alternative. The book is not intended to persuade the reader of the 'correctness' of Marxian political economy; rather it should stimulate debate and challenge much of the mainstream economic theory that is taught in our educational establishments and is still the backbone of the texts most often found on undergraduate reading lists.

Part I
Theory and History

2
Marx's Method

Introduction

Marx's method represents a distinctive approach to the study of political economy and is often considered to be an alternative to methodologies employed in economic analysis that are based on the natural sciences. It is important to note that Marx arrived at economics via philosophy and his analysis has its roots in social theory. As a result, Marxian political economy can be considered to be much more comprehensive in its analysis than other schools of economic thought. However, the distinctive nature of the approach leaves it open to criticism from more 'orthodox' methodologies. In particular, Popper (1972) argues that Marx employs 'historicism' in his view that there is a law of historical development, and this leads Marx to adopt 'economic determinism', which for Popper is not acceptable because human behaviour is individual in character and can therefore change the course of history. However, this charge made by Popper does not stand close scrutiny, as Marx would undoubtedly agree that this could be the case but that, while human beings do make their own history, it is not under conditions of their own choosing. Rather, they are constrained by the institutional and social structures that are associated with the phase of development in which they exist.

Because Marx is concerned with the dynamic process of history, and the fact that he was writing in the nineteenth century, perhaps the best manner in which to view his work is as a framework for analysis that can be transferred to suit the time and the place and therefore must be adapted to the prevailing circumstances. One may suggest that this is precisely the process that was undertaken by Lenin, using the framework for a country that had not reached capitalist maturity, and for

Gramsci in Italy and Lukacs in Hungary. We could also include Mao in China and Castro in Cuba. What all of these have in common is not an inflexible ideology, but indeed exactly the reverse: the commonality lies in the use of a Marxian framework of analysis as the starting point for the understanding of the system within which they found themselves. Indeed, it would be illogical to employ a methodology that has at its heart the importance of history, and then to claim that the theory is predictive of events that themselves will depend upon the course of history, in anything other than the most general manner.

As with all schools of thought, Marxian political economy is not a unique and totally original schema. Marx's thought evolved through a process of acceptance and also of criticism of a variety of existing ideas. The result is unique to Marx, but has its roots in other, earlier strands of philosophy, social theory and economics.

The Hegelian tradition

Marx's earliest writings were devoted to the criticism of the political philosophy of Hegel, and it was this which led Marx to recognize the importance of economics. Although Marx accepted the Hegelian separation of the categories 'man' and 'citizen' and also the division of 'state' and 'civil society', he saw civil society, the area of economic relations, as deviating from the course of political society, caused by the collapse of economic coercion that was central to the functioning of feudalism. Thus, the emergence of 'free' labour became the crucial event in the emergence and development of capitalism. Therefore, the starting point of Marx's thought could be viewed as this separation of the economic and the political, and of the state from civil society. From his beginnings as a political philosopher, he developed his argument as a critique of Hegel's political philosophy and concentrated his thought increasingly on the understanding of the economic mechanism of civil society, which he came to acknowledge as the driving force in the development of societies.

Writing in the early nineteenth century Hegel was concerned with the difference between 'appearance' and 'essence', where appearances, or phenomena, are not necessarily false but may mislead, and essences relate to basic organic relationships that underlie the phenomena that are under investigation (Pheby, 1988, p. 115). Hegel argued that history is not a random sequence of events but rather it is a process that is governed in a comprehensive manner by objective laws. Such objective laws can only be properly understood by viewing history as a whole. This process is not uni-directional but is a dialectical process. Most of the philosophies of the ancient and medieval world contained dialectical forms of reasoning, but in Hegel, the dialectic is a self-differentiating and self-generating process of reason. In the Hegelian system, the truth (the Absolute idea) is the whole and it unfolds through a dialectical progression of concepts and forms of consciousness, from the simplest to the most complex. The progression of concepts appears as incomplete and contradictory, moving on to more adequate concepts which throw up new contradictions.[1] Human history is a vehicle through which the Absolute achieves self-consciousness, but humanity is not the subject of the process.

Hegel, in proposing the use of dialectics, formulated three laws of dialectics. The first was concerned with the transformation of quantity into quality and vice versa, where new qualities develop out of apparently insignificant qualitative changes. Thus, a process of continuous change will not affect the character of something until a certain point when it becomes transformed. The second law of dialectics refers to the unity of opposites. For Hegel motion stems from contradiction, and the contradictory nature of reality forms a coherent unity. Hence, something which may appear to be of only transitory interest is often a single part of an ongoing process of which it forms an essential element. Thus, the fundamental search in political philosophy is for the change and motion that arises from inherent contradictions. The third law is generally described as the thesis – antithesis – synthesis, and is more formally the negation of the negation: the original theory is replaced with an opposite, contradictory theory which is then itself supplanted by a theory which unites elements of both the thesis and the antithesis – the synthesis.

For Hegel, reality can only be understood through examination of the contradictory and organic processes in the totality. Therefore, each stage of development can be explained through contradictions between opposing forces. These contradictions are reconciled in a synthesis, which itself generates new contradictions. According to Hegel, history is essentially a matter of the development of reason and each time and place has its own set of ideas. Hence, the dialectical development of ideas is the motive force of history. The writings of Hegel are however extremely obscure and are capable of many interpretations, and this led to many disputes between various schools of Hegelians, particularly in German philosophy in the 1830s and 1840s. Marx was associated with the school of 'Young Hegelians' who emphasized the dynamic elements in Hegel rather than the conservative interpretation which saw in the Prussian state the apotheosis of reason and the culmination of history (Brewer, 1984, p. 3).

However, although this dynamic element in Hegel was the view of history held by Marx, he did break with Hegel over the 'idealism of the theory', whereby the 'mind' or 'ideas' are primary and physical matter secondary. Marx specifically criticized the 'mystificatory' side of the Hegelian dialectic in his *Critique of Hegel's Philosophy of the Right* (1843) and in the concluding section of the *Paris Manuscripts* (1844). Here Marx followed Feuerbach by comparing Hegelian philosophy conceptually to Christian theology as he considered that both were forms of alienation of man's species attributes. In particular Hegel had projected human thinking into a fictive subject, the Absolute idea, which in turn generated the empirical world.

There has been much debate as to the extent of the Hegelian influence in Marx's work. From Hegel, he utilized the dialectical method, and certainly his earlier writings are much more explicitly Hegelian in influence.[2] However, this is less discernible in *Capital*, which has led some to suggest that the Hegelian influence of Marx was mainly terminological. Sowell has argued that *Capital* was Hegelian only in the very general sense of Marx's emphasis on the dynamics of capitalism (Sowell, 1976, p. 50). Thus, the Marxian dialectic is different in character to that of Hegel:

> My dialectical method is, in its foundations, not only different from the Hegelian, but exactly opposite to it. For Hegel, the process of thinking, which he even transforms into an independent subject, under the name of 'the idea', is the creator of the real world, and the real world is only the external appearance of the idea. With me the reverse is true: the ideal is nothing but the material world reflected in the mind of man, and translated into forms of thought.
>
> (Marx, 1976, p. 102)

However, Marx's thought began as a reaction to the perceived romantic idealism of Hegel, and the important point to note about Hegelianism is that it was concerned with history and social change, these being central to the philosophical attitude. It was the latter that was retained by Marx, and the former that was overturned.

Historical materialism

Thus from Hegel, Marx learned the dialectical method, and this influence is highly pronounced in his early writings and his ideas were mainly expressed in the years 1844–5, producing a new theoretical framework. In 1844 he wrote a rough draft known as the *Economic and*

Philosophical Manuscripts or the *Paris Manuscripts*, in which he focused on the relation between capital and wage labour, arguing that this relation is structural and not personal. At this time Marx was also influenced by Ludwig Feuerbach who was a critic of Hegel, and Marx incorporated Feuerbach's idea of a human essence or species being to suggest that human production is by nature a creative activity. Thus, the subordination of production to the impersonal laws of capital violates the natural relation between producer and product. In essence, as pre-capitalist production gives way to social production, the worker (the producer) becomes remote from the final product and remote from the surplus produced and hence becomes alienated from the product of labour. In the extended discussion on alienation in the *Paris Manuscripts* (1844), Marx refers to the alienation of man who is alienated from work, the products of work and his fellow men. However, Marx did not include separate chapters devoted to alienation in *Capital*; rather it is a concept that appears throughout Volumes I and III in its various guises. For example, in Volume I, Marx discusses alienation as a part of the characteristic of capitalist production as labour is alienated from the labourer by capitalist appropriation (Marx, 1976, p. 716), as alienation of the intellectual potentialities of the worker by the means of production (ibid., p. 799), and alienation as the situation whereby commodities appear as the purchasers of people (ibid., p. 1003). In Volume III, he argues that as the accumulation of capital develops into the growing concentration of capital, it becomes more and more a social power, alienated in terms of becoming a thing through which the capitalist derives power (Marx, 1981, p. 373), and alienation of the worker from the conditions of production (ibid., p. 731).

In 1845 Marx and Engels produced the *German Ideology* which represents the first definitive statement of their theory of history, 'historical materialism', and from 1845 Marx worked to develop the basic framework that was set out in the *German Ideology*.

> Men can be distinguished from animals by consciousness, by religion or anything else you like. They themselves begin to distinguish themselves from animals as soon as they begin to *produce* their means of subsistence, a step which is conditioned by their physical organisation. By producing their means of subsistence men are indirectly producing their material life. The way in which men produce their means of subsistence depends first of all on the nature of the means of subsistence they actually find in existence and have to reproduce. This mode of production must not be considered simply

as being the reproduction of the physical existence of the individuals. Rather it is a definite form of activity of these individuals, a definite form of expressing their life, a definite *mode of life* on their part. As individuals express their life, so they are. What they are therefore, coincides with their production, both with *what* they produce and with *how* they produce. Hence, what individuals are depends on the material conditions of their production.

(Marx and Engels, 1976, pp. 25–6)

This framework began from the simple idea that human beings must produce their means of subsistence in order to exist and to do so they require to work together in a division of labour. Because any stage of development of production is itself a product of history, the development of production is contingent on the development of forms of cooperation and therefore of the development of social organization. Hence, society develops through a succession of stages marked by different forms of property. In the ancient world communal property was based on the exploitation of slaves, in feudal society, feudal landownership was based on the exploitation of serfs, and in capitalism, capitalist private property is based on the exploitation of propertyless wage-workers. Each of these developments of society represents a successively higher state of development of production than its predecessors, but each also generates the conditions requisite for the next.

Although the *German Ideology* contained the core of what was to be the materialist concept of history, the best known summary is in the Preface to the *Critique of Political Economy* (1844):

My inquiry led me to the conclusion that neither legal relations nor political forms could be comprehended whether by themselves or on the basis of a so-called general development of the human mind, but that on the contrary they originate in the material conditions of life, the totality of which Hegel … embraces within the term 'civil society'; that the anatomy of this civil society, however, has to be sought in political economy. … The general conclusion at which I arrived and which, once reached, became the guiding principle of my studies can be summarised as follows. In the social production of their existence, men inevitably enter into definite relations, which are independent of their will, namely relations of production appropriate to a given stage in the development of their material forces of production. The totality of these relations of production constitutes the economic structure of society, the real foundation, on which arises a legal and political superstructure and to which corresponds definite forms of social consciousness. The mode of production of material life conditions the general process of social, political and intellectual life. It is not the consciousness of men that determines their existence, but their social existence that determines their consciousness. At a certain stage of development, the material productive forces of society come into conflict with the existing relations of production or...with the property relations within the framework of which they have operated hitherto...Then begins an era of social revolution. The changes in the economic foundation lead sooner or later to the transformation of the whole immense superstructure...No social order is ever destroyed before all the productive forces for which it is sufficient have been developed, and new superior relations of production never replace older ones before the material conditions of their existence have matured within the framework of the old society.

(Marx, 1977, pp. 20–1)

Thus, the materialist conception of history has at its core the belief that the economic structure explains all other aspects of society and that social and political revolutions are caused by the contradictions that appear between the forces and relations of production. The development of the forces of production occurs in such a manner that the economic relations become no longer appropriate. However, those who take part in these changes do not perceive it in this way and instead they see their conflicts in other terms, which Marx calls 'ideologies'. Although not articulated in the *Preface to the Critique of Political Economy*, for Marx any mode of production involves a division of labour involving class divisions. The development of a class system takes place alongside the development of the productive forces which allow for the production of a surplus product (defined as output in excess of that required to ensure the reproduction of that level of output). The principle class relations are always those in which one or more classes appropriate the surplus produced by the labour of other classes and the central class relations are those of exploitation. The major theoretical dilemma is to specify how exploitation underlies the operation of competitive capitalism, even where there exists a full set of civil liberties. Thus, the relations of production can be interpreted as class relations and these take the form, in legal terms, of property relations. Class relations form the real foundation on which a political superstructure arises and to which correspond definite forms of social consciousness. Hence, the crucial institution is the ownership of property in the means of production because this then allows the exploiting class to gain control of the state. Therefore, the ruling ideas emanate from the ruling-class and hence, the ruling ideas are the expression of the dominant material relations. This property of ideas is described by Marx as 'ideological'. The theory of class also encompasses the principle of historical change which governs the transformation of one mode of production into another. The development of the forces of production leads to them becoming incompatible with the class relations within which they operate. Progress is slowed by the dominant class and is replaced in a process of conflict by another system of class relations allowing further development of social production. The contradictions and subsequent class conflicts are manifested consciously as ideological struggles. Humans therefore make their own history but through false consciousness, through ideologies. In other words, those involved in social production unknowingly create and re-create social structures through their own activity. However, the social structures simultaneously conflict with the potentialities which this activity creates and in resolving these contradictions they do so via the mediation of illusions about their true historical significance. In the *German Ideology* Marx argues that the conflicting classes fail to understand the struggles as they are in reality, but rather see them as a struggle between tenets or principles and, as such, class interests are presented in an ideological framework in such a manner that they appear as though they are the only valid and rational ones (Marx and Engels, 1970, p. 66).

The primacy of the economic structure

For Marx, all aspects of a society are accounted for by the primacy of the economic structure, including the prevailing forms of social consciousness, and it is this quality of the theory of history which justifies its description as materialist. The institutions of society are formed out of the prevailing relations of production and are therefore designed to permit the functioning of the relations of production and the class relations contained within them. Political and legal forms will therefore be different for differing economic structures. In capitalism, it is necessary for wage-labour to be 'free' within the class relations, therefore representative democracy gives the illusion of freedom of action and equality in representation through the parliamentary body. However, this serves only the interests of the dominant class and perpetuates the class relations formed out of the relations of production.

For example, in feudalism such freedom of action and representation is not necessary as the class relations are those of bonded labour, controlled directly by the ruling class.

In the legal domain, the law is said to be accessible by all in capitalism, but in reality is controlled by the ruling class. The guiding principle of the law is to protect property rights and to enforce contracts that are established by the relations of production. Thus the hegemony of the state is maintained through legal relations which change according to the relations of production. Hence, change in society can only be accorded through a change in the relations of production and thus through a change in the economic structure. This change occurs through the dialectical process but is delayed, to a greater or lesser extent, by ideologies which create a veil over the underlying causes of conflicts. Therefore, the state is forever changing to meet the requirements of the relations of production, to conceal the real causes of conflict and to perpetuate the existing economic structure. This is true for Marx also in the legal domain which is apparently quasi-independent, but is also determined by the economic structure within which it operates. Figure 2.1 illustrates this conceptually with the input to the structure being history, to explain how the structure was arrived at, and the outputs are all other aspects of society. Therefore, to understand the individual aspects of a society, one must first comprehend the totality of the structure. That is, superstructures are formed only by the economic structure upon which they are based.

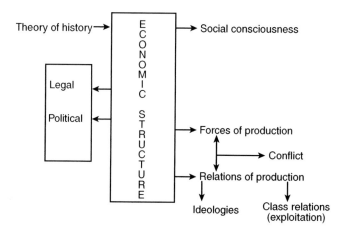

Figure 2.1   Primacy of the economic structure

In economics, Marx studied classical political economy which belongs, principally, to the surplus tradition in that the basic sphere of enquiry was that of the origins, magnitude and growth of the economic surplus. In this, Marx saw classical political economy as the earliest attempt to ground the study of economics in the particular social relations of capitalism, which for Marx gave it relevance and validity methodologically (Howard and King, 1985, p. 64). Blaug has argued that the method of reasoning in *Capital* is the same as that in Ricardo's *Principles of Political Economy* (Blaug, 1997, p. 254). Much of Marx's economic method consists of a critique of Adam Smith and David Ricardo, both in terms of their formulation of societal and economic relations and in their failure, particularly of Ricardo, to apply their own methodological principles in a consistent manner.

> It is the rate of profit that is the driving force in capitalist production, and nothing is produced save what can be produced at a profit. Hence, the concern of the English economists over the decline in the profit rate. If Ricardo is disquieted even by the very possibility of this, that precisely shows his deep understanding of the conditions of capitalist production. What other people reproach him for, i.e., that he is unconcerned with 'human beings' and concentrates exclusively on the development of productive forces when considering capitalist production ... is precisely his significant contribution.
>
> (Marx, 1981, p. 368)

The question that remains is, were Smith and Ricardo forerunners of Marx, or does Marx represent a totally different paradigm? The answer is the subject of a long and protracted debate between historians of economic thought, but is not really of any great significance to the present discussion. It is sufficient here to understand that Marx based his study of economics firmly in the classical tradition, but that his method is not the same as that employed by Smith or Ricardo. What can be suggested, however, is that there are many similarities and many differences between classical political economy and Marx which gives Marxian political economy its richness and its relevance.

Marx's realism

Marx's economic analysis is dominated by the major idea that the sphere of production is fundamental to the economy as a whole and he arrives at this proposition due to his understanding of the nature of science and of scientific enquiry. Marx describes science as the process of producing knowledge by investigating the phenomena that lie behind the superficial appearance of things. In *Grundrisse* this process is described as beginning from the complexity of the superficial world and then constructing the simplest, but highly abstract concepts. Increasing complexity is introduced and developed through the contradictions and interrelations between the concepts until the complexity of the appearances is reproduced. This process of abstraction results in concepts and a logical order of the concepts that is in consonance with material reality and, as such, it does not represent a purely idealist process in which it exists independent of reality. Fine and Harris (1979) discuss this in terms of two hierarchical structures. The first of these is the hierarchy of concepts which are produced in thought in the process of moving from the simple to the complex, or to low from high levels of abstraction. The second structure is the hierarchy of reality which concerns real phenomena and the real relationships of determination between them. Although there is no sense in which the two hierarchies are directly linked in a simple manner, there is a definite and necessary relation between them.

> The existence of a necessary relation between the two hierarchies is given from the fact that the hierarchy of levels of abstraction is not arbitrary. As well as being a theory of reality it is simultaneously a product of that theory and therefore has a definite relation to the reality which is being analysed. This does not provide a guarantee of the 'truth' of the theory, but at the same time it precludes the relativist idea that any hierarchy of concepts is as good as any other.
>
> (Fine and Harris, 1979, p. 11)

Hence, Marx emphasized the importance of a perspective which is not itself empirical, but which is essential for a correct understanding of the empirical. It is also important to note that Marx's position does not allow the total subordination of facts to theory and therefore, his position can justly be regarded as dialectical. At the heart of the schema is the assumption that wholes, or totalities, are of greater importance than the parts of which they consist. As such, each whole is conceived as an array of relations which bestows on the parts a set of properties which cannot be deduced from them separately. It follows therefore, that to fully comprehend any system we do not look to the parts of that system but to the systematic whole and therefore, we require an understanding of the totality in order to gain a complete comprehension of the individual part of the system. The whole has the capacity for internal change and, because human reality is a process rather than a given state, the motive force for change is the contradiction that exists between the parts of the whole that cannot coexist in harmony and it is the tensions that exist between the parts that transform the whole. It follows therefore that human history is always in a state of 'becoming' in which the negativity within the whole is the progressive force.[3]

Marx is not concerned with the explanation of factual matters directly in terms of other facts, but rather he does this using entities which are not directly observable. Hence, there is an intermediate stage between Marx's vision and the empirical facts to be explained. This consists of a theoretical structure which involves elements that are precisely defined, but unobservable. First, it is the accuracy of definition which divides this structure from the vision, and second, it is the non-observability which separates it from that which is to be explained. Such a methodology is not unique to Marx, it is a general approach that is referred to as realism. The main rival to realism is positivism which seeks to explain empirical phenomena through the formation of theories and theories for positivists are defined as being composed of laws which pertain to the associations between observable variables. This rests upon the belief that scientific knowledge can only apply to that which can be observed and therefore, for positivists, theory must be limited to statements regarding empirical events. However, in complete contrast to this approach, Marx formulates the mechanisms of necessity in terms of unobservable categories. The mechanism constitutes the 'essences' or the 'hidden sub-stratum' that lies behind empirical regularities. Crucially, Marx has a specific formulation of realism which is expressed through the fact that his theory is a social theory, where the empirical phenomena are explained in terms of social relations, which themselves have their own laws which govern the character of individuals and the natural entities which they encompass. However, these social relations cannot themselves be reduced to observable entities and it is this aspect of Marx's methodology that has led to it being described as essentially deterministic.

Marx's determinism

The term determinism does not necessarily imply that ideas, choices and decisions do not exist. The essential point is that subjectivities play no independent role but rather they function as transmission belts for the real determinants of human action. It follows that if Marx were to be assumed to take a purely determinist position, he would then have to treat individuals solely as the bearers of social forces. However, at first glance, Marx may appear to contradict himself by regarding humanity as achieving conscious control over its environment (and eventually, in communism, over itself). Thus, conscious human decision-making is elevated to a role which is the exact opposite of that entailed by determinism. Yet elsewhere, Marx appears to deny that self-determination is possible in pre-communist societies and hence, there is a dualism which Marx attributes to history. In fact there is no contradiction. Marx attaches key significance to the role of the proletarian revolution, and the proletarian revolution results from the same forces that caused all other previous social transformations and, as such, it is a determined action. However, there is a unique historical role attached to the proletarian revolution whereby it ends pre-history. It is seen as the first act of history in which human consciousness is the decisive force. Thus, the proletarian revolution has a dual character. It is simultaneously a class revolution and a revolution against the prevailing human condition. This consciousness is an outcome of the social conditions in which the proletariat is placed and its content is a genuine consciousness of an inhuman condition and the causes of that dehumanization. Therefore, it is not subject to false consciousness or the illusory aspects of ideology, as were previous revolutionary classes.

For Marx therefore capitalism is much more than a mode of production which uses 'capital' in the sense of produced means of production. Instead, capitalism is defined in more precise terms which incorporate private ownership in the productive forces. Thus, we can see in Marx's analysis four attributes which together may define capitalism: (a) a system of commodity production; (b) a system of wage-labour; (c) a system of acquisitiveness; and (d) a system of rational organization. But, capitalism is a system in which market exchange coordinates the economic activities that are undertaken by 'free-agents' and as such it is necessary that human labour power becomes a commodity. As such, a system of wage-labour exists in which workers can freely sell the use of their time and therefore, the process that clears the way for capitalism is the process which takes away the labourers' means of production. This process transforms the social means of subsistence and of production into capital, as well as the immediate producers into wage-labourers. Marx describes how the process takes place through the forcible expropriation of the agricultural population through enclosures and state legislation that forces the dispossessed into the labour market, creating conditions which increase mercantile profits through the slave trade, colonization and piracy. This leads to the accumulation of wealth which could be employed in the purchase of the means of production and of labour power. This process Marx calls 'primitive accumulation'. The capitalist mode of production is dynamic, generating rapid economic growth by means of increasing technological knowledge and the extension of the remit of market relations. However, it also contains its own contradictions which cannot be overcome by internal reform. This contradiction takes the form of a growing incompatibility between production which is increasingly social and appropriation which remains private. That is, production becomes ever more interdependent due to the extension of specialization and market exchange, while at the same time, the prevailing property relations ensure that the benefits and motivations remain private. The contradiction is manifested in economic terms in declining rates of profit and rising unemployment rates. These are frequently punctuated and intensified by crises of effective demand failure. Indeed, on this latter point, one could argue that Keynes was only re-emphasizing these issues raised by Marx, but his was only a partial analysis of the Marxian schema.

Summary

Marx's political economy is a distinctive and much more comprehensive framework for analysis in that it can be considered to be applicable to all aspects of social theory. From Hegel we get the important concept of the dialectical method as the basis for Marx's analysis from which developed the theory of history. However, it is not an Hegelian philosophical method, but a method that is derived from the critique of Hegel. Hence, the analysis is dynamic, but founded in class conflict and the primacy of the economic structure, which itself is a product of history. Thus, all aspects of society can be understood only if the development of the productive forces in society are understood. In Marxian political economy the dialectical method may confuse or confound students of economics grounded in the micro and macro courses of undergraduate study, where comprehension of the microeconomic foundations is required before moving on to study the macroeconomic. For Marx, this would be illogical and represent a false premise: full comprehension of any system requires that the systematic whole is the focus of attention, which then allows one to understand the contradictions that exist which give the whole its capacity for change, its dynamic. In this respect, those who employ individualism, falsification and even econometric techniques to study the economy cannot have the basis of their method grounded in reality and hence their conclusions must be without foundation, and be devoid of relevance to economic or social analysis.

3
The Theory of Value

Introduction

For at least the past 120 years the discussion of the source of value has been dominated by the concept of marginal utility, originated by Jeavons in *The Theory of Political Economy* (1871), Menger in *Principles of Economics* (1871) and Walras in *Elements of Pure Economics* (1874). However, prior to the 1870s the debate on the source of value had been dominated by the various interpretations of the labour theory of value. Hence, the question of why goods and services have value and the determination of the magnitude of value, has been a constant theme in economics for over two hundred years. In contrast, the neoclassical school has an emphasis on the concept of subjective marginal utility. Subjective utility is the degree of satisfaction that is obtained by an individual, or household, from the consumption of a good or service. It is said to be quantifiable in the cardinal sense, and implies that individuals acquire goods and services to enhance their own utility. Thus, each individual acts as if they had a set of ordered preferences for different combinations of goods and services, and each individual is the best judge of his or her own utility.[1] It would then be possible to impute a number to the combinations of goods and services that are consumed, and that such a number would represent the utility that was obtained from the bundle of goods and services. It has been suggested that this is a rather 'dubious exercise' outside the assumption laden world of the neoclassical textbook (Hodgson, 1982, p. 42). However, in classical political economy, 'utility' was considered as being fundamental for a thing to have value, but not to regulate its exchange value, which was derived instead from scarcity and the cost of production. For example, for Ricardo:

> The value of a commodity, or the quantity of any other commodity for which it will exchange, depends on the relative quantity of labour which is necessary for its production...Utility...is not the measure of exchangeable value, although it is absolutely essential to it. If a commodity were in no way useful – in other words, if it could in no way contribute to our gratification – it would be destitute of exchange value, however scarce it might be, or whatever quantity of labour might be necessary to procure it.
>
> (Sraffa, 1981, p. 11)

What is generally termed 'the surplus approach', at the core of classical political economy, suggests that the formulation of theories concerning value and distribution should be related to the ability of an economy to produce a surplus, that is, to produce an amount greater than that required for the necessities of production in each production period. The problem, therefore, was to discover how the surplus is created and then distributed in a capitalist economy. In general, the classical political economists, and in particular Marx, consider this to be derived from the ability of the capitalist class to compel the labourer to work longer hours than was necessary for the labourer to produce the necessities of life. Hence, to measure this surplus, a theory of value was required which would allow comparison of the size of the surplus over time and its composition and distribution (Sardoni, 1992, p. 211).

For Marx, value theory was essential to the explanation of capitalist society and therefore, the concept of value was central to his explanation of the prevailing economic and social conditions. In contrast to neoclassical economic theory which covers all possible societies through time and space, Marxian theory has an emphasis on the historical relativity of economic categories. Therefore, value relationships for Marx are specific to a capitalist society and value is a social relationship. For Marx there is an important distinction between the term 'product' and that of 'commodity', in that, products are produced in all economies, but only in capitalism do products take the form of commodities which are produced almost exclusively for exchange.

Value in use and value in exchange

The distinction that Marx adopted in the framework of his theory of value was the classical one between exchange-value and use-value, viewed as two aspects of a commodity. The use-value of a commodity corresponds to the natural properties of the commodity in terms of its capacity to satisfy human wants. Marx describes this particular aspect of a commodity in *Capital*.

> The commodity is, first of all, an external object, a thing which through its qualities satisfies human needs of whatever kind. The nature of these needs, whether they arise, for example, from the stomach, or the imagination, makes no difference. Nor does it matter here how the thing satisfies man's need, whether directly as a means of subsistence, i.e. an object of consumption, or indirectly as a means of production.
>
> (Marx, 1976, p. 125)

Marx makes it clear that the useful properties of things are a product of history and that all useful things are composed of many properties and hence, a thing may be useful in a variety of ways. However, use-value for Marx is not a purely subjective notion and does not therefore reside solely in the mind of the consumer.

> The usefulness of a thing makes it a use-value. But this usefulness does not dangle in mid-air. It is conditioned by the physical properties of the commodity, and has no existence apart from the latter. It is therefore the physical body of the commodity itself, for instance iron, corn, a diamond, which is the use-value or useful thing. This property of a commodity is independent of the amount of labour required to appropriate its useful qualities.
>
> (Marx, 1976, p. 126)

Commodity producers, in exchanging their products, create a quantitative relation between commodities and Marx denotes this relationship between commodities their exchange value. In commodity production the social character of production is expressed through the exchange of commodities and, therefore, such exchanges are concurrently exchanges of the activities of the producers. Hence, the relation between commodities is also a relation between the commodity producers and Marx's concept of value is therefore a representation of the social relation of commodity production. Thus, the public aspect of the commodity is its exchange value. Marx expresses this as follows: 'Exchange value appears first of all as the quantitative relation, the proportion, in which use-values of one kind exchange for use-values of another kind. This relation changes constantly with time and place' (Marx, 1976, p. 126). Therefore, exchange value appears as a set of ratios in which use-values are exchanged for one another in commodity markets.

'Orthodox' economics suggests that a commodity satisfies human wants and that the utility of an object makes it a use-value, independent of the amount of labour required to create its useful properties. As we have seen, at first sight exchange value presents itself as a quantitative relation in which use-values are exchanged and which constantly changes with time and place. However, for Marx, the relation is not as straightforward as this. To illustrate this we can assume that there are two commodities, corn and steel. The proportions in which these commodities are exchangeable can always be represented by an equation, in which a given quantity of corn is equated to some quantity of steel. For example:

$$1 \text{ quarter of corn} = x \text{ tons of steel}$$

Such an equation suggests that in 1 quarter of corn and X tons of steel there exists, in equal quantities, something common to both. The two things must therefore be equal to a third article, which itself is neither corn nor steel. Thus, each of them must be reducible to this third. Leaving aside the use-value, there is only one common property, that is the property of both having been the products of labour. Thus, an article has value only because human labour, in the abstract, is embodied in it. Therefore, it follows that a use-value, or useful article, has value only because human labour in the abstract has been embodied, or materialized, in it. This magnitude can be measured by its duration and labour time finds its standard in weeks, days and hours. We must not confuse price and value. An object may have a price without having value. For example, the price of uncultivated land is without value because no human labour has been incorporated in it.

Hence, the value of a commodity is determined by the socially necessary labour-time contained in it. Socially necessary labour-time is the time required for production, under normal conditions, with an average degree of skill and intensity, using modern machinery. Therefore, the greater the productivity of labour, the less is the labour-time, and the less the value of the commodity and the value of the commodity as such is not fixed, it will change in time and circumstance. Different commodities require different degrees of skill, but skilled labour is simple labour intensified. Hence, commodities in which equal quantities of labour are embodied have the same value. It can now be shown that the distinction between value in use and value in exchange can take the form of a differentiation between two types of labour, that is useful labour and labour in the abstract: useful labour produces use-values which correspond to the different types of use-values produced. Hence, corresponding to different use-values there are different, but specific types of useful labour involved in their production. A complex division of labour exists in a commodity producing society, where different individuals are engaged in different types of work, who then exchange their products. But, the exchange of commodities is not a necessary condition as the division of labour could be present without commodity exchange through a market and, useful labour could continue without the division of labour.[2] However, Marx makes an important distinction by employing the term 'social division of labour' to mean the division between independent producers who sell their products to one another. However, in a commodity producing society, the common feature of different types of useful labour is that they all produce exchange value. Labour itself produces value, which Marx calls abstract labour.[3]

The value of labour power

In capitalism, the labourer has only one commodity to sell, that is labour power. Thus, values are measured in socially necessary units of labour-time and not in terms of labour-time alone, such that the value of an item depends upon the hours that are socially necessary and not on the hours of work that went into the item. Hence, value is a social phenomenon, and not an individual phenomenon as with 'orthodox' economic theory. Because in a capitalist mode of production labour power is a commodity, the capitalist (in the long-run) is obliged to pay for labour power, only the value which is determined by the labour time necessary for its production and reproduction. Hence, its value is equal to its subsistence, where subsistence is defined as a cultural minimum, plus the expenses of education and training. In other words, the labourer's means of subsistence must be sufficient to maintain the labourer in his or her normal state as a labouring individual. Natural wants, such as food, clothing, fuel and housing vary according to climate and other physical conditions. However, the number and extent of these 'necessary' wants are themselves the product of historical development. There is therefore a historical and moral element to this commodity of labour power. The labour power withdrawn from the market, by wear and tear and death, must be replaced by at least an equal amount of fresh labour power, assuming constant technology. Hence, subsistence must include the means to perpetuate through procreation. The value of labour power resolves itself into the value of a definite quantity of the means of subsistence. Therefore, it varies with the value of these means, or with the quantity of labour requisite for their production.[4]

The origin of surplus value

The driving force of the capitalist mode of production is the creation of exchange values, and particularly of surplus value in the form of exchange values, rather than use-values, and the creation of surplus value is a social process. The value process begins with the availability of the commodity labour power and the presence of markets for the materials of production, and values and surplus values are then realized through the selling of commodity output.[5] Productive labour, that is labour that is bought with money capital and enters the production process, not only reproduces the value which it is advanced by means of the wage, it also produces a value above this level – the surplus value. The motivation on the part of the capitalist for hiring labour is in order to make a profit. Productive labour is not defined by the output that is produced, but the labour that is hired for personal service as an item of consumption is defined as unproductive labour as it is exchanged against revenue and no surplus value is created. Hence, labour in the former case takes the form of a commodity and, in the latter, takes the form of a product.[6] There is also a difference in terms of the role of money: whereas money functions as money capital in the case of productive labour, it is a medium of exchange in the case of unproductive labour. Hence, in the creation of surplus value, unproductive labour is inconsequential. Thus, labour power will be a product if it is bought as unproductive labour, but will take the form of a commodity when the labourer sells it for hire to a capitalist.

The creation of surplus value begins when the capitalist arrives at the market with an amount of money (M), and when this is advanced to purchase means of production (MP) and labour power (L), the advancement of money functions as capital. The capitalist purchases labour power for indirect use as a producer of value and while the capitalist holds raw materials, machines and labour power, these commodities take the form of commodity capital (C). Hence, in this process the capitalist has transformed money capital into commodity capital and when the inputs are put into the production process, they are converted into productive capital (P). Thus:

$$M \to \begin{cases} L \\ MP \end{cases} = P$$

Then, the production process converts the inputs into output and this output can be measured in terms of labour content. The output is held by the capitalist who produced it and takes the form of commodity capital (C′). This transformation of the inputs (L and MP) into an output is the production of use-values. When the capitalist sells the output, commodity capital (C′) is converted back into money capital (M′) and the money that had been advanced returns to the capitalist with an additional amount, the profit. Thus:

$$M \rightarrow C \rightarrow C' \rightarrow M'$$
(In general, $M' > M$ and $C' > C$)

Having advanced money capital, the capitalist owns the means of production and therefore the final product also belongs to the capitalist. Therefore, the difference between the costs of production (M) and total revenue (M′) is withdrawn by the capitalist. It would appear as though the entire inputs (L and MP) have contributed to the final output. However, the source of profit is in fact the class relation involved in the buying of labour power revealed as the surplus value originating in the production process through the appropriation by the capitalist as surplus, or unpaid, labour. Labour power is purchased by the capitalist as a commodity in addition to the means of production, and the labourer is therefore at the disposal of the capitalist during the working day to be combined with the means of production in the production process. Hence, the productivity of labour appears as synonymous with the productivity of capital, and appears to sanction the appropriation of profit by the capitalist as being legitimate as all constituents of the productive capital, purchased by the capitalist, have contributed to the creation of profit. Viewed another way, the labourer has restored to the capitalist the wage that was paid, enabling the capitalist to rehire the labourer, such that labour power reproduces its existence as labour power. The cycle can then begin again with the capitalist in possession of M′. Thus Marx writes:

> By turning his money into commodities which serve as the building materials for a new product, and as factors in the labour process, by incorporating living labour into their lifeless objectivity, the capitalist simultaneously transforms value, i.e. past labour in its objectified and lifeless form, into capital, value which can perform its own valorization process, an animated monster which begins to 'work', 'as if it were by love possessed'.

(Marx, 1976, p. 302)

Therefore, we can argue that labour has a use-value to the capitalist that is greater than its exchange value as the latter is the cost of labour, whereas the former is equal to the production which the labourer produces. The larger is the difference between the exchange value and the use-value, the larger will be the surplus that the capitalist appropriates from labour.

The theory of exploitation

Constant capital refers to that portion of the value of machinery and materials which is used up in production and added to the value of the product. Only the value of that portion of constant capital which is used up (depreciation and raw materials) is transferred to the value of the commodity. Variable capital is that part of capital represented by labour power, which in the process of production reproduces the equivalent of its own value.

To explain in more detail the concept of constant capital, we assume that a machine lasts for six days. Then, on average, it loses each day one-sixth of its use value and therefore, parts with one-sixth of its value to the daily product. Hence, means of production never transfer more value to the product than they themselves lose during the labour process by the destruction of their own use-value. We now assume further that a machine is worth £1000 and will wear out in 1000 days. In this case 1/1000th part of the value of the machine is transferred, on average, each day to the product. At the same time, the machine as a whole continually enters as a whole into the labour process while it enters into the process of the formation of value by fractions only. That part of capital which is represented by means of production, by the raw material, auxiliary material and the instruments of labour, does not, in the process of production, undergo any quantitative alteration of value. Marx therefore calls it the constant part of capital.

However, variable capital, the part of capital represented by labour power, undergoes an alteration of value in the process of production. It reproduces the equivalent of its own value, and also produces an excess, surplus value, which may itself vary according to circumstances. This part of capital is continually being transformed from a constant into a variable magnitude. Hence, Marx refers to this as variable capital.

As we have seen, surplus value is the source of capitalist profit and it is obtained by the capitalist from the labourer because the value of labour power (its market price) is only its subsistence and the labourer, working with modern machinery, is able to earn the value of subsistence (the wage) with only a few hours' work out of the working day. It follows therefore, that the value of the labourer's output for the remainder of the working day is appropriated by the capitalist as surplus value. Thus, surplus value is the value created by the labourer, but appropriated by the capitalist. The rate of surplus value can be determined as the capital (K) necessary for the production of a commodity and is made up of two parts, constant capital (c) and variable capital (v). Thus:

$$K = c + v$$

However, as we have seen, variable capital (v) is capable of creating surplus value (s). For example, a labourer may work for ten hours per day and reproduce his or her own value, equal to his or her wage, in only five hours. This is called necessary labour-time. The five extra hours which the labourer works for free for the capitalist is the surplus value created by the labourer but appropriated by the capitalist. Hence, the rate of surplus value can be determined by the equation:

$$\text{Rate of surplus value} = s/v = \text{Rate of exploitation}$$

That is, the rate of surplus value is equal to surplus value over necessary labour-time. Therefore, the rate of surplus value is an exact expression of the degree of exploitation of labour by capital or of the labourer by the capitalist, and therefore surplus value can be increased by the use of machinery. Machinery increases the productivity of labour and thus reduces the labour-time necessary for the labourer to produce his or her own subsistence. It also increases surplus value by making it possible to employ persons of less muscular power. Hence, since a subsistence wage must be large enough to support a household, employing two or more members of a family makes it possible to appropriate more labour-time for the same price. Machinery also prolongs the working day by providing the motive to the capitalist for doing so. In addition, machinery does not tire by use, and to leave it idle is costly, thus providing the incentive to increase its use. Although labour depreciates with use, machinery also depreciates due to the elements (rust for example). This is a further motive for its full utilization. In addition, there is also what Marx describes as 'moral' depreciation (obsolescence due to improvements) which mitigate on behalf of fuller utilization, an increase in the length of the working day. There is, however, a contradiction which drives the capitalist to increase the length of the working day: the more machinery that is employed relative to living labour, the less living labour is available for exploitation. To compensate for this decline in the source of surplus value, the capitalist must utilize the remaining labour more fully. This leads to an intensification of the work of the labourer. The labourer is compelled to work harder during the time that is worked as machinery may be speeded up or discipline tightened.

Summary

The source of value is a question that has dominated the discipline of economics since the eighteenth century, and although it has come to be dominated by the concept of marginal utility, Marx employs a theory of value that is firmly rooted in the surplus tradition of classical political economy. Value theory therefore, must be an essential element in the comprehension of the capitalist mode of production in terms of the specific nature of value relations as a social relationship in which products take the form of commodities for exchange only in capitalism. Within this, use-value relates to those properties of a commodity that satisfy human wants, whereas value in exchange is dependent upon a set of ratios in which use-values are exchanged in commodity markets. The value of an article is therefore found to be dependent upon the fact that human labour in the abstract is embodied in it. This value can then be measured by the socially necessary labour-time that is contained within it. This then allows Marx to introduce the concept of labour power and the creation of surplus value, explaining its origin and thus to argue that the use-value of labour to the capitalist is greater than its exchange value, creating the surplus appropriated by the capitalist from labour, through the process of exploitation.

4

Marx's Critique of Classical Political Economy

Introduction

In his critique, Marx attempted to expose four fundamental errors in the classical law of value. The first error was contained in the confusion between labour and labour power and Marx corrects this in his theory of wages. The second error was the inability of the classical law to explain the origins of surplus value; this Marx corrects in his theory of capital. The third error was the confusion between 'values' and 'prices', which is overcome by Marx in his analysis of the transformation problem. Finally, Marx observed that there was an inability to explain the emergence of rent and his solution to the transformation problem is a necessary prerequisite for the explanation.

The distinction between labour and labour power

> Labour itself has exchange-value and different types of labour have different exchange values. If one makes exchange-value the measure of exchange-value, one is caught up in a vicious circle, for the exchange-value used as a measure requires in turn a measure. This objection merges into the following problem: given labour-time as the intrinsic measure of value, how are wages to be determined on this basis.
>
> (Marx, 1970, pp. 61–2)

This represents Marx's first criticism of Ricardo's version of the labour theory of value. Either labour is sold at its value, in which case the labour theory of value was meaningless, or it did not, and the sale of the most important commodity of all broke the law of value. Hence, it seemed to be logically impossible to adhere to the labour theory of value and to develop a consistent theory of wages at the same time. As such, Marx needed to show that while value depends on the quantity of labour embodied in a commodity, it does not depend on the value of that commodity. In overcoming this logical inconsistency, Marx crucially made the distinction between labour and labour power. Labour is an activity and not a commodity, it is not bought and sold and therefore has no value, since the category 'value' only applies to commodities. What is bought and sold in the 'labour market' is labour power and, having clarified that it is labour power which is the commodity, Marx is able to produce a theory of wages (i.e. of the value of labour power) which is consistent with his theory of value.

Ricardo's theory of wages employs the Malthusian population principle to show how the long-term equilibrium real wage is maintained at the subsistence level. The mechanism for Ricardo is as follows: if real wages increase as a result of an excess demand for labour, then population will grow and labour supply will increase until the real wage returns to subsistence through the forces of supply and demand. This suggests that the long-run supply curve is perfectly elastic at the subsistence level. However, Marx argues that the time-lag involved in the response of the labour supply is far too long. Hence the classical theory of wages is dependent upon a biological law which is supposed to operate in all economies. However, for Marx, the category 'wages' was a historically specific one and therefore meaningful only in the capitalist mode of production. Thus, he attempted to locate a theory of wages which would relate specifically and exclusively to capitalist economies. In addition, he criticized classical political economy for its failure to provide such a law and, in particular, the classical theory of wages isolated the labour market as a special case to which the theory of value does not apply. Ricardo explains the value of all commodities, other than labour power, in terms of a law specific to the social institutions of capitalism, while the 'value of labour' was subject to a quite different analysis. For Marx, this was quite unacceptable.

Marx argues that capitalism is defined by the status of labour power as a commodity and it is this which distinguishes it from feudalism or simple commodity production. Labour power is therefore the most important commodity of all and this left Marx with the need to develop a theory of wages which satisfied two criteria. Marx insisted that since labour power is a commodity like any other, its value must rest on the same factors which determine the value of any other commodity. Hence, Marx attempted to apply the labour theory to distribution itself, and the mechanism by which the long-run equilibrium price of labour power was brought into equality with its value must be rooted firmly in the specific characteristics of the capitalist mode of production. The first criterion is easily satisfied, once the crucial distinction is made between labour and labour power. According to the labour theory of value, the value of a commodity depends upon the quantity of labour (under the prevailing technical conditions) for its production. The labour-time required to produce and reproduce human labour power is simply that necessary to keep the labourer, and the labourer's family, alive and capable of working. It is this which determines the value of labour power and hence, the long-run equilibrium wage. Therefore, Marx, as with Ricardo, has a subsistence theory of wages. Since labour power is not produced for profit by capitalists, this mechanism must be accounted for in some detail, that is how are real wages, on average and in the long-run, maintained at the subsistence level?

The Malthusian ahistorical law of population is replaced by Marx with a factor which is specific to the process of capitalist accumulation: the industrial reserve army of labour (the unemployed). This is also a form of overpopulation, but is quite different from the concept found in classical political economy. Capitalism itself produces a relatively redundant population peculiar to the capitalist mode of production. The forces that produce and reproduce unemployment are inherent in the nature of technical change and the accumulation of capital, which raises productivity through the growth of constant capital at a faster rate than that at which variable capital rises. Therefore, the organic composition of capital, defined as the ratio of constant to variable capital, increases such that capital increases its supply of labour more quickly than its demand for labourers.

There are two further factors that contribute to the industrial reserve army of labour. First, the application of these same technological changes in agriculture causes migration to towns and a high degree of under-employment among those who remain in the rural sector. Second, what Marx describes as the wretchedly exploited and irregularly employed section of the labour force which is still found in domestic industry forming the stagnant part of the industrial reserve army. Hence, the existence of the industrial reserve army means that competition between workers for jobs prevents real wages from increasing in the long run, above the subsistence level. Therefore, Marx's treatment of the theory of wages deliberately and explicitly refers only to capitalism and his theory is wholly consistent with the labour theory of value. Hence, Marx found the distinction between labour and labour power to be necessary to correct the logical flaw in classical political economy, and to allow the reconciliation of the theory of wages with the theory of value. He developed a theory of the value of labour power which is specific to capitalism without the ahistorical naturalism of the Malthusian population principle. Wages are maintained at the subsistence level by the operation of the industrial reserve army of labour, itself an inherent result of capital accumulation. This attack on the classical theory of value through the theory of wage-labour forms the basis for Marx's critique of the classical theory of surplus value.

The theory of capital

> If the exchange-value of a product equals the labour-time contained in the product, then the exchange value of a working day is equal to the product it yields, in other words, wages must be equal to the product of labour. But in fact the opposite is true. *Ergo*, this objection amounts to the problem – how does production on the basis of exchange-value solely determined by labour-time lead to the result that the exchange-value of labour is less than the exchange-value of its product? This is solved in our analysis of capital.
>
> (Marx, 1970, p. 62)

The classical economists insisted that these incomes originated in production and not in exchange, and further, that they resulted from the sale of commodities at, and not above, their value. However, if labour was the only source of value, why does not the entire product accrue to the labourer? In addressing this question Marx contrasts two different types of society: simple commodity production and capitalism. In simple commodity production, commodities exchange in ratios determined by the quantities of labour required to produce them and only the producers consume them.[1] However, in capitalism, labour power itself has become a commodity.

For Marx, 'capital' is above all the expression of the power of the minority class, which monopolizes the means of production, over propertyless labour. He explains it as follows:

> Capital is not a *thing,* any more than money is a *thing.* In capital, as in money, certain *specific social relations of production between people* appear as *relations of things to people,* or else certain social relations appear as the *natural properties of things in society.* Without a *class dependent on wages,* the moment individuals confront each other as

free persons, there can be no production of surplus-value; without the production of surplus-value there can be no capitalist production, and hence no capital and no capitalist!

(Marx, 1970, p. 1005)

Elsewhere he describes it thus: '...capital is not a thing, but a social relation between persons which is mediated through things' (Marx, 1970, p. 932). Associated with this difference in social structure is a difference in income distribution. Non-producers now share in the social product, in the form of rent, interest and profit. But this could be thought of as being consistent with the labour theory of value as it appears to imply, as Adam Smith believed, that the prices of commodities are greater than their labour values because profit is added to them. Marx totally disagreed and in this his distinction between labour and labour power is again crucial to his analysis. Hence the value of labour power is determined by the quantity of labour power necessary to produce the subsistence requirements of the labourer. However, these bear no necessary relation to the product of the worker's labour, which may be very much larger. This is because only part of the working day is required for the labourer to produce enough for the provision of the subsistence needs of the labourer and the labourer's family. During the remainder of the working day, the labourer performs what Marx terms 'surplus labour': the labourer produces for the sole benefit of the capitalist.

The theory of competition

The confusion in classical political economy between 'values' and 'prices' arises in the theory of competition. In classical political economy there are two sides to the problem of a theory of competition. On the one hand, the deviation of day-to-day market prices from the long-run equilibrium due to fluctuations in demand and supply. On this point Marx essentially agreed with Ricardo that it was a relatively minor issue. On the other hand, there is the more serious prospect that long-run equilibrium ('natural') prices, diverge from labour values. Marx observed that these divergences were inescapable if the composition of capital differs while competition tends to equalize the rate of profit between industries. Ricardo attempted to solve this by attributing it to differences in the ratio of fixed and circulating capital. However, he used the term 'value' in an inconsistent manner, using it to mean labour value and at other times equilibrium price. As such he failed to give a satisfactory explanation of the continued operation of the labour theory of value when 'natural' prices and labour values differ. This is the crux of the transformation problem, but it cannot be properly understood without first addressing the theory of capital.

Central to this whole question is the relation between constant and variable capital. Marx assumes a competitive economy where the rate of profit is equal in all sectors, but the organic composition of capital (the ratio of constant to variable capital) is unequal. Marx then shows that labour values and long-run equilibrium prices must, in general, diverge. He attempted to show that these differences modify the operation of the labour theory of value and that they can only be understood with reference to the theory of value which is logically prior to an analysis of equilibrium prices.

As illustrated in Table 4.1, Marx constructs a simple capitalist economy composed of three sectors ('departments'). These produce a means of production (steel), a means of subsistence (corn) and a 'luxury' commodity (gold). The economy produces enough for the same level of output to be maintained in subsequent periods. In addition, there are no landlords, and capitalists consume their entire incomes, that is the rate of accumulation is zero, which Marx calls simple reproduction, with which we shall deal in more detail in Chapter 6. In Department I, the production of 120 tons of steel requires 40 hours of labour and 80 tons of steel. The production of 60 quarters of corn in Department II requires 10 tons of steel and 50 hours of labour. Department III produces 60 ounces of gold for which is required 30 tons of steel and 30 hours' labour. Therefore, the production of one ton of steel requires total labour inputs (direct and indirect) of one hour. Thus, direct labour $= 40/120 = 1/3$, and indirect labour (the labour required to produce the input of steel per ton of steel output) $= 80/120 = 2/3$. Hence, if the labour value of a ton of steel (λ) is:

$$\lambda = 1/3 + 2/3$$
$$\rightarrow \lambda = 1$$

Therefore the value of the total output of steel is $(120).(1) = 120$.

Similarly, a quarter of corn and an ounce of gold have a labour value of one and the output of the two departments is each valued at 60. Hence, constant capital used in each department (entirely consisting of steel) is:

> 80 in Department I
> 10 in Department II
> 30 in Department III

which adds up to 120.

Table 4.1 The transformation of values into prices

(a) Production conditions:

	Means of production		Inputs	Labour	Output
Dept I	80	tons steel	+	40	120 tons steel
Dept II	10	tons steel	+	50	60 qtr corn
Dept III	30	tons steel	+	30	60 oz gold
Total		120		120	

(b) The value system:

	Constant capital (c)	Variable capital (v)	Surplus value (s)	Value (c+v+s)	Rate of exploitation (s/v) (%)	Organic composition of capital (c+v)	Rate of profit (s/c+v) (%)
Dept I	80	20	20	120	100	4	20
Dept II	10	25	25	60	100	0.4	71.4
Dept III	30	15	15	60	100	2	33.3
Total	120	60	60	240			

Table 4.1   *continued*

(c) Marx's price system:

	1 Constant capital (c)	2 Variable capital (v)	3 Cost price (c+v)	4 Average rate of profit	5 = [4.3] Profits	6 = [3+5] Price of production	7 Price minus value	8 Profits minus surplus value	9 Price–value ratio
Dept I	80	20	100	0.33r	33.3	133.3	13.3	13.3	1.11
Dept II	10	25	35	0.33r	11.7	46.7	−13.3	−13.3	0.78
Dept III	30	15	45	0.33r	15	60	0	0	1
Total	120	60	180		60	240	0	0	

Source: Howard and King (1985), p. 99.

The number of hours of living labour employed is:

40 in Department I
50 in Department II
30 in Department III

which adds up to 120. (This will be divided between paid and unpaid components according to the rate of exploitation.)

If we now assume that the rate of exploitation is 100 per cent, we are therefore assuming that the necessary and surplus parts of living labour are equal. Then this gives quantities of variable capital and surplus value as follows:

Department I $(20v + 20s)$
Department II $(25v + 25s)$
Department III $(15v + 15s)$

The sum of variable capital in the three departments $(20v + 25v + 15v)$ equals the labour value of the output of corn. This is because the workers spend all of their income on corn (and they are the sole purchasers). The value of the output of gold (60) equals the sum of the surplus value that accrues to the capitalists $(20s + 25s + 150s)$ and this is because the capitalists spend all of their income on gold. If the labour theory of value holds, then the rate of profit (r) in each department is the ratio of surplus value to the total capital (constant and variable) employed there.

$$r_i = s_i/c_i + v_i \text{ (where } i = \text{Department I, II or III)}$$

There is assumed to be no fixed capital in the model and therefore constant and variable capital turn over exactly once per year and, hence, both consist entirely of circulating capital.[2] Marx believed that fixed capital made little difference to the analysis as this was just a simplification.

The rate of profit in each sector is represented by:

Department I $= 20/(80 + 20)$ $= 20.0\%$
Department II $= 25/(10 + 25)$ $= 71.4\%$
Department III $= 15/30 + 15$ $= 33.3\%$

Hence, there is an intimate and inverse relationship between these rates of profit and the organic composition of capital (c/v), in the three sectors:

Department I $= 80/20$ $= 4.0$
Department II $= 10/25$ $= 0.4$
Department III $= 30/15$ $= 2.0$

Therefore, the higher is the organic composition of capital, the lower is the rate of profit. However, in a mature competitive capitalist economy, these differences in profit rates cannot persist. This is because capitalists will abandon unprofitable industries for sectors which offer higher profit rates and it is this movement of capital that ensures that rates of profit become equal, and indeed capital movement will continue until the equalization of profits has occurred. This implies the establishment of long-run equilibrium prices (or 'prices of production') which diverge from labour values in a predictable manner and profits are distributed according to the number of shares – the investment in social production.

Marx carries out the necessary transformation of values into prices and of surplus values into profits in Table 4.1(c) as follows. *The average rate of profit* is the ratio between aggregate surplus value and aggregate capital (constant and variable): this is $60/(120+60)=0.33r$ (column 4). *The capital stock* is calculated using constant plus variable capital for each of the departments, and this also equals cost price, and this is shown as $(100+35+45)=180$ (column 3). If we multiply each department's cost price by the average rate of profit, we arrive at the *profit paid to the capitalists* (column 5). Finally, if we add the profits to cost price, we have the *price of production*.

We can observe that in Department I, which has an above average organic composition of capital, the price of production is greater than its value. That is, the ratio of price to value is 1.11 (column 9). Also, it has profits greater than surplus value ($+13.3$) (column 8). However, in Department II, the reverse is true as it has a relatively low organic composition of capital (0.4), and a price of production lower than value at 0.78 (column 9). Profits, at 11.7, are less than surplus value (25), which equals -13.3 (column 8). In Department III we have the special case where the organic composition of capital is equal to the average of the whole economy. As such, the organic composition of $120/60=2$ is the special case where the price of production is equal to value $(60=60)$ and profits are equal to surplus values $(15=15)$. In addition, we can see that for the whole economy, the sum of values is equal to the sum of prices $(120+60+60=133.3+46.7+60=240)$ and aggregate surplus value is equal to aggregate profit $(20+25+15=33.3+11.7+15=60)$.

These equalities form the foundation of Marx's argument that the labour theory of value is required to determine the prices of production and the rate of profit. Thus, 'transformation' is a redistribution of surplus value from industries with a low organic composition to those with a high one and the magnitudes to be redistributed are quantities of embodied labour. Hence, values are logically prior to prices of production and surplus values are prior to profits. Only when competition is sufficiently strong, and the mobility of capital sufficiently vigorous, is the equalization of profit rates between departments a possibility. In earlier stages of development, prices and labour values are identical and rates of profit differ between industries. Therefore, the amount of profit that accrues to an individual capitalist is not equal to the quantity of surplus value extracted from the workers employed by that capitalist. This would only be the situation in the special case where the organic composition of capital is equal to the social average, as in the example of Department III. In general, equal capitals yield unequal surplus value, but equal profits. The outcome is that both sides are mistaken. The capitalist attributes profit to the powers of capital, missing the social origins of profit in surplus value and surplus value in surplus labour. The workers believe that every hour of their work is paid labour and do not see the unpaid part of the working day from which surplus value is derived.

The theory of rent

The fourth error in classical political economy concerns the explanation of the emergence of rent. Whereas Adam Smith saw rent as one of the components of the value of the output, David Ricardo argued that the existence of rent is not incompatible with the labour theory of value. For Ricardo, the value of corn is determined by the quantity of labour required to produce it under the least favourable conditions. Hence, intramarginal land, requiring a lower labour input to produce the same output of corn, yields most rent to the landlords. Therefore, it follows that, the more fertile the land in relation to that at the margin of cultivation, the higher will be the rent. Rent, for Ricardo, therefore, is a purely differential payment, and no rent is paid at the margin.

Marx agreed with the logic of this argument but suggests that it is too restrictive because rent could be paid at the margin without inconsistency with the labour theory of value as long as the transformation from values into prices is taken into account. The question is: if a farmer makes the same profits as all other capitalists, then labour-time has been appropriated, but where on top of this does the rent come from? Why should surplus labour in agriculture resolve itself into profit and rent, but in industry it is just profit alone? The answer for Marx is that agriculture operates with a lower organic composition of capital and the prices of production are therefore lower than the value of the corn. However, land is not a commodity in the Marxian sense because it cannot be reproduced by human labour. The monopoly of land ownership enables the landowner to squeeze that part of surplus labour that would form excess profit. But it is not that the landed proprietor can force the price of the commodity above its value, quite the reverse is the case: monopoly makes it possible to maintain the value of the commodity above its average price, selling the commodity at its value and not above. To exemplify this, Marx assumes that agriculture and industry use the same total quantity of capital equal to 100. However, it is divided between constant and variable capital in different proportions: 80(c) : 20(v) in industry and 60(c) : 40(v) in agriculture. Marx also assumes a rate of exploitation of 100 per cent. It follows therefore that the value of output would be:

$$\text{Industry:} \quad 80c + 20v + 20s = 120$$
$$\text{Agriculture:} \quad 60c + 40v + 40s = 140$$

Then, the values would be transformed into prices of production in order to equalize the rate of profit in both sectors. Both would sell at 130, and the same average rate of profit (30 per cent) would be paid in both. Hence, agricultural output would sell at less than its value. It should be noted however, that this is only possible if land is not privately owned. Therefore, in capitalism, landlords are able to maintain the price of agricultural output at a level equal to its value. Thus, corn sells at 140 and the landlord takes 20 of the 40 units of surplus value in rent. The capitalist farmers retain 20, giving them the same rate of profit as the industrial capitalists. Hence, for Marx, the theory of rent is not a law of nature, as it was for Ricardo, but a social law. The landlord is a parasite of capitalist society who could be abolished without adverse consequences for the operation of the system as a whole. As modern technology is applied to agriculture, the organic composition of capital will rise to the social average, at which point value would then be no greater than the price of production and absolute rent would disappear.

Hence, we can see that there are a number of essential differences between the theory of rent as presented by Marx, and the arguments of Ricardo, such that, agricultural productivity is not required to fall as accumulation proceeds. This is due to the fact that the lower organic composition of capital in agriculture means that, although productivity in that sector may rise more slowly than in industry, it does rise over time. Although rent does not form part of the price of production of agricultural output, it does represent a constituent part of its final selling price, which otherwise would be equal to the lower price of production. This suggests that Ricardo was mistaken in his argument that rent is determined by price, rather than being a determining factor in price.

The declining rate of profit and Say's Law

Marx's criticisms of the classical theory of economic development concentrates on two major aspects of that theory: the Ricardian analysis of the declining rate of profit and the validity of Say's Law in the capitalist mode of production. On the declining rate of profit, Marx's analysis is based on his criticisms of the classical theory of value. Having illustrated why Ricardo's theory of rent was incorrect, Marx shows that in failing to distinguish between constant and variable capital, Ricardo had confused the rate of profit (r) with the rate of exploitation (ε) and had therefore concluded that the declining rate of profit relies upon a fall in the productivity of agricultural labour, such that, to continue to produce the labourer's subsistence, an ever increasing proportion of the working day must be devoted to the production of this subsistence. However, Marx realized that modern industry would develop using technology which would increase the organic composition of capital, causing an increase in the numbers of the industrial reserve army of labour, and as the rate of profit can be shown to be a relationship between the rate of exploitation (ε), and the organic composition of capital (k), if there is a tendency for the organic composition of capital to increase more rapidly than the rate of exploitation, then the rate of profit (r) must fall. Thus, if:

$$r = \frac{s}{c+v}$$

Then:

$$r = \frac{(s/v)}{c/v} + 1$$

The rate of exploitation is:

$$\epsilon = \frac{s}{v}$$

The organic composition of capital is:

$$k = \frac{c}{v}$$

Therefore:

$$r = \frac{\epsilon}{k} + 1$$

Hence, if k rises faster than ε, r will decline.

The crucial point of this analysis is that the decline in r has resulted from an *increase* in labour productivity, the exact opposite of that suggested by Ricardo.

In his criticism of Say's Law, Marx attacks the proposition that there exists an endogenous mechanism which automatically guarantees that there will be a level of aggregate demand sufficient to realize the whole of the surplus value that is embodied in commodities when they are presented in the market.[3] Marx argues that Say's Law, that 'supply creates its own demand', is correct, but only in a barter economy. However, in a money-using, market economy, supply no longer creates its own demand as it is possible to sell without buying and to save the proceeds of a sale, thus aggregate supply may exceed aggregate demand. In essence, Marx's critique of Say's Law is an obvious anticipation of Keynes's criticisms in this area and, indeed, Marx has been cited as anticipating the dual decision hypothesis of Clower (Junankar, 1982, p. 141).

Summary

In his critique of the classical law of value Marx was able to address the four fundamental errors that he identified as lacking in logic and consistency. Out of this emerged the theory of wages, the theory of capital and the explanation of the difference between values and prices, as illustrated in the transformation of value and surplus value into prices and profits using the theory of competition. Hence, Marx shows that while value depends on the quantity of labour embodied in a commodity, it does not follow that it must depend on the value of that commodity and crucially does this through the distinction between labour and labour power, the latter being a commodity in the capitalist mode of production that is bought and sold in the same way as with any other commodity. This then allows Marx to formulate a theory of wages that is completely consistent with the theory of value, and which does not depend upon the ahistorical Malthusian population principle, as used by Ricardo, but a mechanism that is specific to capitalism. The industrial reserve army of labour is produced by capitalism and performs for capitalism the function of preventing real wages from increasing above the subsistence level in the long run. Probably the most controversial and hotly debated aspects of Marx's work is the so-called transformation problem, which we will examine in much greater detail in the next chapter.

5
The Transformation Problem – Some Complicating Detours

Introduction

Much controversy continues to surround the interpretation, the relative importance and the accuracy of Marx's formulation of the transformation of values into prices and of surplus values into profits, which is mainly to be found in Chapter IX of *Capital*, Volume III. A great deal has been written on this subject since it first appeared and the debate will assuredly continue far into the future. In the chapter presented here, we will examine Marx's discussion of the transformation procedure before investigating the critiques and counter-critiques that have ensued. It is not that this is the most important aspect of Marx's political economy, indeed many would suggest that it has constituted an unwelcome and misplaced diversion, but it remains the one area that has caused Marxian economists the most difficulty in terms of a complete refutation of 'orthodox' interpretations of the operation of a capitalist economy. It has often been seized upon by non-Marxians as the 'chink in the armour' of Marxian political economy.

It is for this reason that we should understand the debates that surround this issue, and the developments that have taken place during this century, in terms of the theorizing apropos the problem of transformation. We can divide such theorizing into two main camps. The first is what we may call the 'Fundamental Flaw' thesis as proposed by Bohm-Bawerk (1896), Samualson (1957), Seton (1957), Steedman (1977) and others. The second, the 'Marx needs to be understood properly' thesis, is associated with, among others, Morishima (1973), Yaffe (1973), Shaikh (1977), Dumenil (1980), Foley (1982) and Kliman and McGlone (1988).

Marx's procedure

In Chapter IX of the third volume of *Capital*, Marx begins by re-emphasizing that the organic composition of capital depends on the proportion between labour power and means of production applied, and also on the prices of those means of production. He highlights in particular that this must be considered in *percentage terms*. He assumes a rate of exploitation of 100 per cent and, at this point in the analysis, assumes that the depreciation of the constant capital has no effect on the rate of profit, and therefore, that the constant capital enters as a whole into the annual product. It is then assumed that the amount of surplus value realized in different spheres of production is proportional to the size of the variable capital in each sphere. Marx shows that he understands that variations in turnover times will alter the results, but at this stage in the analysis he ignores this effect for simplicity of exposition.

Therefore (as shown in Table 5.1) he examines five spheres of production with different organic compositions, each with total capital of 100. Thus the average organic composition is $78v + 22v$, the average surplus value is 22, and the average rate of profit is 22 per cent. Hence, the price of each 25 per cent of the total product for each sphere of production is 122, and the product of each sphere would have to be sold at 122. However, Marx explains that if all cost prices were to be taken as 100, wrong conclusions would be reached and therefore, we must take account of the different compositions of constant capital relating to its fixed and circulating components. In addition, the fixed components may depreciate at differing rates and, therefore, impart different quantities of value to the product during the same production period. However, this is of no matter concerning the rate of profit as cost price $(c + v)$ is less than the value of the product $(c + v + s)$ and the same is true for used capital (c') as $(c' + v) < (c' + v + s)$.

In Table 5.1, the surplus value is evenly distributed among the five spheres of production and the divergences of price to value are cancelled out when adding average profit (22) on the capital advanced (100), with some sectors selling at above value, others selling at below value. Marx explains that this is an important result as it illustrates that it is only since they are sold at these prices, notwithstanding their different organic compositions of capital, that the profit rates are equal at 22 per cent.

The prices of production are derived from the average of the different rates of profit in the spheres of production, added to their cost prices, and the prerequisite of the prices of production is the existence

Table 5.1   Marx's transformation procedure

Capital	Rate of surplus value (s/v)	Surplus value (s)	Value (c+v+s)	Rate of profit	Used up constant capital (c')	Value of commodities (c'+v+s)	Cost price of commodities (c'+v)	Rate of profit	Divergence of price from value	Price of commodities (cost price+ av. profit)
I 80c+20v	100%	20	120	20	50	90	70	22%	2	70
II 70c+30v	100%	30	130	30	51	111	81	22%	−8	81
III 60c+40v	100%	40	140	40	51	131	91	22%	−18	91
IV 85c+15v	100%	15	115	15	40	70	55	22%	7	55
V 95c+5v	100%	5	105	5	10	20	15	22%	17	15
Total 390c+ 110v		110		110%		422			0	0
Average 78c+ 22v		22		22%		84.4			0	

of a general rate of profit, such that, the profit rates in each sphere are already reduced to their average rates. Hence, 'the production price of a commodity equals its cost price plus the percentage profit added to it in accordance with the general rate of profit, its cost price plus the average profit' (Marx, 1981, p. 257). Due to the differing organic compositions of capital in the different spheres of production, capitals of the same amount (here 100), produce different surplus values, depending on the percentage of variable capital in total capital. Thus, the rates of profit are balanced out to arrive at an average of the different rates, the general rate of profit.

Marx then gives an example of the calculation of the prices of production. It is assumed that of a total capital of 500, 100 is fixed capital, 10 per cent of which is the depreciation of a circulating capital of 400. If we further assume that the average profit is 10 per cent, then the cost price is:

$$10c + 400 (c + v) = 410$$

Therefore:

$$\text{Price of production} = 410 \text{ (cost price)} + 50 \text{ (10\% profit)}$$
$$= 460$$

Hence, while each capitalist receives the capital value required to produce their commodities, they do not receive the surplus value, and thus the profit, that has been produced in their particular sphere of production. He explains this in terms of the example of the shareholders of a joint stock company, assuming that the dividends are distributed evenly for each 100 units, and according to the number of shares owned by each shareholder. Hence, while the cost price is determined by the outlay in each respective sphere of production, the profit is determined by that profit which falls on average to each capital invested, as an exact divisor of the total social capital invested in total production.

Thus, the cost price of the commodity of an individual capitalist is specific, but the profit added to the cost price is independent of that particular sphere of production – it is an average per 100 units of capital advanced (i.e. an average percentage of total capital). Again, to illustrate the point in more accessible terms, Marx assumes that the five spheres of production belong to one person. The cost prices would differ for each commodity, and the profit produced in each sphere could be counted as profit on total capital, with an exact divisor falling to each of the capitals of 100. Hence, cost prices would differ, but the proportion of the sale price arising from the profit added per 100 units of capital would be the same. It follows, therefore, that the total price of the commodities would be the same as their total value contained in the commodities. Thus, the sum of the prices of production in society as a whole is equal to the sum of their values.

Marx then turns to the problem that arises if we consider that productive capital is bought on the market and therefore, is likely to contain in its price already realized profit, and thus the production price of one sphere of production, such that the profit of one sphere of production enters into the cost price of another sphere. 'But if the sum of the cost prices of all commodities in a country is put on one side and the sum of profits or surplus values on the other, we can see that the calculation comes out right' (Marx, 1981, p. 260).

Assume that there are four commodities w, x, y, z. Commodity w may contain in its cost price, the profits of x, y and z. Making this calculation, the profits of w will be absent from its own cost price, as will the profits of x, y and z be absent from theirs. Thus, none of them includes their own profit in cost price. If there are n spheres of production, each making a profit (π), then the cost price (ψ) is:

$$\psi = n\pi$$

Hence, if the profits of one sphere go into the cost price of another, these profits have already been accounted for as to the overall price of the final product, and as the commodity is a productive capital, its price of production does not go into the cost price of another commodity. If a sum π enters into the cost price of a commodity for the profit of the producers of productive capital and a profit of π_1 is added to this cost price, then

$$\text{Total profit } (R) = \pi + \pi_1$$

Thus the total cost price of the commodity is then its cost price minus R (total profit), hence

$$\psi + R = \psi + \pi + \pi_1$$

As the product of any capital can be seen to consist of one part that replaces capital and another part that represents surplus value, when too much surplus value goes into a commodity, too little goes into another, with divergences from value in prices of production cancelling each other out. 'With the whole of capitalist production, it is always only in a very intricate and approximate way, as an average of perpetual fluctuations which can never be firmly fixed, that the general law prevails as the dominant tendency' (Marx, 1981, p. 261). Thus, for the system as a whole, the difference in turnover periods of the different sectors becomes atomized because the general rate of profit is derived from the average rate of profit of the different sectors and the differentiation between turnover periods is, in turn, crucial in the determination of the rate of profit in each sector of production. Marx then explains that his construct of the formation of the general rate of profit had assumed a total capital of 100 in each sphere of production to highlight the *percentage* differences in the rates of profit, and also the differences in the values of commodities produced by capitals of 100 units. But, the surplus values produced in each sphere actually depend upon the mass of the total capital employed, due to the role of the organic composition in the production of surplus value. To illustrate this, Marx assumes four differing organic compositions of capital in four capitals, or sectors. He then shows how the total value produced will vary depending upon the size of total capital in each of the sectors. Thus, the general rate of profit is not only formed out of the different *rates* of profit in the different sectors of production, but also their relative weights in the formation of the average. By relative weights, Marx is concerned with the relative size of the capital in each sector, in relation to the total capital invested. In addition, the rate of profit will depend upon how much of the total capital is invested in those sectors where the organic composition of capital is relatively high or low in comparison with the social average. Hence, the general rate of profit is determined by the organic composition of capital in different sectors of production, and the distribution of total capital in these different sectors (as illustrated in Table 5.2).

Marx now explains that part of the value of commodities has 'split away' as the cost price (ψ) and the production price had developed as a transformed form of value. He illustrates this as follows. Assuming an annual rate of exploitation of 100 per cent (s' = 100%), and the organic composition of average social capital is $80c + 20v$, then the average annual rate of profit will be 20 per cent. As such, the price of production of the commodities will be ($\psi + 20$). For the sectors of production that have below the average organic composition, $(80-x)c+(20+x)v$, the annual profit will be ($\psi + 20 + x$), x *more* than the price of production. Where the organic composition is higher than the social average, $(80+x)c+(20-x)v$, the annual rate of profit will be $(20-x)$ and the commodity value will be ($\psi + 20 - x$), x *less* than the price of production. Assuming no difference in the turnover of capital, only in the case where the organic composition of capital was equal to the social average ($80c + 20v$) would the value of the commodities be equal to their price of production.

Table 5.2   The transformation of profit into average profit

(a)

Capital	v	c	s	
A	25	75	25	25
B	40	60	40	40
C	15	85	15	15
D	10	90	10	10
			90	90

$$\text{Av. } \pi \; \frac{90}{4} = 22\tfrac{1}{2} \; \frac{90}{400} \times 100 = 22.5\%$$

(b)

Capital	c + v	v%	v	s
A	200	25	50	50
B	300	40	120	120
C	1000	15	150	150
D	4000	10	400	400
	5500			720

$$\text{Av. rate of profit} = \frac{720}{5500} \times 100 = 13.09\%$$

Hence, the determination of the cost price of a commodity for a buyer now involves the price of production, and may enter into the determination of the price of another commodity. Because, as we have seen, the price of production may well diverge from value, the cost price of a commodity, containing the price of production of other commodities, can also therefore, be above or below that segment of its total value that is produced by the value of the means of production that have gone into its formation. 'It is necessary to bear in mind this modified significance of the cost price, and therefore to bear in mind too that the cost price of a commodity is equated with the value of the means of production used up in producing it, it is always possible to go wrong' (Marx, 1981, p. 265).

However, Marx insists that, notwithstanding the above, the cost price of commodities will always be smaller than their values, because even where there exists a divergence between a commodity's cost price and the value of the means of production contained in its formation, it will be of no matter to the capitalist, because the cost price will be independent of the capitalist's production, whereas the outcome of the capitalist's production is a commodity which contains surplus value. This surplus value is an excess value over and above its cost price. Thus, 'As a general rule, the principle that the cost price of a commodity is less than its value has been transformed into the principle that its cost price is less than its price of production' (Marx, 1981, p. 265).

In other words, while the value of a commodity depends upon the total of paid and unpaid labour contained within it, the cost price is dependent only upon the amount of paid labour contained within it. However, the price of production is dependent upon the total of paid labour and a certain amount of unpaid labour which is an amount independent of its sector of production. Marx illustrates this with the equation:

$$P = \psi + \psi \pi'$$

This is interpreted as, the price of production is equal to the cost price plus the cost price times the general rate of profit. Therefore, if the cost price of a commodity is 300 and the general rate of profit is 15 per cent, the price of production can be calculated as:

$$P = \psi + \psi \pi'$$
$$P = 300 + 300 \times \frac{15}{100}$$
$$P = 345$$

Marx then extends the analysis to take account of the dynamic nature of the system by explaining in what circumstances the prices of production in a particular sector may change in magnitude: first, the general rate of profit may change, through changes in other sectors of production; second, value in the sector may change due to technical innovation in the sector, or changes in the value of commodities that enter as constant capital in its production process; third, a combination of each of these changes. An alteration in the general rate of profit takes place only after a prolonged period of time, during which the rates of profit in the particular sectors of production change constantly. Hence, in the shorter period, a change in the prices of production can be explained by an actual change in commodity values, caused by changes to the total amount of labour-time required for the production of those commodities. However, in terms of the total social capital, the sum of values of the commodities produced by it will be equal to the value of the constant capital, the value of the variable capital and the surplus value produced. Therefore, if the rate of exploitation is constant, then the rate of profit can only alter if (a) the value of constant capital changes, (b) the value of variable capital changes, or (c) if both the values of constant and variable capital changes. In each of these cases, the change in the organic composition of capital means that the general rate of profit will change. Thus, an alteration in the general rate of profit assumes a change in the value of those commodities which enter into the production process as constant and variable capital, or a relaxation of the assumption of a constant rate of exploitation.

Marx then suggests that, although the rate of profit can vary with the rate of surplus value being unchanged, except in total, as the capitalist is only interested in the former, the real origin of surplus value is hidden from the capitalist. But, the difference is between the *rate* of profit and the *rate* of surplus value and not between profit and surplus value, which are of the same magnitude in the totality. The fact that becomes disguised in the process of production is that surplus value, and therefore profit, originates, not from the total capital, but from only that part of total capital that is variable capital. 'In actual fact, therefore, surplus value denies its own origin in this, its transformed form, which is profit; it loses its character and becomes unrecognizable' (Marx, 1981, p. 267).

It is a matter of accident only if the surplus value that is actually produced in a particular sector of production is equal to the profit contained in the sale price of the commodity, and in general profit and surplus value will differ. However, the individual capitalist has no interest in the process as a whole and is interested only in the surplus value that is created in his/her own sector of production as one of the determinants of the average rate of profit. The actual character of profit and its origin are thus concealed by the difference in magnitude between profit and surplus value in the sectors of production as a result of the transformation of values into prices of production. The capitalist is not concerned with the total labour involved in the production of the commodity, rather he/she is only concerned with that part of labour paid for as means of production. Thus the concept of value does not enter into the capitalist's account of the formation of profit. The crucial point of this analysis, for Marx, is that the establishment of a general rate of profit, *if observed from the point of view of the individual sectors of production*, is not determined by the value formation in these sectors, but is formed externally to them.

> All economics up till now has either violently made abstraction from the distinctions between surplus value and profit, between the rate of surplus value and the rate of profit, so that it could retain the determination of value as its basis, or else it has abandoned, along with this determination of value, any kind of solid foundation for a scientific approach, so as to be able to retain those distractions which obtrude themselves on the phenomenal level.
>
> (Marx, 1981, p. 269)

Changes in the general rate of profit are slow because changes in individual sectors of production will tend to cancel each other out and, therefore, the impact of individual changes will impact on the general rate of profit only as the organic composition of capital changes in the individual sectors of production. It is this separation of individual sectors and the general rate of profit that masks, for the capitalists, the origin of profit. Thus increasing the constant portion of the total capital appears, for the individual capitalist, to be a rational decision. Given the previous analysis, however, it is clear that if the portion of cost price which represents constant capital rises in a particular sector, this is the portion that comes out of the circulation process and goes into the commodity's production process from the outset enlarged. But, if the productivity of labour increases, the quantity of labour required to produce a certain amount of commodities changes. Hence, the portion of the cost price representing the value of variable capital may remain the same and hence go into the cost price of the total product with the same magnitude. However, each of the individual commodities, whose sum comprises the total product, now contains more or less labour (paid and therefore also unpaid), that is, also more or less of the outlay for this labour, a greater or smaller portion of the wages. Thus, the *total* in wages paid by the capitalist is unchanged, but not if it is computed on the basis of each individual commodity. This is because the commodity's cost price is changed in respect to the variable capital contained in it, as variable capital is the source of surplus value. Marx assumes $v = £100$ for 100 workers and that 100 workers produce 200 items, denoted as 200C. Hence, 1C (ignoring constant capital) costs $= £100/200 = 50$ pence, since $£100 = 200C$. Now assume that there is a change in the productivity of labour, in that it doubles.

As far as cost price consists simply of labour, now £100=400C. Hence, 1C now equals £100/400=25 pence. If productivity were reduced by 50 per cent, then the same labour would produce only 200C/2, and since

$$200C/2 = £100 \rightarrow 1C = £200/200 = £1.$$

Marx concludes the chapter with an appraisal of what the preceding analysis shows in terms of the implications for the capitalist mode of production.

> The changes in the labour-time required for the production of the commodities, and therefore in their value, now appear in connection with the cost price, and therefore also with the price of production, as a different distribution with the same wages over more or fewer commodities, according to whether more or fewer commodities are produced in the same labour-time for the same wages. What the capitalist sees, and therefore the political economist as well, is that the part of the paid labour that falls to each item of the commodity changes with the productivity of labour, and so too therefore does the value of each individual article; he does not see that this is also the case with the unpaid labour contained in each article, and the less so, as the average profit is in fact only accidentally determined by the unpaid labour absorbed in his own sphere. The fact that the value of commodities is determined by the labour they contain now continues to percolate through only in this crudified and naive form.
>
> (Marx, 1981, p. 272)

Critiques and 'complete' solutions

Bohm-Bawerk (1896) asserted that the price–value divergence was a contradiction in Marxian value theory and that the theory that surplus value was the origin of profit could not stand because of this divergence, giving the impression of an important anomaly in Marx's theory. However, in *Theories of Surplus Value*, it is evident that Marx was fully aware of the significance of the divergence in price and value and that this divergence caused the obscuring of value relations. In fact, this divergence is an essential element in the behaviour of prices in a capitalist mode of production. Bortkiewicz confirmed this by demonstrating that the theory of profits arising from surplus value is correct as the rate of profit and the prices of production are shown to be functions of the rate of exploitation, the organic composition of capital and the rate of turnover.

Perhaps a more serious problem concerns the two invariance conditions in Marx, that the sum of total value is equal to the sum of total prices of production and that the sum of surplus values equals the sum of total profits. We can write these as follows:

$$\Sigma(c+v+s) = \Sigma(c_p + v_p + \pi)$$
$$\Sigma s = \Sigma \pi$$

If Marx's value rate of profit is written as:

$$r = \frac{\Sigma s}{\Sigma(c+v)}$$

and the price rate of profit is:

$$r_p = \frac{\Sigma \pi}{(c_p + v_p)}$$

Then:

$$r = r_p$$

However, it is argued that the constant and variable capital components have not been transformed, and remain in labour values. Because some departments produce means of production, some of the departments' outputs become inputs into other departments and, therefore, will sell at their price of production. It is argued therefore, that these commodities should enter the schema in terms of prices of production and not as labour values, otherwise the transformation procedure is incomplete. Marx was in fact fully aware of this problem and, as we have seen, explains this in *Capital*, Volume III (cf. Marx, 1981, pp. 259–69). Bortkiewicz demonstrated that, in general, using numerical examples, it is impossible to satisfy both of Marx's invariance conditions, and that the price and value rate of profit would, in general, be unequal (Howard and King, 1992, p. 230; Howard and King, 1989, p. 61). Thus, the position after Bortkiewicz's articles[1] appeared to be that prices of production are derivable from values, but both of Marx's invariance conditions cannot be satisfied. Bortkiewicz uses the assumption of simple reproduction, but this was extended by Seton (1957), which showed that prices could be derived from labour values in more complex cases of a multi-sector economy which involved n commodities, used as inputs in n industries. In the same year, Samualson presented an article in the *American Economic Review* employing the framework of linear economics to suggest that the transformation problem was pointless as labour values are not required to determine prices of production. Samualson concludes that the theory of value, according to Marx, only explains the deviation of prices from values in terms of a truth being equal to an error plus a variation. This article was much more critical to the totality of the Marxian schema with its attack on the formulation of the labour theory of value, suggesting that, as with Ricardo, the labour theory of value only provides an accurate theory of price when profits are zero (Samualson, 1957). Samualson wrote again in 1971 and 1974, seeking to establish two main propositions: first that the divergence in values and prices is a trivial matter, and second that the value calculus is a 'complicating detour' as prices and profits can be derived directly, given a subsistence wage rate.

This strand of criticism employs mathematical apparatus to reformulate Marx's theories, and in particular the transformation problem. Morishima (1973) deals with a variety of aspects of Marx's theory, including accumulation, crisis and value theory, but in particular, he attempts to analyse the transformation problem in both simple reproduction and in its dynamic context. There is much similarity between Morishima's analysis and that of Bortkiewicz, although no reference is made to Bortkiewicz in Morishima's book. The rate of profit and prices can be shown, according to Morishima, to be functions of the rate of exploitation, rate of turnover and the organic composition of capital, and the link between the rate of profit and the rate of surplus value is exposed and called the Fundamental Marxian Theorem.[2] This theorem states that a necessary and sufficient condition for there to be positive profits is that the rate of exploitation be positive.

In the aftermath of the publication of Sraffa's *Production of Commodities by Means of Commodities* (1960), Samualson attempted to use the Sraffian analysis against Marxian value theory. Sraffa's analysis was to 'solve' the transformation problem by sidestepping the 'problem' by using data on the conditions of production and income distribution, to derive commodity prices and the rate of profit. This appeared to confirm the earlier criticisms of Marx by Bortkiewicz, Samualson and others, concerning the logical priority of values. In 1971, Samualson reaffirmed his position that the labour theory of value was a 'complicating detour' in the light of Sraffa's work and argued that the general rate of profit and prices of production could be derived directly from information on the conditions of production and the distribution of income, and that Sraffa had actually confirmed his views expressed in his earlier 1957 paper (Samualson, 1971). In 1975, Steedman suggested that Sraffa had, through his analysis, revealed the existence of cases where the labour values of commodities may not, as Marx had implied, be positive. If this analysis is correct, then Marx's transformation cannot be undertaken because labour values may not be defined, or they may be zero, and as such, Marx's analysis cannot find prices of production. In addition, if labour values can be negative, as Sraffa suggests, then overall, this undermines the Fundamental Marxian Theorem.

From its origins with Bortkiewicz at the beginning of the century to the debate of the 1970s, the transformation problem had, it appears, been transformed. That is, from a problem of 'solving' for inputs to a problem that encompassed the quantitative relation of values to prices and the qualitative considerations surrounding the purpose of the transformation process itself.

The first attempt to 'rescue' Marx from this attack came in 1977 with Shaikh's, 'Marx's Theory of Value and the Transformation Problem' (Schwartz, 1977, pp. 106–39), in which it was claimed that Marx's transformation procedure in Volume II of *Capital* represented the first stage of a process which would ultimately provide the correct prices of production. This was severely criticized by the Sraffians[3] and Howard and King described Shaikh's analysis as the 'least successful attempt to vindicate Marx' (Howard and King, 1992, p. 276).

What has become known as the 'new solution' is associated with Dumenil (1980) and Foley (1982, 1986), although this has been endorsed by Lipietz (1982) and Glick and Ehrbar (1987). The 'new solution' essentially entails a redefining of the value of labour power as the value of money multiplied by the money wage, rather than the labour embodied in the wage-goods consumed by the labourer. However, while one of the invariance conditions of Marx is satisfied in the 'solution', that the sum of surplus value equals the sum of profits, the other is not, as the rate of profit in the value system is lower than that in the price system. However, it has been pointed out that in this construct, one cannot move from values to prices step by step and the 'new solution' only provides a mapping procedure from one to the other. (Hunt and Glick, in Eatwell et al., 1990). As such, it does not properly address the criticism of Samualson that employing labour values is a 'complicating detour'.

Naples (1989) suggests that the critiques of Marx's approach have tended to assume equilibrium, which involves market-clearing, uniform profits and stationary prices and have also tended to ignore the crucial distinction between labour and labour power.[4] The outcome is that, on the one hand, Marx is found to be incorrect in arguing that the profit rate is caused by exploitation and, on the other hand, Ricardo is found to be correct in his assertion that only wage and capital goods sectors affect the profit rate. Thus, by ignoring the distinction between labour and labour power, those who claim to have disproved the exploitation theory of the rate of profit have done so from an inaccurate view of Marx's analysis, by giving unwarranted priority to equilibrium, thereby substituting an equilibrium methodology for Marx's methodology. Naples argues that Bortkiewicz essentially assumed that the economy was in long-run equilibrium and abstracted from historical time whilst using gold as the numeraire, as opposed to Marx who denominated prices directly in value units as socially necessary labour-time. As such, Marx's theory does not represent Ricardo's theory with the addition of an exploitation equation, rather it is a fundamentally different construct of the origin of profits and, therefore, a uniform rate of profit was 'becoming' in capitalism as the outcome of the behaviour of individual capitalists as profit maximizers. Hence, to treat prices as stationary over time is not legitimate in a Marxian context and the use of long-run equilibrium should be rejected.

Summary

Saad-Filo (1997) considers the proposition that much of the literature concerning the transformation problem actually represents alternative approaches to that of Marx and because they either view the relation between values and prices in conflict with Marx, or indeed address totally different issues, they cannot claim to correct the transformation as presented by Marx himself. Indeed, Marx's intent in Chapter IX of *Capital*, Volume III, as we have seen, is not to mathematically derive prices from values, or indeed profits from surplus values, but to show how, in the capitalist mode of production, the value of labour power is transformed into the wage and surplus value is transformed into profit, being derived from the exploitation of labour. Such an interpretation would appear to provide a logical and coherent understanding of Marx's purpose and would suggest that the controversies that have arisen over this particular aspect have been, at the least, misplaced, and at the extreme, mischievous. And for the purpose of the overall exposition of the derivation of profits in a capitalist mode of production, Marx indeed presents a 'complete' solution. Marx is interested to show how and why profits deviate from surplus value but are determined by it and that price is only the outward form of value as a reflection of value in circulation. Thus, those who have maintained that there is a fundamental flaw in the Marxian schema have themselves engaged in a 'complicating detour' taking with them on their journey many of those who wished to argue that Marx had been misrepresented.

6
The Dynamics of Capitalism

Introduction

Essential to the Marxian analysis is the dynamic nature of capitalism and its ability to produce and to reproduce the capitalist relations of production. The reproduction of capital is a circular process in which commodities which embody surplus value are produced and sold. In addition, labour power and the means of production are bought to renew the process. Marx explains this by utilizing two models of a capitalist economy, one in a stationary state general equilibrium and another of a growing economy, to make manifest the role that money plays in the growth process. However, it is important to understand how this dynamism arises as a historical process that begins with the transition from feudalism to capitalism, the process of primitive accumulation and the appropriation of land from the peasant.

The stage theory of development

In the *German Ideology*, Marx and Engels argue that to exist, human beings must produce the means of subsistence and, in order to do this successfully, they must work together in a division of labour. In addition, a stage of development of production must be itself a product of history, in the sense that it must be an outcome of the achievements of past generations. Thus the development of productive forces must involve the development of the division of labour, forms of cooperation and of social organization. Hence, society develops through a succession of stages which are differentiated by distinct forms of property. In the ancient world, communal property was based on the exploitation of slaves, whereas in feudalism, it is the exploitation of serfs that forms the basis of the system. In capitalism, private property of the capitalist and exploitation of propertyless wage labourers define the relations of production. These stages represent successively higher levels of development of the productive forces and, crucially, each stage generates the conditions that are required for the next. However, the dynamic is present in each stage and, as such, each stage of development passes, itself, through various stages in its movement towards the next stage. Each transformation is associated with a new structure of social relations upon which social reproduction is based.

Primitive accumulation

Primitive accumulation refers to the historical process by which the capitalists were able to gain ownership of the means of production in the capitalist mode of production and in Chapter 26 of *Capital*, Vol. I Marx argues that it is necessary to understand how the mass of capital and labour power comes to be held in the hands of the commodity producers. Because the relations of production in capitalism are those of the class relations between those who own the means of production and those who do not, it is essential to the analysis as a whole to explain the process whereby primitive accumulation precedes capitalist accumulation. In other words, it is the process by which the capitalists come to own the means of production and hence provide the conditions necessary to move to the capitalist mode of production. Therefore, capitalism requires the class of owners of the means of production who buy the labour power of others, and also a class of free workers who sell their labour power. Thus, Marx shows how the economic structure of capitalism arises from the economic structure of feudal society within the dialectical method of investigation, the dynamic process of historical development. Hence, the emancipation of the serfs necessarily includes the dispossession of the means of production into the hands of a minority class. Marx argues that

> ...these newly freed men became sellers of themselves only after they had been robbed of all their means of production, and all the guarantees of existence afforded by the old feudal arrangements. And this history, the history of their expropriation is written in the annals of mankind in letters of blood and fire.
>
> (Marx, 1976, p. 875)

On the other hand, the capitalist has to displace the feudal lords who owned the sources of wealth. Because of the nature of Marx's method of analysis and the pre-eminence of history, he makes the important point that although the expropriation of the peasant is the basis for the movement to the capitalist mode of production, the history of expropriation will be different in both time and place, but Marx suggests that it takes its 'classic form' in England. Hence, Marx relates how the feudal retainers were disbanded at the end of the fifteenth century and beginning of the sixteenth century, producing a mass of free labour[1] and that by the seventeenth century around 24 per cent of the land had been enclosed. The reformation of the sixteenth century is also cited by Marx as increasing the size of the landless labourers as the estates of the Catholic Church were given away or sold, confiscating the property of those under church tithes and redistributing the lands of a very large feudal owner of the land in Britain at that time.

Enclosures

It has been argued that the technical changes that occurred in agriculture and industry in the eighteenth century were aided considerably by the enclosure of the open field (cf. Mingay, 1997). However, the extent and importance of enclosures, in terms of their economic and social consequences, are still a matter of intense debate among economic historians. It is possible to suggest, however, that enclosure was a prerequisite for many of the improvements that took place, and indeed, the perceived wisdom of the time was that the open field system was economically inefficient and was only defensible on social or cultural grounds. Although there appears to be little doubt that enclosure did not always result in technological improvements, it was still the most important single development in terms of extending the cultivable area and in improving the use of the land. The cultivated area was increased because of the elimination of the commons that had occupied a traditional and necessary place in the old rotation patterns as rough grazing land. It is also argued that enclosure made all other innovations in agriculture, and ultimately industry, possible.

Marx believed that enclosure was partly contrived to provide labour for industry by producing a surplus population.

> The bourgeois capitalist favoured the operation, with the intention, among other things of converting the land into a merely commercial activity, extending the area of large-scale agricultural production

and increasing the supply of free and rightless proletarians driven from their land.

(Marx, 1976, pp. 884–5)

In addition, Marx saves his most vitriolic attack to the final paragraph of Chapter 27, arguing that:

The spoilation of the Church's property, the fraudulent alienation of the state domains, the theft of the common lands, the usurpation of feudal and clan property and its transformation into modern private property under circumstances of ruthless terrorism, all these things were just so many idyllic methods of primitive accumulation. They conquered the field for capitalist agriculture, incorporated the soil into capital and created for the urban industries the necessary supplies of free and rightless proletarians.

(Marx, 1976, p. 895)

The view of agricultural improvement that remained orthodox until the 1920s was that of a picture of a functioning and balanced common land system which was destroyed by enclosure, driving the peasantry from their land and laying the foundation of agrarian capitalism dominated by a three-tier social structure of the landlord, the large tenant farmer and the landless labourer.[2] This view was reinforced by a popular sense of a lost rural idyll of bygone days. However, this assessment was strongly criticized by a number of economic historians who argued that the positive side of enclosure had been underestimated and, in particular, the large gains in grain production and increases in labour productivity that took place following enclosure had not been seriously considered in the formulation of the orthodox view. Nevertheless, in the 1950s and 1960s a new orthodoxy arose: Chambers (1953) concluded that the enclosure acts had the effect of reducing, but not of destroying the English peasantry, a thesis taken up by Mingay (1968), Beckett (1977) and Turner (1980). By contrast, in 1992, Allen argued that the economic benefits were limited and that a labour surplus accumulated in the countryside, finding an outlet in the spread of hand trades, and helping to swell the growth of London. Neeson (1993) also concluded that, in most Northamptonshire villages, enclosure destroyed the peasant economy. The debate is not settled by any means, it continues to provide economic historians with a subject that appears to be inexhaustible in its propensity for argument. However, within this debate, Marx has been criticized for his supposed exaggeration of the importance of enclosures to the process of the capitalization and com- mercialization of agriculture. In fact, enclosure for Marx was an impor- tant factor in the process of primitive accumulation, as evidenced in Part Eight of *Capital,* Volume I. Hence, in the context of Marxian polit- ical economy, it is a part of the dynamic, one factor in the capitaliza- tion of agriculture and the migration of labour to the urban sector and factory employment.

'Recent' debates

Proto-industrialization is seen as a phase in the development of modern industrial economies that preceded industrialization proper and is widely associated with Franklin F. Mendels (1972). In his article, Mendels studied Flanders and argued that pre-industrial society preceded and prepared modern industrialization proper. The rural labour force became involved in domestic industry, producing for supranational mar- kets, and gradually the population became liberated from an agrarian resource base as labour, previously unused due to seasonal underem- ployment, found employment throughout the year. It was necessary therefore, for production to expand, for specialization into regions of rural industry and for commercial agriculture. It was argued that proto- industrialization broke down the traditional regulating mechanisms of agrarian society, such as inheritance systems and other institutional controls, which had previously adjusted population growth to the available resources. This produced a self-sustaining proto-industrial spi- ral which generated labour, capital, entrepreneurship, commercial agri- culture and supraregional consumer markets, all of which were required for factory industrialization.

There are, however, several schools of thought in this area. For exam- ple, Levine (1977), studied two villages in Leicestershire, and while he agreed that proto-industrialization revolutionized demographic behav- iour, the associated population explosion led to the proletarianization of the workforce, breaking down the social structure and landowner- ship pattern of the traditional rural society. This created a large group in society who had no land to live from and therefore had to work for wages. This, he argues, created the preconditions for capitalism and industrialization. Mokyr (1976), however, rejects most of Mendels' argu- ments. He was convinced that proto-industrialization provided cheap, surplus labour which fuelled European industrialization by means of the mechanisms described by W. A. Lewis in the dualistic growth model. Thus, Mokyr argues that surplus labour was provided not by agriculture, but by proto-industry. Kriedte, Medick and Schlumbohm (1981) combine the models of Mendels and of Levine to turn the theory of proto-industrialization into a general model of European social and economic change in the period between the Middle Ages and the nineteenth century. Hence, it represents the second phase of a transformation process from feudalism to industrial capitalism. The first phase was the increasing differentiation of the agrarian class structure as agriculture moved into the commercial sector. Once proto-industries had arisen and become established in the countryside they could not expand into the towns due to the fact that the town guilds restricted their growth. Thus, they led to a transformation of the organization of industrial production through a succession of different stages of development: first, the workshop system (Kaufsystem) where rural producers retained autonomy over both production and selling; second, 'putting-out' (Verlags-system), where increased penetration of merchant capital into production took place, leading to the greater dependency of producers on the merchants until they no longer had independent access to markets, either for their raw materials or for the selling of the finished product; third, the concentration of production into centralized manufactories with the mechanized factory system.

In 1982, Mendels redefined proto-industrialization to stress several key characteristics. He argued that it was a regional phenomenon, but produced for external markets, providing employment in the countryside and creating a symbiosis of rural industry with the regional development of a commercial agriculture, creating a dynamic element whereby proto-industrialization produced economic growth over time through the industrial employment of rural workers. The effects are suggested as being four-fold: first, it led to population growth and the fragmentation of land; second, it created profits that could be used to purchase capital for factory industrialization; third, it provided merchants with the skills and experience required for factory industrialization; and fourth, it caused the commercialization of agriculture, which in turn led to urbanization and factory industrialization (Mendels, 1982).

Hence, the proto-industrialization thesis essentially examines the transition between the feudal stage and the capitalist stage, showing how the dynamic process produces changing relations of production and, although it is not based in a Marxian framework of analysis, it certainly supports the Marxian position and can be viewed as giving additional credence to the Marxian theory of history. Proto-industrialization of itself is not a sufficient argument to justify an acceptance of the Marxian model and, in particular, it cannot fully explain the rise of commercial capital. Indeed, Marx discusses three further factors that were at the genesis of the capitalist mode of production in England in the eighteenth century. Marx considers the growth of commercial capital in terms of the role of colonization, the slave trade and the National Debt.

International trade

The development from a pre-industrial to an industrial state necessarily entailed the exploitation of opportunities from international trade through the exchange of goods in overseas markets that are in excess supply in the domestic market for scarce commodities in the home economy. In such a situation it is possible to widen the market and to increase the level of domestic output. Thus, it is argued that foreign trade encourages specialization and allows an economy to develop skills and techniques of economic organization, while reaping the rewards of economies of scale, giving an incentive to greater productive activity. However, in the eighteenth century when most countries produced the vast majority of their own basic requirements, international trade tended to be limited to luxuries and those goods which were localized by their geographical incidence, for example tobacco, sugar, fruit and minerals. Hence, for pre-industrial Europe, the most obvious way in which to achieve economic growth was to extend the range of its trading relationships and to open up markets in other continents. The consequences of European extension were the numerous attempts to open up European trading horizons throughout the fifteenth, sixteenth and seventeenth centuries. The level of purchasing power in Africa, Asia and Latin America was low and they were indifferent to the goods that European traders had to offer. However, strategically, Britain was in a very favourable position as Atlantic trade had been opened up before 1750 and English plantations in the Caribbean had greatly extended the range of commodities which English merchants could sell in Europe. As with spices and tea in the Far East, the Caribbean products of sugar, cotton and tobacco were valuable commodities that were unobtainable in Europe and were rapidly becoming necessities of life. Thus there emerged a re-export trade which developed into a complex network of trading transactions centred on the City of London. In this network, the Caribbean islands, administered by a British plantation elite on the basis of a slave society, constituted the most valuable and intimate link.

In this process of multi-angular trade, weapons, hardware and spirits from Britain along with calicoes from India, were shipped to West Africa where they were exchanged for slaves, ivory and gold. The slaves were sold in the Caribbean for sugar, mahogany, tobacco and raw cotton, while the gold and ivory were shipped to the East to be exchanged for teas, silks, spices and calicoes. Tropical goods were sold in Europe for timber, hemp, iron and grain. On all of these transactions British merchants accumulated capital. Marx comments on this, arguing that:

> Liverpool grew fat on the basis of the slave trade. This was its method of primitive accumulation...While the cotton industry introduced child-slavery into England, in the United States it gave the impulse for the transformation of the earlier, more or less patriarchal slavery into a system of commercial exploitation. In fact the veiled slavery of the wage labourers in Europe needed the unqualified slavery of the New World as its pedestal.
>
> (Marx, 1976, pp. 924–5)

Thus, the capitalist class emerged through the opening up of the world market.[3] Much debate has taken place on the question of whether the external conquest that allowed this to occur was the main cause of the development of capitalism in Europe, or whether it merely accelerated the process which was by then already under way. A reading of *Capital* would suggest that Marx sees colonial expansion as an important part of the whole, but it must be viewed in that light – the whole, the development of capitalism, was not dependent upon one factor and each factor was interdependent. Hence, Marx can argue in Chapter 32 of *Capital*, Volume I, that:

> ...the combination embraces the colonies, the national debt, the modern tax system and the system of protection. These methods depend in part on brute force, for instance the colonial system. But they all employ the power of the state, the concentrated and organised force of society, to hasten as in a hothouse, the process of transformation of the feudal mode of production into the capitalist mode, and to shorten the transition. Force is the midwife of every old society which is pregnant with a new one. It is itself an economic power.
>
> (Marx, 1976, pp. 915–16)

Having shown that the process of economic development is a dynamic one as society is transformed in stages from one mode of production to another, we turn to the explanation of the dynamics of the capitalist mode. To illustrate this Marx employs two models, simple reproduction and extended reproduction.

Simple reproduction

This is a general equilibrium model of an economy in a stationary state. However, unlike the traditional general equilibrium model, money is not just a 'veil'. In fact, money plays a crucial role in intermediating all transactions, and money capital plays an important role in the process of capitalist production. In contrast to the traditional general equilibrium theory, Marx analyses the domination of the capitalist class over the working class. The model is a two-sector, two-class model of a monetary economy and the questions that Marx examines are threefold. First, if an economy is to continue in a stationary state, what transactions must take place between and within classes? Second, what transactions must take place between and within departments? Third, what role does money play in this process? The model which Marx analyses is the circular flow of a macro-economy, that is the movement of social capital. Therefore, Marx poses the question in these terms: 'How is the *capital* consumed in production replaced in its value out of the annual product, and how is the movement of this replacement intertwined with the consumption of surplus value by the capitalists and of wages by the workers?' (Marx, 1978a, p. 469). In other words, in aggregate, where does the money come from to realize the surplus value?

For Marx, it is crucial to show that, since surplus value is created in production, the process of circulation is consistent with the realizing of the surplus value. His answer is extremely elementary: the circular flow of income and the velocity of circulation allows this realization of surplus value. In order to illustrate this, Marx makes a number of necessary simplifying assumptions:

(a) There are only two classes: capitalists and workers, and there are no unproductive activities, other than the consumption of the capitalists.

(b) The organic compositions of capital are constant over time, but may differ from each other. Thus, there is no technical change in the model.

(c) Even though the organic compositions of capital are different, goods exchange at their values (the transformation problem is ignored) and each capitalist uses only their own capital and there is no borrowing or lending between the departments. Hence, there is no tendency for the equalization of profit rates between departments.

(d) The production process is described as a 'point-input, point-output' process as the inputs are made at the beginning of the production period, and outputs are obtained at the end of the period with each department's technology said to be 'productive'.

(e) There are constant returns to scale, due to the assumption in (b) above that there is no technical change.

(f) There are two departments: department I producing capital goods and department II producing consumption goods. However, department II consists of two subdepartments: (i) necessities (consumed by capitalists and workers) and (ii) luxuries (consumed by capitalists alone). Marx further assumes that the output of department I cannot be consumed and that of department II cannot serve as a means of production.

(g) There is unit turnover of capital, that is all fixed capital wears out in the course of the production period.

(h) Capitalists' net savings and investment are zero, such that their whole income is spent on consumption goods and replacement investment takes place only within the department.

(i) The wage is at subsistence level, therefore workers do not save.

(j) The rate of exploitation is constant and equal in the two departments.

(k) The economy is closed, there is no foreign trade.

$$C_1 + V_1 + S_1 = W_1 \text{ (department I)} \tag{6.1}$$
$$C_2 + V_2 + S_2 = W_2 \text{ (department II)} \tag{6.2}$$

Equation 6.1 states that constant capital of C_1 plus variable capital of V_1, produces an output of W_1 which exceeds the value of inputs by the amount of surplus value S_1, in the capital goods department. Equation 6.2 states the same for department II. Hence, the capitalists of each department have money capital with which they advance the wages payment for variable capital and constant capital. Therefore, money plays the role of the store of value (as money capital) and the medium of exchange in purchasing constant and variable capital. However, it must be noted that for a stationary state economy there is no net increase in its capital stock, and production continues at the same rate from year to year. In a two-departmental economy, we require that the production of each department be unchanging. Hence, the capitalists of department I produce capital goods so that they, and the workers, must trade with department II to provide them with the basic necessities and to provide capitalists with luxury goods. In other words, department I provides $V_1 + S_1$ of capital goods to department II and purchases consumption goods of (equal) value of C_2. The capitalists of department I spend C_1 within their own department on maintaining capital intact (replacement investment) in order to maintain a constant rate of production in the future. They spend their surplus value, S_1, on the purchase of consumption goods from department II. The workers in department I sell their labour power to the capitalists of that department and then spend V_1 on buying consumer goods from department II. Department II capitalists spend their surplus value, S_2, within the department. The workers of department II sell their labour power to 'their' capitalists and then purchase from them, consumption goods to the value V_2. To maintain their capital intact, the capitalists of department II have to buy capital goods worth C_2 in value from department I capitalists. Therefore, assuming a stationary state and voluntary and fair exchange, equilibrium requires that $V_1 + S_1$ of department I's capital goods are exchanged for C_2 of department II's consumption goods. This is illustrated in equation 6.3.

$$C_1 + \underline{V_1 + S_1} = W_1$$
$$\underline{C_2} + V_2 + S_2 = W_2$$

6.3

Equilibrium requires:

$$C_1 + C_2 = W_1 = C_1 + V_1 + S_1$$

6.4

(demand for capital goods)   = (supply of capital goods)
or by elimination:

$$C_2 = V_1 + S_1$$

6.5

Similarly:

$$V_1 + S_1 + V_2 + S_2 = W_2 = C_2 + V_2 + S_2$$

6.6

(demand for consumption goods) = (supply of consumption goods)
or by elimination:

$$V_1 + S_1 = C_2$$

6.7

Thus, both conditions reduce to the same equilibrium condition.

The equilibrium condition simply states that the value of capital goods sold by department I must equal the value of consumption goods sold by department II. These intra- and inter-departmental trades permit the realization of surplus value created in the two departments via the use of money as a medium of circulation. Hence Marx argues that:

> It is therefore literally correct, in the present case, that the capitalist himself cast into circulation the money into which he converts his surplus value, i.e. by means of which he realizes it, and, what is more, by spending this on means of consumption.
>
> (Marx, 1978a, p. 496)

$$4000 \ C_1 + \underline{1000 \ V_1} + \underline{1000 \ S_1} = 6000 \ W_1$$
$$\underline{2000 \ C_2} + 500 \ V_2 + 500 \ S_1 = 3000 \ W_2$$

6.8

The underlined components in 6.8 are those which are exchanged between departments. In department I, the $4000 \ C_1$ consists of means of production which are produced by department I itself. The $1000 \ V_1$ and $1000 \ S_1$ consist of consumption goods which are produced by department II. Conversely for department II, the $500 \ V_2$ and the $500 \ S_2$ consist of consumption goods produced by department II itself and the $2000 \ C_2$ consist of means of production produced by department I. Therefore, department I must obtain from department II a quantity of consumption goods sufficient to provide for the consumption of capitalists. Department II must obtain from department I a quantity of means of production, sufficient to replace the constant capital used up in its production. In equilibrium, these requirements must be equal, and in the example of 6.8, they are at 2000. Hence in an economy with free and fair exchange, capitalists create surplus value in the production process and then realize it in the process of circulation through the means of money acting as a means of exchange. The creation and realization of surplus value has therefore been masked by the process of circulation.

Extended reproduction

Marx then proceeds to analyse the role of money in a growing economy. Here he is interested in showing how surplus value created in an economy is realized and then provides for capital accumulation and therefore growth. The focus is *not* on growth, but on how money accommodates the growth process via its role in capital accumulation.

That is, a growing economy requires additional money for circulation and this additional money comes via two sources: (a) increased gold production and (b) increased velocity of circulation.

As in the case of simple reproduction, surplus value created in production is realized in the process of circulation via the inter- and intra-departmental trade flows, as capitalists advance money capital, buy labour power and constant capital. The surplus value created is partly consumed and partly saved. The savings are initially accumulated as latent (or virtual) money capital, that is a temporary hoard for accumulation. Any sudden changes in hoarding will disrupt the circular flow and lead to under/over-production. The model that Marx employs is that of balanced growth equilibrium, where we retain all of the assumptions of simple reproduction except assumption (h), i.e. capitalists' net savings and investment are zero, and this is replaced by: (i) department I capitalists consume half of their surplus value and invest the remainder in department I; (ii) department II capitalists invest in department II as much as is required to remain in equilibrium and as such can be described as passive adjusters; (iii) the investment in each department is such as to leave the organic composition of capital unchanged. In addition, the assumption that the wage rate is at subsistence such that workers do not save is extended to assume an infinitely elastic supply of labour at the subsistence wage rate.

Hence, the capitalists of department I use their surplus value, S_1, for the consumption of wage and luxury goods, S_{13}, for adding to constant capital in their department, ΔC_1 or S_{11}, and for adding to variable capital in their department (ΔV_1 or S_{12}) so as to keep K_1 constant. Therefore:

$$K_1 = \frac{C_1}{V_1} = \frac{C_1 + \Delta C_1}{V_1 + \Delta V_1} = \frac{\Delta C_1}{\Delta V_1}$$

$$S_1 \equiv S_{11} + S_{12} + S_{13} \equiv \Delta C_1 + \Delta V_1 + S_{13} \qquad 6.9$$

Similarly in department II:

$$K_2 = \frac{C_2}{V_2} = \frac{C_2 + \Delta C_2}{V_2 + \Delta V_2} = \frac{\Delta C_2}{\Delta V_2}$$

$$S_2 \equiv S_{21} + S_{22} + S_{23} \equiv \Delta C_2 + \Delta V_2 + S_{23} \qquad 6.10$$

Algebraically:

$$C_1 + V_1 + \Delta C_1 + \Delta V_1 + S_{13} = W_1$$
$$C_2 + V_2 + \Delta C_2 + \Delta V_2 + S_{23} = W_2 \qquad 6.11$$

Equilibrium requires the output (supply) of capital goods to equal the demand.
Therefore:

$$C_1 + \Delta C_1 + C_2 + \Delta C_2 = W_1 = C_1 + V_1 + \Delta C_1 + \Delta V_1 + S_{13} \qquad 6.12$$
$$\text{(Demand)} \qquad\qquad \text{(Supply)}$$

or:

$$C_2 + \Delta C_2 = V_1 + \Delta V_1 + S_{13} \qquad 6.13$$

Similarly for the consumption goods department:

$$V_1 + \Delta V_1 + S_{13} + V_2 + \Delta V_2 + S_{23} = W_2 = C_2 + V_2 + \Delta C_2 + \Delta V_2 + S_{23} \qquad 6.14$$
$$\text{(Demand)} \qquad\qquad\qquad \text{(Supply)}$$

or:

$$V_1 + \Delta V_1 + S_{13} = C_2 + \Delta C_2 \qquad 6.15$$

This inter-departmental trade can be shown as:

$$C_1 + \Delta C_1 + V_1 + \Delta V_1 + S_{13}$$
$$C_2 + \Delta C_2 + V_2 + \Delta V_2 + S_{13} \qquad 6.16$$

Numerically:

Initial Period – Year 0

	C	V	S	W	K	
Dept I	4000	1000	1000	6000	4	6.17
Dept II	1500	750	750	3000	2	
				9000		

Department I accumulates $1/2\ S_1 = 500$, of which:

$$\Delta C_1 = 4/5 \times 500 = 400$$
$$\Delta V_1 = 1/5 \times 500 = 100 \qquad 6.18$$

Department I capitalists consume $1/2\ S_1 = 500 = S_{13}$.

Department II capitalists accumulate just enough constant capital so that demand and supply of capital goods are equal, which is:

$$6000 - 4400 - 1500 = W_1 - (C_1 + \Delta C_1) - C_2 = 100 = \Delta C_2 \qquad 6.19$$

To keep K_2 constant, department II must have $\Delta V_2 = 50$, thus department II capitalists' consumption is:

$$750 - 100 - 50 = 600 = S_{23} \qquad 6.20$$

We now turn to consumption demand:

(a) *Demand by workers for consumption goods*:

$$\text{Dept I } 1000\,V_1 + 100\,\Delta V_1 = 1100$$
$$\text{Dept II } 750\,V_2 + 50\,\Delta V_2 = 800$$
$$\text{Total demand for workers} = 1900 \qquad 6.21$$

(b) *Demand by capitalists for consumption goods*:

$$\text{Dept I } 500\,S_{13}$$
$$\text{Dept II } 600\,S_{23}$$
$$\text{Capitalists' total demand} = 1100 \qquad 6.22$$

Therefore, aggregate demand for consumption goods is:

$$1900 + 1100 = 3000 = \text{Supply of}$$
$$\text{consumption goods by dept II} \qquad 6.23$$

Hence:

$$\text{Dept I } 4000\,C_1 \rightarrow 4400\,C_1;\ 1000\,V_1 \rightarrow 1100\,V_1$$
$$\text{Dept II } 1500\,C_2 \rightarrow 1600\,C_2;\ 750\,V_2 \rightarrow 800\,V_2 \qquad 6.24$$

Therefore at the end of year 0 (the beginning of year 1):

	[C]	[V]	[S]	[W]	[K]
Dept I	4400	1100	1100	6600	4
Dept II	1600	800	800	3200	2
				9800	

6.25

At end of year 1 (the beginning of year 2):

	[C]	[V]	[S]	[W]	[K]
Dept I	4840	1210	1210	7260	4
Dept II	1760	880	880	3520	2
				10780	

6.26

In the first year, department I grows at a rate of 10 per cent and department II grows at a rate of 6.67 per cent. In year 2 both departments grow at a balanced rate of 10 per cent. Given the peculiar assumptions that are made, it is not surprising that the model converges rapidly to a balanced growth path. However, Marx uses this to illustrate how, even under 'pure' conditions of balanced growth, money and circulation allow for the realization of surplus value. This surplus value is then used for capital accumulation and, therefore, leads to a growing economy. If this were a growth model, there would be many criticisms. The implied investment behaviour is rather strange, because even though the value profit rates differ, capitalists only invest in their own department. This conflicts with Volume I of *Capital*, where competitive behaviour leads to the equalization of the profit rate. Another question that the model raises is that of why capitalists maintain a constant organic composition of capital. In *Capital*, Volume I, Marx argues that capitalist development leads to technological change and an increasing organic composition of capital. Also, why does the rate of profit remain constant over time in the model? This is inconsistent with the tendency towards a falling rate of profit over time outlined in *Capital*, Volume III. Finally, why do the capitalists of department II act so obligingly as to maintain equilibrium by acting as 'passive adjusters'?

These criticisms would be valid if Marx were analysing a growth model. However, Marx was not concerned with growth as such. He is attempting to illustrate that, even assuming the best possible case for 'bourgeois' economics (an equilibrium model of a stationary state or growing economy), surplus value is created in production and is realized in exchange (circulation). Marx was at great pains to show how capitalists could get more back from a system than they put into it. The surplus value could not be the result of a process of circulation since in aggregate, one person's gain is another person's loss: a zero-sum game. The surplus value is created in production but goes through the circulation process, thus disguising the exploitation from all its participants, from the workers and from the capitalists. Hence, Marx did not believe that the capitalist system would grow at a steady state equilibrium. The purpose of this analysis is to outline the several weak links in the chain of circulation which will increase the possibility of crisis.

Summary

From the stage theory of development it is important to note that although each economy will not necessarily follow the same pattern of development, nor the same timescale, all economies will pass through the stages. It therefore follows that stages of development cannot be skipped because the structures and relations required by one stage are provided by the contradictions that became apparent in the previous stage. For example, the collapse of the Soviet Bloc is often used by political analysts and others to suggest that Marx and Engels were incorrect in their assertions in the *Communist Manifesto*. However, one should argue that indeed the collapse of the state socialism of the Soviet Bloc actually proves that Marx was correct in that the former Soviet Union did not pass through the mature capitalist stage of development and therefore could not successfully make the transition to socialism. Hence, the collapse vindicates the Marxian analysis.[4] The dynamics of the development process in this stage theory are shown to be relevant in the context of the capitalist mode of production by Marx's use of the two models of a capitalist economy, one in a stationary state and the other in a growing economy. It is also important to re-emphasize the point that Marx was not attempting to analyse the growth process, it is a tool that is employed to illustrate that value is logically prior to price and that surplus value is created in production and is logically prior to profit which is realized in the circulation process. Hence, the dynamics that are evident in the capitalist mode of production are a product of the inherent contradictions of the previous stages and of the antithesis of capitalism itself.

7
Capital Accumulation and Technical Change

Introduction

Capital accumulation for Marx is promoted by competition, which compels individual capitalists to invest and accumulate in order to survive. In addition, those firms which grow faster will benefit from economies of scale and increasing returns through an expansion of their market share and subsequent higher profits. However, the process of capital accumulation does not proceed in a smooth and orderly manner because when expected profits are low, capitalists halt the process of investment and accumulation and hence precipitate a general crisis involving unsold goods and high unemployment. Therefore, accumulation is a cyclical process in which forces unique to capitalism work to reassert the cycle of accumulation and investment. As unemployment rises, the real wage falls and profits rise, leading to a new cycle of accumulation and investment. The dynamic nature of the capitalist mode of production is identified with several elements that are inherent to the system and Marx shows how the system itself involves the capitalist imperative to accumulate and the competitive process leads to the requirement to innovate and to introduce labour-saving techniques into the production process. This ensures the rising productivity of labour and therefore economic growth. However, this dynamic brings with it the seeds of its own destruction, and Marx is able to illustrate why the very success of the capitalist mode of production will lead to its eventual demise as this success is based upon conflict and contradiction. This itself is described as the 'inner logic' of capitalism, the continuous reduction in the socially necessary labour-time required to produce commodities as the competitive process forces the introduction of labour-saving technology, reducing the quantity of labour that is absorbed by each commodity.

The role of the capitalist

The amount of surplus value that is created is dependent upon the length of the working day and the intensity of exploitation. The amount of profit that is realized by the capitalist class as a whole, as well as by an individual capitalist, depends upon the competitive process, working through the sphere of exchange (circulation). Then, the capitalists must choose how to allocate their profit between capitalist consumption and accumulation. The allocation for accumulation is further subdivided into additions to constant capital and additions to variable capital. Thus, by 'accumulation', Marx refers to spending on constant capital and spending on variable capital. In Marx's model, capitalists are assumed to be profit maximizers and therefore are treated similarly to 'bourgeois economics'. They strive continuously to minimize costs and maximize profits through increases in the exploitation of labour and by continuously introducing new and more efficient machinery. Marx explains it thus in *Capital*, Volume I:

> As the conscious bearer of this movement, the possessor of money becomes a capitalist. His person, or rather his pocket, is the point from which the money starts, and to which it returns. The objective content of the circulation we have been discussing – the valorization of value – is his subjective purpose, and it is only in so far as the appropriation of ever more wealth in the abstract is the sole driving force behind his operations that he functions as a capitalist, i.e. as personified and endowed with consciousness and will. Use-values must therefore never be treated as the immediate aim of the capitalist; nor must the profit on any single transaction. His aim is rather the unceasing movement of profit-making. This boundless drive for enrichment, this passionate chase after value is common to the capitalist and the miser; but while the miser is merely the capitalist gone mad, the capitalist is a rational miser. The ceaseless augmentation of value, which the miser seeks to attain by saving his money from circulation, is achieved by the more acute capitalist by means of throwing his money again and again into circulation.
>
> (Marx, 1976, pp. 254–5)

Marx identifies *total* profits with *total* surplus values. However, this is not the case for an individual capitalist, where profits are not equal to the surplus value created in that capitalist's enterprise. It is worth noting at this point that the discussion of accumulation takes place in different spheres of abstraction in the volumes of *Capital* for different motives: in Volume I, Marx assumes that equal organic compositions of capital, and therefore prices, equal values. In Volume II, Marx's discussion of accumulation is secondary to his concern with studying the process of circulation, and thus exchange. In Volume III, it is argued that Marx's discussion of accumulation should be in terms of price, but he constantly identifies surplus value with profits for an individual capitalist, as well as for the capitalist class as a whole, where this would be acceptable.

However, it is the case that, assuming a constant rate of exploitation, a capitalist is able to increase the surplus value created by increasing *variable* capital, that is, by employing more labour power. Therefore, the question needs to be addressed as to what gives the capitalist an incentive to increase the *constant* capital? First of all, given fixed coefficients in the production process, an individual capitalist must expand constant capital proportionately with variable capital in order to retain a constant organic composition of capital.[1] Hence, what is it that sets the limit to the process of expansion for the individual capitalist? Neoclassical theories of investment argue that the existence of a concave production function, and hence diminishing returns, sets a finite limit to the size of the firm. However, for Marx, capital accumulation (in terms of additional expenditure on constant capital and variable capital) is constrained by the capitalist's realized profits, the choice that the capitalist makes as to how much to consume and the propensity to borrow and the availability of borrowings. Marx points to the development of joint stock companies, which increased the ability of larger companies to raise much larger and increasing amounts of money capital. In terms of the choice between capitalist consumption and accumulation, as the capitalist gets wealthier he/she wishes to consume more and accumulate less. Thus there arises a conflict between consumption and accumulation. Marx does not fully explain how this conflict is resolved, but assumes a marginal propensity to consume (save) that is constant over time. In addition, as well as a capitalist desire to maximize profits, they wish to increase their control (and therefore power) over the workers. Therefore, there is also a sociological objective of the capitalist.[2] Therefore, given a constant marginal propensity to consume out of surplus value, does the capitalist accumulate all of the remaining surplus value? If this is the case then there should be no effective demand (realization) problems. As such Say's Law would hold, supply creates its own demand. But Marx attacks Say's Law, as did Keynes. Therefore, in the short run, there are periods when the capitalist does not automatically invest all surplus value that remains after consumption and this will cause realization (effective demand) problems. However, in the long run, capitalists will invest all their surplus value remaining after capitalist consumption and the underlying reason for this, for Marx, is sociological. There exists a sociological imperative, i.e. it is the function of a capitalist in a capitalist economy to accumulate. Hence the oft-quoted phrase from *Capital*, Volume I, 'Accumulate, accumulate! That is Moses and the prophets!...Accumulation for the sake of accumulation, production for the sake of production' (Marx, 1976, p. 742). It is the capitalist system that impels the capitalist to accumulate, and the capitalist must accumulate to survive because of competitive forces. Therefore, we can now state the capitalist's objective: to maximize profits, to increase their power over workers and to survive in a competitive economy.

Marx argues that because production is a continuous process, it is the case that the elements that are involved in the production process must be continuously reproduced, that is due to the fact that labour power and the means of production are constantly consumed, they must therefore all be constantly replaced. Given this necessity, it follows that if the capitalist were to consume the surplus value that is produced in its entirety, then production will only continue at a constant level because capital of the same magnitude would be advanced in each production period, resulting in simple reproduction. In fact, however, beginning with a certain amount of capital, the capitalist class restore their advances, plus surplus value and can therefore consume the surplus value and retain enough capital to begin the process again. This is due to the fact that the workers have only their labour power to sell and the wages paid in return for this labour power are simply enough to meet their consumption requirements, and they therefore must offer their labour power for sale in the next production period. Hence, in the production process the social and material conditions for the production of surplus value have been reproduced.

This analysis is in direct opposition to those bourgeois theories of capitalist accumulation which extol the virtues of abstinence of the capitalist class and suggest that profit is the reward to the capitalist for avoidance of the temptations of luxury:

> ...whenever he [the capitalist] valorizes their value as capital by incorporating labour-power into them instead of eating them up, steam engines, cotton, railways, manure, horses and all; or, as the vulgar economist childishly conceives, instead of dissipating 'their value' in luxuries and other articles of consumption.
>
> (Marx, 1976, p. 745)

Marx argues that both Adam Smith and David Ricardo were correct in their analysis that the part of the surplus that is spent on the employment of extra productive workers should be envisaged as accumulation, but the employment of unproductive workers, for example domestic servants, counts as consumption, while the hoarding of money counts as neither accumulation nor consumption. However, Marx asserts that they were incorrect in their assumption that accumulation consists wholly of the advancement of wages to extra workers, because this is tantamount to overlooking the additional means of production that is required to expand production.

Given the fact that the capitalist will divide the surplus value between consumption and accumulation, it would follow that the level of accumulation is dependent upon the amount of surplus value. Hence, if wages can be forced downwards, or if labour becomes more productive, then accumulation will increase. However, as productivity rises, the value of commodities will fall, enabling the capitalist to purchase a greater number of commodities with the same amount of surplus value. In addition, as the number of workers increases, the same rate of surplus value will correspond to a greater mass of surplus value. The outcome is that the purchasing power of the capitalist consistently rises, increasing both accumulation and luxury consumption.

Determination of the level of accumulation

The level of accumulation depends upon the amount of surplus value because surplus value can be divided between consumption and accumulation. The amount of surplus value is in turn determined by the rate of exploitation and therefore more accumulation is possible if wages are forced down or labour becomes more productive or more intense. However, as productivity is increased, the value of commodities falls such that, an equal amount of surplus value will allow the capitalist to purchase more commodities. Hence the purchasing power of the capitalist is constantly increasing, permitting an increase in both luxury consumption and accumulation. Marx explains this in the following passage:

> With a given degree of exploitation of labour power, the mass of surplus-value produced is determined by the number of workers simultaneously exploited; this corresponds, although in varying proportions, with the magnitude of the capital. Thus, the more that capital increases by means of successive accumulations, the more

does the sum of value increase that is divided into a fund for consumption and a fund for accumulation. The capitalist can therefore live a more pleasant life, and at the same time 'renounce' more. And, finally, the more the scale of production extends, along with the mass of the capital advanced, the greater the expansive capacity of its driving forces.

(Marx, 1976, p. 757)

The 'good' or successful capitalists aim to maximize their profits and to accumulate in order to increase their capital stock.[3] Operating in a competitive system, the innovating capitalist can reap the short-term benefits and therefore the capitalist is continuously expanding the production of commodities for exchange. However, Marx suggests that capitalists will accumulate in order to counteract the downward trend in the rate of profit, such that when the rate of profit falls below the 'normal level', the capitalists will augment accumulation and introduce innovations. 'Improvements, inventions, greater economy in the means of production, etc. are introduced not at times when prices rise above their average level but when they fall below it, i.e. when profit falls below its normal rate' (Marx, 1969b, pp. 26–7). However, in the long run, the rate of profit will depend on the rate of accumulation. In the same manner, bursts of accumulation occur when the wage rate increases, substituting capital for labour, but in the long run, wages are dependent upon accumulation:

... the rate of accumulation is the independent, not the dependent variable; the rate of wages is the dependent, not the independent variable. Thus, when the industrial cycle is in its phase of crisis, a general fall in the price of commodities is expressed as a rise in the relative value of money, and, in the phase of prosperity, a general rise in the price of commodities is expressed as a fall in the relative value of money.

(Marx, 1976, pp. 770–1)

Thus, the cyclical nature of accumulation is inherent in the competitive nature of the system and is driven by innovation and the profit level.

Technical change

Marx outlines a set of concepts that are essential for an understanding of the process of capital accumulation in Chapter 25 of *Capital*, Volume I.

He refers to the value composition of capital, to mean the ratio of constant to variable capital, measured in values, and the technical composition of capital as the same ratio, but measured in terms of use-values, that is, the mass of means of production relative to the living labour that is employed. Because the technical composition of capital cannot be measured quantitatively (that is, one cannot be divided by the other as means of production and labour are quantitatively different), Marx employs the organic composition of capital, defined as, the value composition of capital, determined by its technical composition. Hence, changes in the organic composition show how the value composition would have altered if the values of individual commodities employed as means of production, and the value of labour power, had remained as constants. However, in the capitalist mode of production, as the productivity of labour increases, so too does the technical, and therefore the organic, composition of capital. Hence, as accumulation proceeds and individual capitals grow, competition causes centralization, as smaller capitals are forced out through the lower costs of the large capitals.

Accumulation and innovation are bedfellows because, in essence, capital accumulation is linked inseparably to technical change. It follows that accumulation not only brings in new types of machinery, but it also ushers in new methods of production, and an increasing division of labour. All technology is described as being of the 'embodied' variety, that is, new capital goods embody the latest technology. Thus, the accumulation of fixed capital and innovation are synonymous. It also follows that an individual capitalist will attempt to increase productivity through the substitution of constant capital in place of labour power and hence, production of the commodity progressively takes place using smaller amounts of labour embodied than those of competitors. But the reaction of the competitors has to be to follow suit. Hence, the organic composition of capital can reasonably be assumed to be increasing during the course of capitalist development. This reflects the tendency, inherent in capitalism, for technical change to be biased towards labour-saving innovations, and an immediate implication of this is that since the organic composition rises, the equilibrium growth path is not balanced. In fact, department I (the capital goods sector) will be producing an increasing proportion of total output. This also means that the rate of exploitation is not constant and, given the subsistence wage, the relative share of workers in net output declines. As in the reproduction models, Marx assumes that all surplus value takes the form of industrial profits, but now ignores the distinction between the two departments. Although technical change in capitalism is assumed to be predominantly labour-saving, Marx does recognize that labour using innovation may exist. However, the overall net effect is expected to be in the direction of labour-saving over the long period, hence, increasing the productivity of labour. Therefore, if technological change is predominantly labour-saving, the employment of labour power will grow less rapidly than does constant capital and hence, the demand for labour power is a function of the accumulation of capital. Since accumulation increases the organic composition of capital, the growth in demand for labour power *must* be slower than the growth of constant capital. In addition, since the value of a commodity is the social average, the innovating capitalist can capture 'excess' surplus value. The output is sold according to social value, which is greater than the individual innovator's value, and then, competition will force other capitalists to introduce the same methods of production. This will therefore reduce the social value of the commodity and hence, remove the 'excess' surplus value of the innovator. Therefore, the capitalist system is a dynamic system with continual change taking place.[4]

Technical change makes the existing machinery obsolete and reduces the economic life of machines in general, thus raising the value of the constant capital employed. It follows therefore, that this process will increase the rate of unemployment, not due to deficiencies in aggregate demand, but it exists when all existing capital is fully staffed. During the process of accumulation there is an increasing division of labour in industrial production. The larger firms accumulate at a faster rate due to the fact that they have greater amounts of profit. Due to increasing returns to scale, the larger capitalists have an advantage over smaller firms and, in addition, because the larger firms accumulate at a faster rate, they produce with technologically superior machines. Hence, the small firms are forced into bankruptcy by, technically superior, large firms. Therefore, increasing accumulation leads to the tendency towards increasing concentration, that is, increasing monopoly, and as larger capitalists accumulate and grow larger and become more powerful, they take over, or merge with, the smaller capitalists.

Marx emphasizes the point in Volume III of *Capital*:

> No Capitalist voluntarily applies a new method of production, no matter how much more productive it may be or how much it might raise the rate of surplus value, if it reduces the rate of profit. But every new method of production of this kind makes commodities cheaper.
>
> (Marx, 1981, p. 373)

It is the effect of the competitive process that causes a reduction in the value of commodities, the actions of the capitalists, as a class, attempting to increase the productivity of labour. Individually, the capitalists strive to introduce new, labour-saving, techniques of production in order to sell the commodities above their price of production, and even above their value, as competitors use techniques with higher costs of production. To remain in business other capitalists must introduce these new techniques which has the effect of reducing the labour-time necessary to produce the commodities and hence reducing the value of the commodities. Therefore, as individuals, the capitalists are striving to increase their surplus value, and thus their profits, but as a class, the competitive process ensures that in fact the opposite occurs. This is the logical outcome of the capitalist mode of production.

However, this is not the only mechanism by which capitalism moves towards crisis. The need to ensure that wages remain at the subsistence level in the long term requires of the system a level of unemployment, an amount of the reserve army of labour, not only to effect the subjugation of the workforce, but also to maintain the power of the capitalist, as a class, over labour to increase the rate of exploitation. However, the effect of this need for unemployment leads to a realization crisis as the capitalists are unable to realize their profit out of surplus value in the circulation process as fewer and fewer members of the labouring population are able to afford the products offered for sale by the capitalists. Hence, while the introduction of new techniques of production reduce the value of commodities and add to the reserve army of labour, the demand for those same commodities is falling as the market for labour tightens, not through any biological law of population change, but as a logical outcome of the capitalist mode of production.

The cause of unemployment

There are several interrelated causes of unemployment in a capitalist economy but at the forefront is the increasing organic composition of capital over time. In the initial stages of capitalist development the growth of the supply of labour power to the capitalist sector occurs through the decline of the pre-capitalist sector. However, since the productivity of the capitalist sector is higher than that of the pre-capitalist sector, more labour is released than can be absorbed in the expansion of the capitalist sector. This process is reinforced over time with the tendency towards increasing concentration, which reduces the number of capitalists, while increasing the size of the proletariat. The rate of technical change, and its form, is conditioned by the relative scarcities of the appropriate inputs. Hence if in any period, there is an excess demand for labour, so that wages increase and the rate of profits falls, the application of labour-saving technology will be accelerated, thus reducing the demand for labour power. In addition, because the organic composition of capital rises over time, the demand for labour power will be falling relatively as a greater part of capital is used to purchase means of production and less in the purchase of labour power. The reserve army of labour allows the total domination of capital over labour. It is the *key* economic force which keeps the real wage down to subsistence level, ensuring that the techniques of increasing the productivity of labour increase the rate of exploitation and, thus, the relative share of the capitalist class in net output. At the same time, the concentration of capital occurs such that the increasing relative share of net output appropriated by the capitalist class accrues to the surviving capitalists, causing an increasing polarization of the class structure.

Within the general term, the reserve army of labour, Marx outlines the different parts into which it can be divided, the floating, the latent and the stagnant. The floating form is made up of unemployed workers who previously have been employed by capital and already reside in the industrial districts and the industrial cycle successively forces large numbers of workers into the reserve army and then recruits them back into employment. Marx identifies this section of the reserve army as the most readily available to capital when required. The latent surplus population arise from the introduction of capitalist agriculture which creates large underemployment in the rural sector and hence ensures that new workers are always available to the urban sector. Those who are employed on an irregular basis and can command only very low wages when they are employed are categorized as the stagnant reserve army, forming what Marx describes as an inexhaustible reservoir of disposable labour power.

What Marx refers to as the industrial reserve army is therefore a pool of unemployed, or underemployed workers, that is in a continuous state of change in both size and composition. Both the demand and the supply of labour are affected by capital accumulation: on the supply side, capital accumulation is a labour-saving process which causes workers to become unemployed, and on the demand side, unemployed workers reduce their demand for a set of commodities, leading to a fall in price and a decrease in the production of that set of commodities, and therefore to an increase in unemployment in that sphere of production. However, it must be noted that one effect of this process may be that the demand for labour in the machine producing sector will partially offset this reduction in employment. The overall effect therefore depends on the organic composition of capital in the machine producing sector, as well as the rate of exploitation in that sector. On this point Marx argues that capital accumulation leads to a rising organic composition of capital and therefore the process as a whole leads to an increase in the size of the reserve army of labour.

Summary

Marx analyses the laws of motion of the capitalist economy by looking at the dialectical nature of capital accumulation. Each individual capitalist, in attempting to increase profit, accumulates and introduces technological change. Other capitalists are forced, by competition, to imitate and thus negate the advance of the innovator. Hence, the competitive system perpetuates this process. However, the dialectical process leads to a negation of the competitive system itself, i.e. capital accumulation destroys the competitive system and brings increasing monopoly. This is the so-called 'inner logic' of capitalism, whereby it is the very success of the system that effects its inherent contradictions bringing forth the crisis of capitalism.

8
The Tendency for the Rate of Profit to Fall and the Realization Crisis

Introduction

For Marx, the law of the tendency of the rate of profit to fall is an essential element in the laws of motion of a capitalist economy. It occurs in a dynamic context as technological change leads to the increasing productivity of labour with the increase in capital accumulation leading to an increasing organic composition of capital which effects a fall in the rate of profit. This in turn leads the capitalists to accumulate and innovate to prevent the fall, leading to centralization and concentration of capital. The law is composed of two opposing forces that are contradictory and the resolution of these contradictions is what creates the movement within the system. The realization crisis is a problem that is discussed throughout the history of economic thought either in explicit or implicit terms as underconsumption theory or problems associated with the lack of effective demand and is therefore not unique to a Marxian analysis. However, the manner in which Marx sets his discussion of the problems of realization is firmly set in the specific nature of the capitalist relations of production. Hence, the crisis occurs as a result of commodity production being motivated by accumulation rather than use-value, the dynamic nature of the system which involves economic change and disrupts the pattern of production, and the increasing division of labour produced by capitalist commodity production.

The tendency for the rate of profit to fall

Marx assumes profits to be rents, interest and industrial profits, hence when Marx refers to a falling rate of profit, it is perfectly feasible for the rate of industrial profits to be rising, i.e. the average rate may fall as rent and interest fall, while industrial profits are rising. Marx also identifies total surplus values with total profits, but this is true only if there is no transformation problem. However, this does not detract from his argument. Once we accept that there is a transformation problem we need to distinguish the value of the rate of profit, r(V) from the prices of production rate of profit, r(P) and also the rate of profit in terms of market prices, r(MP). Therefore:

Value rate of profit

$$r(V) = \frac{S(V)}{C(V) + (V)} \qquad 8.1$$

Prices of production rate of profit

$$r(P) = \frac{S(P)}{C(P) + V(P)} \qquad 8.2$$

Rate of profit in market prices

$$r(MP) = \frac{S(MP)}{C(MP) + V(MP)} \qquad 8.3$$

Capitalists do not see r(V) or r(P); they only observe r(MP) and respond to this. The law of the falling rate of profit is a long-term relationship and applies to r(V) or r(P). The law assumes that the rate of exploitation is constant and in Marx's words, '... this gradual growth in the constant capital, in relation to the variable, must necessarily result in a *gradual fall in the general rate of profit*, given that the rate of surplus value, or the level of exploitation of labour by capital, remains the same' (Marx, 1981, p. 318). Hence, there is a tendency for the organic composition to rise due to the substitution of labour power by machines. Thus, if surplus value is assumed to be constant and the organic composition of capital increases over time, then r(V) must fall. A capitalist accumulates and innovates and sells below the market price, but above the price of production. Thus, the rate of profit rises until competition forces imitation and eventually lowers the equilibrium price, causing a fall in the rate of profit.

The progressive tendency for the general rate of profit to fall is thus simply *the expression, peculiar to the capitalist mode of production, of* the progressive development of the social productivity of labour. This does not mean that the rate of profit may not fall temporarily for other reasons as well, but it does prove that it is a self-evident necessity, deriving from the nature of the capitalist mode of production itself, that as it advances the general average rate of surplus value must be expressed in a falling general rate of profit.

(Marx, 1981, p. 319)

Therefore, the falling rate of profit is due to the competitive nature of the capitalist economy and is independent of the inclination of the capitalist, and by attempting to maximize profits in fact the opposite occurs.

As we have seen, accumulation is generally accompanied by centralization and concentration and therefore, although there is a fall in the rate of profit, *total* surplus values and *total* profits increase. This is the case because although the capitalist uses relatively more constant capital, absolutely more labour power is used. However, it does not necessarily follow that a greater number of workers are employed because more labour power may be extracted from a reduced number of workers through an increase in the rate of exploitation by increasing the intensity of work, by prolonging the length of the working day or by decreasing the value of labour power.

Therefore, the law of the tendency of the rate of profit to fall, of necessity, employs the concept of the composition of capital. However, for this purpose the concept has to be defined with much greater clarity and the distinction made between three notions of the composition of capital. This has not always been the case in the literature and the distinction has not always been fully appreciated.[1] Marx employs the technical composition, the value composition and the organic composition in his discussion of the law of the tendency of the rate of profit to fall. The technical composition of capital (TCC) is the ratio of the mass of means of production consumed per production period to the mass of wage goods. That is, the mass of means of production that can be processed into final commodities in a given labour-time. This cannot be measured by a single index as it is a ratio of material, physical quantities, 'a heterogeneous bundle of use-values (the material inputs) and a quantity of labour' (Saad-Filo, 1993, p. 131). The value composition of capital (VCC) is defined as an expression for the same ratio but measured in terms of the current values of means of production and wage goods consumed and therefore, is the ratio of constant to variable capital. Finally the organic composition of capital (OCC), is expressed as c/v in the same way as the VCC but because the technical composition is always increasing as more productive techniques are employed, the increase in productivity reduces the values per unit of means of production and wage goods at differential rates. Therefore, while the VCC is based on these constantly changing values, the OCC abstracts from the changes. Hence, changes in the OCC are directly proportional to changes in the TCC, but changes in the VCC are not.

> The composition of capital is to be understood in a twofold sense. As value it is determined by the proportion in which it is divided into constant capital ... and variable capital ... As material, as it functions in the process of production, all capital is divided into means of production and living labour. This latter composition is determined by the relation between the mass of the means of production employed on the one hand, and the mass of labour necessary for their employment on the other. I call the former the value composition, the latter the technical composition of capital. There is a close correlation between the two. To express this, I call the value composition of capital, in so far as it is determined by its technical composition and mirrors the changes in the latter, the organic composition of capital. Whenever I refer to the composition of capital, without further qualification, its organic composition is always understood.
>
> (Marx, 1976, p. 762)

Therefore, Marx makes the distinction between the OCC and the VCC, making the distinction between two dialectically related processes as the increasing OCC is associated with a rising TCC and increasing productivity, while there is a consequent reduction in the *values* of commodities that are associated with that increase in productivity. Hence, the OCC is associated with the total value of the constant capital to the total labour-time necessary to transform the inputs. Marx explains this as:

> [t]he ratio between different elements of productive capital ... [may be]..determined...[b]y the organic composition of productive capital. By this we mean the technological composition. With a *given productivity* of labour ....the amount of raw material and means of labour, that is the amount of constant capital – in terms of its *material elements* – which corresponds to a definite *quantity of living labour* (paid or unpaid), that is, to the *material elements* of *variable* capital, is determined in every sphere of production.
>
> (Marx, 1972, p. 382)

However, the analysis of capital from the perspective of its organic composition presents a significant problem, because the value of a bundle of means of production is the product of the unit values of its constituent parts by the amounts used up, it would appear impossible to ascertain whether alterations in a certain OCC have resulted from changes in the TCC, or from changes in the value of the means of production that have been used up. But for Marx, this does not represent a problem as the definition of the OCC means that it cannot change if the TCC is constant even though changes take place in the value of the components of capital. Marx then explains that

> ... if one assumes that the organic composition of capitals is given and likewise the differences in their organic composition, then the value ratio can change although the technological composition remains the same... The organic changes and those brought about by changes of value can have a similar effect on the rate of profit in certain circumstances. They differ however in the following way. If the latter are not due simply to fluctuations of market prices and are therefore not temporary, they are inevitably caused by an organic change in the spheres that provide the elements of constant or of variable capital.
>
> (Marx, 1972, pp. 383–6)

Hence, Marx understands that, for a given process of production, changes that take place in the value-ratio between the constant capital and the quantity of variable capital may arise from either the variation in the value of the inputs, or from technological changes in production.

Marx regards the value rate of profit as:

$$r = \frac{s}{c+v} = \frac{(s/v)}{(c/v)} + 1$$

and then maintains that if c/v rises, whilst s/v does not increase sufficiently, then the rate of profit will fall. Fine and Harris suggest that in *Capital*, Volume III, Marx appears to suggest that the law of the tendency of the rate of profit to fall is an inevitable outcome of accumulation, but argue that it can only properly be understood if the emphasis is placed upon the *tendency* part of the law, and should not be misinterpreted as suggesting that the rate of profit *will* fall (Fine and Harris, 1979, p. 61).

Hence, while the law outlines the process by which the rate of profit will fall, there are, however, countervailing forces at work. The rate of exploitation may not be constant over time, and increasing the intensity of work will have the effect of increasing the rate of exploitation and negating the fall in the rate of profits. Also, the depression of the wage below the value of labour power can be achieved when the reserve army of labour is large. Thirdly, cheapening the elements of constant capital leads to increased productivity which will reduce the value of constant capital. Fourthly, relative overpopulation through capital accumulation and redundancies in employment and the introduction of new industries with relatively low organic compositions slows down the falling rate of profit. Finally, foreign trade may lower the value of labour power, for example through cheaper food imports, and may lower the value of constant capital (raw materials) which will raise the rate of profit. Therefore, with the operation of such countervailing forces, the 'law' becomes a tendency.

However, it could be argued that there is no reason why technological change should be labour-saving. But it is relatively easy to show that it is, in terms of the need to have control or power over labour through the threat of redundancy and through the threat to employed labour that is posed by a large and increasing reserve army of labour. More formally, it can be argued that the rate of profit should be defined in the price system, but because of the transformation problem we do not know the organic composition of capital in the price domain. Neo-Ricardians argue that technological change leads to an increase in the rate of profit in the price system, assuming a real wage that is constant. Hence, for a given real wage, if technological change lowers the unit cost of production (in the price system), then at the new equilibrium set of prices, the rate of profit (in the price system) is either unchanged or it will increase. However, Marx did not assume a constant real wage and hence, if the real wage rises as technology changes, the rate of profit will fall. In addition, in the Ricardian model there is no allowance for the competitive nature of capitalist accumulation and innovation. If it were to be taken into account then collectively this would result in a lower rate of profit due to the 'anarchic nature of capitalism'.

Glyn has demonstrated, using postwar growth patterns in advanced capitalist economies, that a close relationship exists between capital accumulation and profitability, and also a stronger relationship between accumulation and economic growth than neoclassical theory has suggested. In addition, he argues that attempts to restore profit levels in the 1980s after the slowdown of the 1970s were successful due to the increase in unemployment, which significantly reduced the bargaining power of labour (Glyn, 1997).[2]

The realization crisis

The realization problem is not unique to Marx. Indeed it was first considered by Ricardo and Sismondi, and the theory of effective demand
associated with Keynes also has a bearing on the problem (Kenway,
in Eatwell et al., 1990, p. 326). The problem is essentially one of
whether there exists enough demand for the commodities that have
been produced, and Ricardo suggested that nobody will produce without the intention to sell while nobody will sell in the absence of wish-
ing to buy something else. 'Productions are always bought by
productions, or by services; money is only the medium by which the
exchange is effected' (Sraffa, 1981, pp. 291–2). Marx is highly critical of
this argument and indeed suggests that it is wrong, because it over-
looks the specific nature of capitalist production. In particular, money
is not only a medium of effecting exchange, but it is also a means of
payment and thus, a change in payment patterns may generate a situation whereby commodities must sell at below their prices of production. In addition, Marx suggests that following a serious disruption in
monetary exchange, deviations from the equilibrium level of activity
will be increased. He argues that as price relations command the
process of reproduction, this is 'halted and thrown into confusion'
when there is a general fall in prices. This causes the function of money,
as a medium of payment, to become paralysed. At the same time the
credit system collapses, which together lead to sudden depreciations,
stagnation and the disruption of reproduction (Marx, 1981, p. 363).
However, Marx distinguishes between the factors that establish the possibility of crises and those which actually bring them about. The purchase and the sale of commodities become separated only with the use
of money and this is the basis of Marx's argument for the generation
of crises. These crises only repeatedly occur in the capitalist mode of
production and Marx suggests three reasons as to why this
is the case. First, the dominant motive for commodity production
in capitalism is not for use-value but for the accumulation of wealth
in the abstract. Hence, the effects of problems in the realization of
value are amplified in capitalist commodity production. Second,
because capitalist commodity production is dynamic, it continuously
produces economic change which tends towards disruption of the
established pattern of reproduction, and increases the capacity for
the realization crisis to lead to failure of the system. Third, because capitalist commodity production increases the division of labour and
intensifies specialization, the disruption to the system that is caused by

a realization crisis will intensify the crises over a much more extensive area.

In explaining cyclical fluctuations, Marx places great emphasis on the role of variations in profits and the expectations of profits held by the capitalists. He outlines the circumstances in which such fluctuations will occur, dividing these into two categories: the randomly distributed shocks that are exogenous to the system, and endogenous factors internally generated by the capitalist mode of production. The greater emphasis is placed upon the latter category to explain cyclical fluctuations and is itself divisible into two endogenous determinants. First, the production of surplus value experiences difficulties which generates a crisis through the falling rate of profit. Second, a lack of purchasing power makes it impossible to realize the surplus value that has been produced, again reducing the rate of profit. In *Capital*, Volume III, Marx argues that immediate exploitation and the realization of that exploitation require different conditions. Immediate exploitation is restricted solely by the productive forces of society, while the realization is restricted by the proportionality of different branches of production and the power of consumption within the framework of antagonistic conditions of distribution which reduce consumption of the majority to a minimum. Additionally, it is restricted by 'the drive to accumulation, the drive to expand capital and produce surplus value on a larger scale' (Marx, 1981, pp. 352–3). The motivation for this arises from within the capitalist mode of production itself through the imperative to change the method of production through competition to avoid bankruptcy. However, as productivity rises it comes into conflict with the framework of the relations of consumption.

Underconsumption theories argue that crises occur as a consequence of a deficiency in the effective demand for commodities for one of a number of possible reasons and in Marxian theory is best expressed in Luxemburg (1963) and Baran and Sweezy (1966). The similarities between such theories and the arguments of Keynes in the *General Theory* (1936) are obviously apparent. Marx discusses the concept of effective demand but in terms of the form which the crises take rather that the underlying cause. Indeed, in *Theories of Surplus Value*, Volume III, Marx appears to reject the underconsumption theories of Sismondi, Chalmers and Malthus, preferring to see crises as occurring at determined periods rather than in terms of secular stagnation. Thus, for Marx, although the creation of surplus value is the object of production, it is only the first action in the process of making profit.

The second action is the sale of commodities on the market, limited by the consuming power of society which is reduced to a minimum by the process of exploitation, competition and accumulation. Hence, periodic underconsumption (overproduction) reduces the realization of surplus value under the conditions of consumption and distribution that are characteristic of capitalist production. This overproduction and failure of the capitalist to realize profit cannot continue without recurrent disarrangement. Hence, it is underconsumption due to its capitalist form that is the cause of all real crises and therefore is the inability of society to consume what it produces. As Clarke (1994) points out, some commentators have stressed the role of the supply of labour power in a theory of crisis founded on overaccumulation, but in fact in Volume III of *Capital*, Marx maintains that the primary determinant of the pattern of accumulation is not the rise and fall of wages. This is because this movement of wages is but a mechanism through which the capitalists are compelled to develop the forces of production. Thus, for Marx the development of the crisis cannot be explained by the supply of labour, although rising wages do play a role in its formation.

The process of accumulation is hastened by a fall in the rate of profit, while accumulation accelerates the fall in the rate of profit. In addition, the fall in the rate of profit increases the momentum of the concentration of wealth in the hands of fewer capitalists. Additional accumulation is constrained by the fall in the rate of profit and endangers the mechanism of capitalist development by bringing about speculation, crises and surplus capital and population. Continuous capital growth is accomplished by the expropriation and pauperization of the great mass of producers and this means that there is unceasing conflict between the historical task of capitalism, to create and re-create productive capacity, and the conditions of social production corresponding to it, the tendency to effect a decline in the rate of profit. In addition, the concentration of capital into a relatively small number of hands brings about new crises as large capital concentrations with modest rates of profit can accumulate more rapidly than small capitals with high rates of profit. The expropriation of profitable investment outlets by capital forces small capital into speculative channels and the consequence is a 'so-called plethora of capital', which plainly indicates that this is an expansion of capital which cannot survive the deterioration in the rate of profit because it is not sufficiently large. The net consequence is both unemployed labour and unemployed capital.

The mechanism involved is that as accumulation takes place the TCC rises such that each worker will use more raw materials and therefore there will exist a greater mass of means of production. Consequently, the value of the elements of capital will fall as their measure increases. Hence, the OCC will not increase to the same extent as the TCC, although it is assumed that the OCC will continue to rise with the growing scale of capitalist production. With the tendency to greater concentration of ownership of capital there is also the tendency to centralization of ownership which accelerates the socialization of production and the rise in the OCC. This rising OCC expresses the tendency of capitalist production to develop the productivity of social labour through the development of the forces of production and results in the extension of the market onto a world scale through the concentration and centralization of capital. However, this process of capital accumulation does not proceed smoothly, being interrupted by periodic crises and overaccumulation causing bankruptcy of outdated capitals and an expansion in the reserve army of labour.

Marx also crucially highlights the role of credit in terms of the cycle that is generated by the capitalist mode of production, and the inherent contradictions that are fundamental to the system. He identifies the basis of the periodicity of the business cycle as being located in the replacement of fixed capital. Indeed in a footnote to Chapter 30 of Volume III of *Capital,* Engels suggests that:

> The acute form of the periodic process with its former ten-year cycle seems to have given way to a more chronic and drawn-out alternation, affecting the various industrial countries at different times, between a relatively short and weak improvement in trade and a relatively long and indecisive depression. Perhaps what is involved is simply an extension of the cycle's duration. When world trade was in its infancy, 1815–47, cycles of approximately five years could be discerned; between 1847 and 1867 the cycle was definitely a ten-year one; might we now be in the preparatory phase of a new world crash of unheard of severity?
>
> (Marx, 1981, p. 620)[3]

The important aspect for Marx is that the 'constant revolutionizing of the means of production leads to the 'moral depreciation of machinery'. During the turnover cycle capital is bound by its fixed component and this is the basis for the periodic crises. A gestation lag exists whereby capital is advanced in the purchase of means of production and wages, but it may be some time before commodities arrive on the market. Hence, there will be a period where demand exceeds supply and the demands for advances of capital will put pressure on the money markets.

> Since elements of productive capital are constantly being withdrawn from the market and all that is put into the market is an equivalent in money, the effective demand rises, without this in itself providing any element of supply. Hence prices rise, both for the means of subsistence and for the material elements of production ... .Wages generally rise, even in the formally well employed sections of the labour market. This lasts until the inevitable crash, the reserve army of workers is again released and wages are pressed down once more to their minimum and below it.
>
> (Marx, 1981, pp. 390–1)

In considering the reproduction of capital *as a whole* the major problem that emerges is that fixed capital investment is discontinuous in that, the demand for new means of production differs from period to period and disproportionalities emerge between branches of production. As the capitalist accumulates money over a period of time, this is spent on fixed capital investment which in turn creates a period in which money is withdrawn from circulation, creating barriers to realization as money is no longer fulfilling its role as a means of circulation.

Summary

Marx argues that there is an inherent tendency for the rate of profit to decline during periods of prosperity into periods of depression and, therefore, recurrent crises and depressions are inevitable in capitalism. However, the law of the tendency for the rate of profit to fall is an inevitable outcome of accumulation. It is a tendency due to the possibility that countervailing forces may be at work to increase the rate of exploitation or to force the real wage down when the reserve army of labour is large. This itself presents problems for the capitalist mode of production as profit cannot be realized from surplus value due to the process of exploitation, competition and accumulation. Hence, the crisis of realization is itself an outcome of the relations and forces of production, the very mechanisms that produce surplus value.

9
Michal Kalecki and Piero Sraffa

Introduction

Michal Kalecki and Piero Sraffa are not only two of the most successful critics of neoclassical economic theory in the twentieth century, but both approach their respective critiques from an essentially Marxian perspective. Both also, having demonstrated the paucity and logical inconsistency of neoclassical economics, attempted to apply the framework of Marx to contemporary capitalism.[1] However, their analyses and their conclusions can be seen as having very different implications for the Marxian schema.

Michal Kalecki (1899–1970)

Kalecki was self-taught in economics after his early formal study as an engineering student at Warsaw and Gdansk polytechnics. His studies were interrupted by family poverty. In 1933 he published 'An essay in the theory of the business cycles' (in Polish) which outlined the main points of what became known as Keynes's theory. Kalecki was in Sweden when the *General Theory* was published, and read a copy of the book that he had intended to write. However, he never made any reference in public to his priority of publication. After reading the *General Theory* he came to England and began to challenge the young Keynesians on several weak points in Keynes's analysis, forcing them to reconsider. He joined the Department of Economic Affairs at the United Nations as deputy-director in 1946, but was forced to resign in 1946 due to McCarthyism, returning to Poland to concentrate on work directed at helping to improve planning methods and techniques in socialist Poland (Sawyer, 1985, pp. 3–7).

In his early writings on capitalism, he shows a Marxian insight into many of the problems facing capitalism in the 1930s, but the main thrust of his work on capitalism concerns the contradictions which manifested themselves in persistent excess capacity, self-generating business cycles, stagnation tendencies and labour unemployment, seeing these as intrinsic to the functioning of capitalism. A major point of divergence between Kalecki and Keynes is their respective understanding of the role played by the state in capitalist economies. Kalecki saw serious socio-political constraints on full employment and the maintenance of full employment would require a permanent budget deficit. In *Political Aspects of Full Employment* (1943) he argued that the assumption that a government will maintain full employment in a capitalist economy, if it only knows how to do it, is a fallacious argument. Big business will oppose such a policy and their opposition will be due to a dislike of government intervention in employment. Under 'free markets' the level of employment depends upon the 'state of confidence' and if this deteriorates, private investment falls, resulting in falling output and employment. This gives the capitalists a powerful, indirect control over government policy. Hence, budget deficits are regarded as perilous, and they argue for 'sound finance' to make the level of employment dependent upon the 'state of confidence'. As such, it is the government's job to maintain the 'state of confidence', which is always in the interests of capital. Kalecki also argued that big business has a dislike of government spending and the subsidizing of consumption which stems from a dislike of public investment which competes with private business – 'crowding-out'. As far as the subsidizing of consumption is concerned this is opposed on moral grounds: 'The fundamentals of capitalist ethics require that "You shall earn your bread in sweat" – unless you happen to have private means' (Kalecki, 1972, p. 78). Finally, big business has an aversion to social and political changes that result from the maintenance of full employment because under a regime of full employment, the 'sack' loses its role as a disciplinary measure. The social position of the 'boss' is undermined and self-assurance and class consciousness of the working class would increase and this in turn would lead to strikes and disputes. Kalecki argues that full employment would not affect profits as price increases would be more likely than falling profits to pay for wage increases. However, ' "discipline in the factories" and "political stability" are more appreciated by the business leaders than are profits' (Kalecki, 1972, p. 78). He suggests that 'class interest' tells us that lasting full employment is unsound from their point of view and unemployment is an integral part of the capitalist system. Hence, Kalecki adopts the Marxian perspective that the autonomy of the state is only relative to the power of the individual factions of the capitalist class. State activity is aimed to produce and reproduce the class relations of capitalism and is part of the very structure of the system.

In his discussion of the political business cycle, Kalecki maintains that in a slump, public investment, financed by borrowing, will be undertaken to prevent mass unemployment. However, if the government attempts to continue the policy to maintain the high level of employment reached in the following boom, they will meet with the opposition of the capitalists. The capitalists want the disciplinary tool of unemployment and their pressure induces the government to return to the 'orthodox' policy of cutting back the budget deficit, which leads to a slump, requiring the reintroduction of public investment. Therefore, the 'political business cycle' would not secure full employment, except at the top of the boom.

Kalecki's approach shows a Marxian insight in terms of the continuing crisis of capitalism. In 'is a capitalist overcoming of the crisis possible' he makes the distinction between a structural crisis of capitalism and a medium-term recessionary phase of the business cycle and therefore to miss this distinction results in over-optimism about the stability of capitalism (Kriesler and McFarlane, 1993, p. 219). Kalecki suggests that the recessionary phase of a cycle can be overcome within the framework of a capitalist system, but structural crises cannot. The decisive factor will be not the economic but the social one, the position taken by the working class. 'Three Systems' (1934) is concerned with the general theoretical question of what the specific conditions are, under which a change in money wages will cause a change in real wages and, therefore, a change in the share of wages in national income. He utilizes reproduction schemas and focuses on inter-sectoral flows and discusses the relations between the wages of the producer goods sector and the surplus of the consumer goods sector within the implicit framework of Marx's equations of extended reproduction. In the other systems, Kalecki deals with relations between interest rates, the level of output, investment and the velocity of circulation of money. He is interested in the relationship between the wage bill of the producer goods sector and the surplus of the consumer goods sector and concludes that, a balance is necessary at the end of the period, when the consumer goods sector finds a market, generated in the capital goods sector, which is just large enough to dispose of its surplus, to provide a situation where there is no unintended accumulation of inventories (stocks) of consumer goods. It must be noted that he is not concerned with how a neoclassical style equilibrium is established, but as with Marx, he is interested in the balance of the relationship. In fact, Kalecki did not rely on any notion of equilibrium. He argues that periodic crises emerge because 'investment is not only produced but also producing' (Osiatynski, 1990, p. 554). Investment spending as a source of effective demand brings prosperity, but it is a 'double-edged sword', because investment is at the same time an addition to capital equipment, competing with an older generation of capital equipment:

$$K_{t-1} + I_t = K_{t1} \qquad\qquad 9.1$$

'The tragedy of investment is that it calls forth the crisis because it is useful. But it is not the theory that is paradoxical but its subject – the capitalist economy' (Osiatynski, 1990, p. 554).

Unlike the Hicks model of the cycle, where amplitudes of the cycle are contained by a ceiling (labour and output bottlenecks) and a floor (autonomous investment), Kalecki does not ever have firms getting to the feasible peak of the boom (full employment), owing to excess capacity hangover. The turning point is determined by the relationship between the rate of profit and investment. Therefore,

> [w]hen investment reaches its top level during the boom the following situation arises: profits and national income, whose changes are directly related to those of investment, cease to grow as well, but capital equipment continues to expand because net investment is positive. The increase in productive capacity is thus not matched by the rise in effective demand. As a result, investment declines, and this causes in turn a fall in profits and national income.
>
> (Osiatynski, 1991, pp. 417–18)

A key element therefore in Kalecki's economic dynamics is the determination of investment. For the neoclassicals the causal relationship is from savings to investment, but for Kalecki, as with Keynes, the direction of causality is reversed. However, here again, Kalecki differs from Keynes in certain key respects: Kalecki makes much of the distinction between the investment decision and the resulting investment, the 'gestation lag', that is, the time lag between them arising from the time necessary to take orders and for equipment to be built, allowing for changes in 'entrepreneurial reactions'. He also incorporates financial constraints into his analysis of investment whereby gross investment by firms out of current profits becomes an important influence on the investment decision. Other influences that he identifies are changes in profits per unit of time and changes in the stock of fixed capital. However, although this appears to be similar to the accelerator model, the accelerator is too simplistic and totally inadequate because it does not take account of the other determinants of investment that Kalecki outlined, it does not agree with the facts and output may actually increase without an actual increase in existing capacity, i.e. when large reserve capacity exists.

Gross real profits for Kalecki are determined by the capitalist's consumption and investment decisions, thus the phrase most often associated with Kalecki, 'the workers spend what they get and the capitalists get what they spend'.[2] When total profits and capitalist's consumption and investment are determined in real terms, so are the levels of output and employment in the sector manufacturing producer goods and in the sector producing the capitalist's consumption goods. Then, the microeconomic factors which determine the distribution of income (degree of monopoly, mark-up) will have their impact, not by affecting gross profit directly, but through real wages which will influence the level of national output via their impact on the wage-goods sector.

In *The Business Cycle* (1943), Kalecki assumes that there is no budget deficit, that there exists a current account balance and that workers do not save. The level of economic activity is determined by investment and investment is determined, with a time lag, by the level of economic activity and the rate of change in this level. It follows therefore, that investment, at a given point in time, is determined by the level and rate of change of investment at some earlier point in time:

$$\frac{\mathrm{I}}{\Delta \mathrm{I}} \rightarrow \frac{\mathrm{II}}{\mathrm{g}} \rightarrow \frac{\mathrm{II}}{\Delta \mathrm{I}} \rightarrow \frac{\mathrm{III}}{\mathrm{g}} \rightarrow \frac{\mathrm{III}}{\Delta \mathrm{I}} \rightarrow \dots \qquad 9.2$$

(where g = the rate of economic activity)

This provides the basis for Kalecki's analysis of the dynamic economic process and enables him to show that this process involves cyclical fluctuations. The analysis proceeds as follows. The fluctuations in the degree of utilization of capital equipment are of a similar order as those experienced in aggregate output. Thus, a considerable proportion of capital equipment lies idle (under-utilized) in the slump. Even on the average, the degree of utilization throughout the course of the business cycle will be substantially below the maximum attained during the boom. Fluctuations in the utilization of the available labour will parallel those in the utilization of capital equipment and thus not only is there mass unemployment in the slump, but average employment over the course of the cycle is considerably below the peak that is attained in the boom. Hence, the reserve of capital equipment and the reserve army of labour are typical features of a capitalist economy, at least through a considerable part of the cycle. In his *Outline of a Theory of the Business Cycle* (1933), Kalecki considers the interrelated changes of investment orders, the gross accumulation of capital and the volume of capital equipment which produce the business cycle. He considers that the fluctuations of the gross accumulation, which result from this mechanism, must also be reflected in the fluctuations of the aggregate production (output). Gross real profits are, on the one hand, an increasing function of gross accumulation whereby an increase in gross accumulation leads to an increase in profits. On the other hand, they can be expressed as the product of the volume of aggregate production and of profit per unit of output. Thus, the relation between changes in the gross accumulation, which is equal to the production of invest-ment goods (change in capital stock = change in investment) and those of the aggregate production, materializes in the following manner: when the production of investment goods increases, the aggregate produc-tion increases directly in step, but in addition, there is an increase due to the demand for consumption goods on the part of workers newly engaged in the investment goods sector. The consequent increase in employment in the consumption goods sector leads to a further increase in demand for consumption goods. The levels of aggregate production and of the profit per unit of output will ultimately increase to such an extent that the increment in real profits is equated to the increment of the production of investment goods. However, Kalecki argues that we need to take account of the changes in the consump-tion of the capitalists. This consumption is dependent, to a certain degree, on aggregate profits and will therefore rise together with gross accumulation. The increase in capitalist consumption will exert the same influence as that in the production of investment goods, i.e. the production of consumption goods for capitalists expands. This leads to an increase in employment, and this raises again the demand for con-sumption goods for the workers, causing a further increase in produc-tion. The aggregate production and the profit per unit of output will ultimately increase to such an extent as to assure an increment in real profits, equal to that of the production of investment goods and capi-talist consumption. The conclusion that the increase in capitalists' con-sumption in turn increases their profits is counter-intuitive, in that the common conviction is that the more that is consumed, the less that is saved. Such an approach would be correct with regard to an individual capitalist; however, it does not apply to the capitalist class as a whole. If some capitalists spend money, either on investment or consumption goods, their money passes on to other capitalists in the form of profits. Therefore, investment or consumption of some capitalists creates profits for others and, indeed, the capitalists as a class gain exactly as much as they invest or consume, and if, in a closed system, they ceased to invest or consume they would not make any money at all. Hence, capitalists, as a class, determine their own profits by the extent of their investment and personal consumption. 'In a way they are "masters of their own fate"; but how they "master" it is determined by objective factors, so that fluctuations of profits appear after all to be unavoidable' (Kalecki, 1971, p. 13).

Piero Sraffa (1898–1983)

Sraffa was born in Turin and studied at Turin university from 1916 to 1920. His friendship with Antonio Gramsci started in 1919,[3] but he was forced to leave Italy during the 1920s due to articles published in the *Manchester Guardian* on European reconstruction and on the banking crisis in Italy published in the *Economic Journal* which annoyed Mussolini.[4] He attacked Alfred Marshall's theory of value in 'The laws of return under competitive conditions' (*Economic Journal*, 1926) which established his reputation as a theorist of some considerable brilliance. He accepted a position at Trinity College, Cambridge in 1927, where he remained until his death, and influenced Maurice Dobb and Joan Robinson, while among his students were Ronald Meek, Pierangelo Garegnani and Luigi Pasinetti. Sraffa set in train great controversies with his *Production of Commodities*, but took no part in the subsequent debate.

The *Production of Commodities by Means of Commodities* was published in 1960 and led directly to the 'capital controversies' which fatally undermined those forms of neoclassical theory which had always been most aggressive towards socialism and socialist economics. For example, J. B. Clarke (late nineteenth century) argued that the remuneration of land, labour and capital is explained by each factor's relative scarcity and its productive contribution to output: Sraffa demonstrated that this was logically incoherent in that factors of production do not receive their marginal products, in particular the productivity of capital played no role in explaining profits. Bohm-Bawerk (Austrian school) had reduced produced means of production to a series of dated 'original' factors of production, land and labour: Sraffa showed that this could not be the case where production processes used fixed capital. In addition, even with circulating capital technologies, Bohm-Bawerk's theory of accumulation and distribution was fatally flawed. Neoclassical economists, such as Paul Samualson, quickly accepted that this offensive against Clarkian and Austrian analysis had been successful. However, they maintained that the leading form of their theory – Walrasian general equilibrium – remained unscathed. In particular, they were able to make this claim because the Sraffian analysis, as we shall see, is set in an equilibrium framework.

Sraffa sets out to essentially solve the problem faced by Ricardo, that of the existence of an invariable measure that is invariant to changes either in the rate of profit or the wage rate. Beginning with a Ricardian long run equilibrium, Sraffa assumes the labour is homogeneous and is the single non-reproducible input of the system, whose amount is given. In all industries there are fixed input coefficients and therefore production satisfies the condition of constant returns to scale.[5] Each industry produces a single commodity using a single technique, that is a combination of working capital and homogeneous labour. Initially he employs a simple system of simultaneous input–output equations, using one for each commodity, and then shows how, with a system in a stationary equilibrium with wages at the subsistence level, both relative price and the rate of profit can be simultaneously determined. However, an arbitrary change in the subsistence wage would change the structure of relative prices. Therefore, he introduces a 'standard commodity' which can express the relative price without the distortionary effects of the wage level or the rate of profit. The 'standard commodity' consists of only those outputs that have been combined in the same proportions as the reproducible non-labour inputs of manufacture. As such, this represents the 'standard system' which is unique to any economic system, such that the ratio of net outputs to inputs of the 'standard system' and the proportion of net output that accrues to wages will determine the rate of profit in the economy as a whole. There is an important distinction to be made between a 'basic' commodity, one which enters directly or indirectly into the production of all other commodities (including itself), and a 'non-basic' commodity which only enters into final consumption. The 'standard commodity' is comprised only of basics which enter into its production in a 'standard ratio' (in the same proportion as they enter into their own production). Thus, the standard commodity represents 'the interconnected, undecomposable core of an economy, made up as it is entirely of basics, which is surrounded by a detachable belt of nonbasics' (Blaug, 1997, p. 136). Thus, depending on whether the rate of profit or the rate of wages are given exogenously, then one can find both relative prices and the other variable (the rate of profit or the rate of wages). This is because they depend only on the technical conditions of production involved in the production of the 'standard commodity' and as such, the standard commodity represents the invariable measure of value.

Sraffa attempts to show how the transformation problem is a 'complicating detour' in Marx's analysis and encompasses joint production technologies, single-product activities, fixed and circulating capital, the use of produced commodity inputs, the use of non-produced inputs such as land, and the existence of alternative production processes. In each case, Sraffa illustrated how equilibrium prices could be derived directly from information concerning conditions of production and the distribution of income:

$$a_{11}+a_{12}+ \ldots a_{1n}+l_1 \rightarrow b_{11}+b_{12}+ \ldots b_{1n}$$

$$a_{21}+a_{22}+ \ldots a_{2n}+l_2 \rightarrow b_{21}+b_{22}+ \ldots b_{2n}$$

$$a_{n1}+a_{n2}+ \ldots a_{nn}+l_n \rightarrow b_{n1}+b_{n2}+ \ldots b_{nn} \qquad 9.3[6]$$

Here:

> a_{ij} represents inputs of the commodity j in the process i;
> b_{ij} represents the corresponding outputs;
> l_i represents the amounts of direct labour used.

Hence the system incorporates joint production, since there can be more than one output from each process. It also allows there to be items of fixed capital; some of the a_{ij} may represent machines of various types and ages, in which case they would also be represented on the right-hand side of the arrow by appropriate b_{ij}, thus signifying that the process reproduces them as machines which are one period older. In other words, a durable capital good is treated as a set of disparate commodities, differing by stage of obsolescence, so that the older goods which remain at the end of the production period are treated as by-products of this process. Some of the a_{ij} and b_{ij} may be zero, since not all processes will necessarily utilize all inputs and produce every output. Some may be single-product processes where all b_{ij}, except one, will be zero. However, on Sraffa's assumptions, prices can be derived *directly* from the conditions of production, supplemented by information on the distribution of income, that is the level of the wage, or the rate of profit.

In price terms:

$$(a_{11}p_1 + \ldots a_{1n}p_n)(1+r) + l_1w = b_{11}p_1 + \ldots b_{1n}p_n$$
$$(a_{21}p_1 + \ldots a_{2n}p_n)(1+r) + l_2w = b_{21}p_1 + \ldots b_{2n}p_n$$
$$(a_{n1}p_1 + \ldots a_{nn}p_n)(1+r) + l_nw = b_{n1}p_1 + \ldots b_{nn}p_n \qquad 9.4$$

Here:

p_i represent equilibrium prices;
w   represents the wage;
r   represents the rate of profit.

This incorporates Sraffa's usual treatment of wages as paid in arrears at the end of the production period, so that the 'wage fund' is *not* part of the capital on which profit accrues. Provided either the wage or the rate of profit is taken as exogenous, all commodity prices and the value of the other distributive variable (either the rate of profit or the wage) can be determined. This may be seen intuitively by noting that there are n processes of production and $n+1$ endogenous variables. Therefore, since one p can be eliminated by taking it as the unit of price measurement (setting its value to unity), we have sufficient information to solve all other prices and the other distributional magnitude. Hence, labour values are derived magnitudes which depend upon exactly the same factors as do prices. Marx himself worked from labour values to prices of production.

In value terms:

$$a_{11} + l_1 + \ldots a_{1n}l_n + l_1 = b_{11}l_1 + \ldots b_{1n}l_n$$
$$a_{21} + l_1 + \ldots a_{2n}l_n + l_2 = b_{21} + l_1 + \ldots b_{2n}l_n$$
$$a_{n1} + l_1 + \ldots a_{nn}l_n + l_n = b_{n1}l_1 + \ldots b_{nn}l_n \qquad 9.5$$

Here, labour values (l_i) can be determined *only* from the information on input–output relations contained in 9.3. Marx's journey therefore, according to Sraffa, involves a detour which is redundant from the point of view of quantitative value theory. Marx's procedure is to move from the conditions of production and income distribution, through a detour into labour values and surplus values, to prices of production and profits. Sraffa's more direct route misses out the calculation of values and surplus values, but has the same destination:

Marx:	Conditions of production	$\rightarrow$	Values	$\rightarrow$	Transformation algorithm	$\rightarrow$ Prices of production
	Real wage		Surplus values			

Sraffa:	Conditions of production			Prices of
	Real wage		$\rightarrow$	production

Therefore, Sraffa's solution to the transformation problem is one where the problem is sidestepped in favour of more fundamental issues of deriving commodity prices and the rate of profit from data on conditions of production and the distribution of income. Marx invariably treated labour values of produced commodities as positive magnitudes, but Sraffa's analysis revealed the existence of contrary cases. The consequences of this are dramatic: labour values may not be defined, or they may be zero, so that Marx's transformation cannot be undertaken. In this case his route to prices of production may not exist. Also, Sraffa suggests that labour values may be negative. This undermines the Fundamental Marxian Theorem which states that, positive profits imply, and are implied by, positive surplus value. In fact, however, Sraffa shows that a positive rate of profit may be associated with a negative or zero rate of exploitation and positive profits can coexist with negative or zero surplus value. These are counter-intuitive results. If direct labour is utilized in all production processes, how can outputs fail to have well defined labour values and how could these values be anything other than positive?

Taken as a whole, Sraffa's *Production of Commodities* has an ambiguous relation to Marxian political economy. The theory of value is shown to be valid *only* for special cases, and Marx's own exposition of his theory of exploitation is shown not to be general. However, Sraffa's treatment is not comprehensive, and indeed, can be used to 'rescue' one form of Marx's theory of exploitation. In addition, some Sraffians argue that since Sraffa's paradigm is within the same 'surplus tradition' of economics as that of Marx, Marxian economics is actually strengthened by his work, because of the defects of Marx's own specific form of surplus economics. Overall, the qualitative labour theory of value emerges essentially unscathed. Production is an inherently *human* process, notwithstanding the title of Sraffa's book. Beneath the phenomena of exchange can be found a social division of labour. Because producers relate to each another through the medium of commodity exchange, they are also alienated from each other and their perceptions of social reality are distorted by the resulting fetishism of commodities. This is why labour occupied a privileged place in political economy.

However, Sraffa highlights two important problems. First, Marx argues in Volume III of *Capital* that the transformation problem could be solved, that the sum of profits equalled total surplus value and that the uniform rate of profit which prevailed in a regime of prices of production was thereby predetermined by the ratio of surplus value to the value of constant plus variable capital. Sraffa shows that this is not, in general, correct and is valid only with special assumptions. Once joint production, fixed capital and alternative processes are allowed for, it is almost always false. Second, Marx maintained, also in Volume III of *Capital*, that prices and profits could only be derived from labour values which thus had logical priority. Sraffa shows that this is also false, hence the 'complicating detour' was unnecessary.

However, it can be argued that the labour theory of value is not necessary for a theory of exploitation. Profits arise, as Marx himself explained, because of the capitalist class monopoly over the means of production in an economy which produces a surplus. The class monopoly is the ability of capitalists to deny access to the means of production which they own. Since the majority of the population cannot survive without such access, capitalists can establish an effective claim on part of what is produced. Generally, profits can be expressed in quantities of surplus labour, but this is only one possible scale of measurement and is therefore not essential to the theory of exploitation. Discussion has since centred on attempts to salvage Marx's theory of value, but Sraffians have maintained that Marxian political economy has actually been strengthened by exposing the defects in Marx's original formulation and showing that they are irrelevant to the more general approach that underpins it.

We may disagree with the Sraffians in their general conclusions in that they have essentially an equilibrium methodology, whereas Marx was correct in the need to think in terms of history, not equilibrium. In the Sraffian construct the existence of general equilibrium prices and the general equilibrium profit rate is assumed. This is illegitimate if one wishes to show how the variables (that are taken as given), rate of profit and the wage, come into existence and therefore the *meaning* of the variables in the economic system.

Part II

History and Contemporary Relevance

10
Monopoly Capitalism

Introduction

Monopoly capitalism pertains to the stage in the development of capitalist development when the process of concentration and centralization of capital has led to the emergence of oligopoly in significant sectors of the economy. Although a theory of monopoly capitalism has been presented by other theorists, it is an expression employed among Marxian economists that has been associated with the stage of capitalism that began in the final quarter of the nineteenth century and attained full maturity in the latter half of the twentieth century. Marx understood that in a system where commodities are produced by industries that all consist of a large number of firms all of whom respond to price and profit signals that are induced by market forces, such a system would be inherently unstable and lacking in permanence. However, in the capitalist mode of production competition forces firms to cut costs and to expand their production, necessitating perpetual accumulation and the introduction of new technological and organizational methods. Marx explains this as follows:

> [N]ot only are accumulation and the concentration accompanying it scattered over many points, but the increase of each functioning capital is thwarted by the formation of new capitals and the subdivision of the old. Accumulation, therefore, presents itself on one hand as increasing concentration of the means of production, and of the command over labour; and on the other hand as repulsion of many individual capitals from one another.
>
> (Marx, 1976, pp. 776–7)

Theories of monopoly capitalism

Marx understood that pressures exist that are endogenous to the capitalist mode of production that will propel it away from free competition. Thus:

> The battle of competition is fought by the cheapening of commodities. The cheapness of commodities depends, all other circumstances remaining the same, on the productivity of labour, and this depends in turn on the scale of production. Therefore the larger capitals beat the smaller ... [W]ith the development of the capitalist mode of production, there is an increase in the minimum amount of individual capital necessary to carry on a business under its normal conditions. The smaller capitals, therefore, crowd into spheres of production which large scale industry has taken control of only sporadically or incompletely. Here competition rages in direct proportion to the number, and in inverse proportion to the magnitude, of the rival capitalists, whose capitals partly pass into the hands of their conquerors, and partly vanish completely.
>
> (Marx, 1976, p. 777)

However, notwithstanding this, there are a variety of explanations that have been advanced as to what actually distinguishes one state from another, and the basis upon which such periodization can be undertaken. The forerunner in this field was Rudolf Hilferding who published his *Daz Finanzkapital* in 1910. This represented an attempt to coalesce the concentration of capital and corporate finance into Marx's theoretical structure through the process of capitalist accumulation. He found that prices under the conditions of monopoly are indeterminate and, therefore, unstable. Intrinsically, his proposition was that whenever concentration allows the capitalist to attain profits that are higher than the average, both their customers and their suppliers are obliged to introduce counter combinations in order for them to appropriate part of the additional profit for themselves. This suggests to Hilferding that monopoly will 'spread in all directions from every point of origin' and therefore that there is no absolute limit to cartellization, and in fact cartellization will be found to have a tendency to spread continuously until finally there exists a 'general cartel'. This general cartel will be the consciously controlled society in its 'antagonistic form' (Sweezy, 1990, p. 298). However, the history of twentieth century capitalism, although exhibiting the strong tendency toward concentration, also contains counter-tendencies which have precluded the formation of the general cartel. These counter-tendencies can be found in the establishment of new firms and the break-up of existing firms as new technologies and new products replace outdated techniques and commodities. This itself is an outcome of the dynamism of the competitive process in capitalism, but as the system matures production even of these new outputs has the tendency to become concentrated in the hands of fewer and fewer firms through merger and takeover.[1]

In many ways, Lenin's *Imperialism, The Highest Form of Capitalism*, which was published in 1916, followed the logic of Hilferding's argument extremely closely, suggesting that competition becomes transformed into monopoly on the basis of economies of scale and superior technology, but that industrial capital falls prey to finance capital. Hence, Lenin outlines several tendencies that had become apparent in the development of capitalism in this period: the concentration of production and capital creating monopolies that play a decisive role in economic life, the banks playing an ever increasing and leading role in economic decision-making through the merging of finance capital with industrial capital, the growing importance of the export of capital, the formation of the international capitalist monopoly, and the division of the world among the larger capitalist powers (Brewer, 1980, p. 109). The most important tendency within capitalism, for Lenin, was the dominance of finance capital, and he emphasized the rise of a class of rentiers who own money capital, but play no part in production.[2] Lenin suggests that as competition becomes gradually eliminated, there will be a tendency towards decay and stagnation as the pressure to innovate declines and therefore, the world for Lenin was divided by the tendency for capital export to produce an extension of the capitalist relations of production around the globe, and the tendency for power to be concentrated in the hands of blocs of finance capital directed to a parasitic rentier class.

Work by Baran and Sweezy (1966) attempted to explain the mechanisms that exist under monopoly capitalism in terms of the political, ideological and cultural superstructure. Thus they treat subsequent developments, such as the welfare state, as attempts to overcome the contradictions of monopoly capitalism. In particular, the increase in state expenditure to overcome demand deficiency is an attempt, not to benefit the working class, but to negate the pressures placed on the capitalist class by the emergence of monopoly capitalism (Baran and Sweezy, 1966). This work was an attempt to synthesize the theories of

Kalecki (1939) and Steindl (1952). Kalecki had developed the proposition of macroeconomic effective demand failures in a framework of imperfect competition and Steindl examined this in the context of long-term stagnation in the advanced industrial capitalist economies. Hence, Baran and Sweezy were able to develop an approach which suggested there to be a tendency for the potential economic surplus to rise, while there was a problem of the absorption of that surplus. As productivity growth permits production costs to fall relative to prices, the potential surplus rises, but this potential fails to be realized fully because investment spending will stagnate when the excess productive capacity is not removed through price competition. Therefore, monopolistic conditions lead to a lack of effective demand as the inducement to invest is weakened, while the profit share is maintained and hence the growth of consumption is restricted. Others, for example Cowling (1982), approach this question by suggesting that monopoly capitalism is a state that is independent of political representation, multinational corporation growth or the existence of a welfare state. He begins by developing Kalecki's idea of the degree of monopoly and then by relating the theory to the developments in industrial organization and managerialist theory. Cowling also argues that the effect of greater internationalization on mark-ups depends upon the existence of significant asymmetries in competition between the foreign and domestic markets within which the firms operate. As such, where there exists protection in the domestic market they anticipate greater benefits from price-cutting abroad than would otherwise be the case and, therefore, greater internationalization of production can introduce greater downward pressure on wages, which in turn depresses aggregate demand.

However, such approaches have been criticized for the narrowness of their analysis (cf. Fine and Murfin, 1984). Fine and Murfin argue that the monopoly capitalism model rests on the interaction between demand and supply and therefore it is difficult to consign empirical effects to these factors. They criticize Cowling for making no attempt at empirical estimation in these terms, and for the absence of production in his theory, which leads to exploitation being located in the market place through workers paying monopoly prices for consumption goods. For Marx, however, exploitation takes place in the production process as workers are forced to work longer than is required to produce wage goods. The central theme of monopoly capitalism is therefore contained in the generation and absorption of the surplus, which itself is a consequence of the production process.

The increasing concentration of capitalism

It is quite evident that concentration, defined as the absolute increase of the size of the firm, has increased substantially over the period of the twentieth century and has done so in measurable terms at the local, national and international level. This arises from accumulation causing internal growth of the firm. Sawyer shows how Marx makes a clear distinction between concentration and centralization, with centralization being the process whereby new companies are formed out of the amalgamation of two or more companies, or through the takeover of one company by another (Sawyer, 1989, p. 151). Taken together, these effects lead to increasing monopolization of particular industries and a consequent reduction in competition, yet the mechanism by which this phenomenon is produced is the competitive process itself. There are several elements of the competitive process that lead to monopoly capitalism that are generated from the technical change that is engendered. The existence of economies of scale, arising from the introduction of new techniques, pressurizes firms to invest to reduce costs and this becomes cumulative as firms strive to introduce more, and newer, capital equipment and techniques of production to further reduce costs. With all firms attempting to grow in this manner a conflict arises as some are successful in achieving increased efficiency and profitability, while others will lose out and decline. The outcome is a move towards a monopolistic structure as firms cease to exist under the pressure of competition and the level of concentration increases. Expansion of the firm is also a consequence of the search for new areas for investment and for new markets, which expands the capitalist sphere of production. In this imperative for expansion comes the inevitable conflict between firms, as the availability of new markets is limited in the short run. However, in the longer term, competition produces greater concentration and centralization alongside the continued expansion of firms and this means that, not only have concentrations and centralization occurred in national economies, but there has been a continual geographical expansion in the capitalist mode of production.

In 1905, the hundred largest manufacturing firms in Britain accounted for only 15 per cent of the total output, and although the degree of concentration in manufacturing in other major economies was less at this time than in either Britain or the United States, large companies did exist in the form of the *zaibatsus* in Japan and the cartels in Germany (Alford, 1996, p. 217). In 1930, the share of the largest hundred manufacturing companies in Britain was 20 per cent and remained at the same level until 1953. However, the share had risen to 41 per cent by 1970 (Millward, in Floud and McCloskey, 1994b, p. 157). By the end of the Second World War, large North American companies were commonly found to be multidivisional, and while such a structure was relatively rare in Britain, manufacturing industry in Britain still held the position of being the most concentrated in the world (Alford, 1996, pp. 217–18). Finally, in terms of industrial concentration measured by employment, the three largest firms in manufacturing industry accounted on average for 26.3 per cent of employment in 1935, 26.3 per cent in 1951 and 32.4 per cent in 1958, increasing to 41 per cent in 1968 (Millward, in Floud and McCloskey, 1994b, p. 157). Most commentators in this area suggest that the increase in industrial concentration was caused by merger and takeover activity, rather that just through an increase in the size of plant.[3]

Merger and takeover in history

The first merger wave in the United States began in 1897 and continued until 1904 and contained mostly horizontal mergers leading to monopolies, or near monopolies, in the steel industry (US Steel), the tobacco industry (American Tobacco), the chemical industry (DuPont) and in the manufacture of agricultural machinery (International Harvester). It is argued that the creation of national markets through improvements in the infrastructure led to intensified competition and allowed the expansion of firms into markets beyond regional borders. This wave was mainly financed by investment bankers who were becoming increasingly aggressive in their attitude to takeovers and it only came to a halt with the economic downturn of 1904. The second wave commenced in 1916 when investment bankers again played a prominent role in the provision of finance to fund the deals, which were again mainly horizontal mergers with approximately 30 per cent being of the vertical type. The second wave ended with the onset of the depression as the stock market crashed in October 1929, following which the number of mergers and acquisitions then remained at a relatively low level until the mid-1960s when, it is argued, the conglomerate era began.

   This third wave began in 1965 and continued until the stock market downturn of 1969 and saw the introduction of the Monopolies and Mergers Act of 1965, which required the Board of Trade to refer cases to the Monopolies and Mergers Commission if the merged concerns were to have at least a third of the market share, or at least £10 million of assets, or £5 million for one of the parties involved. During the period 1965–73, 875 mergers were considered by the Board of Trade, but only 18 of these went to the Monopolies Commission, with only six being prohibited (Millward, in Floud and McCloskey, 1994b, p. 158). The fourth wave began in 1984 and although the increase in the number of mergers was only 0.39 per cent, the $ value of the deals rose at 67 per cent. This wave appeared at the time to exhibit a number of unique characteristics, including the use of leveraged buyouts, the use of aggressive takeover tactics and junk-bond financing. Thus, this was the first wave that could be characterized as involving large-scale hostile takeover battles (Gaughan, 1994, p. 3).

In Britain, the nature of the target companies appears to have changed somewhat in the 1980s as the larger companies, which had been shielded from the threat of takeover by their size in the 1960s and 1970s, became vulnerable to rival bids from smaller companies using the leveraged bid. In 1986 alone 695 British firms changed ownership (50 per cent higher than in 1985) and between 1973 and 1986, 2184 British firms were taken over (Gray and McDermott, 1989, pp. 4–5). According to UNCTAD, during the 1980s there was a massive increase in mergers leading to a universal trend towards liberalization and deregulation. Indeed, the extent of the merger boom is amply illustrated with the fact that the transactions involving US companies are estimated to be in the order of over $1.3 trillion in total. In Britain the total was 57 billion ECUs in 1985–8 and in Japan 3330 mergers and transfers of business were filed with the Fair Trade Commission in 1991 (an increase of over 900 on 1989) (UNCTAD, 1993, p. 12). The distinctive feature of the 1980s wave is said to have been the very large value, their cross-border character and the predominantly horizontal nature of the mergers, and it was apparent in almost every sector (ibid.).

Gray and McDermott suggest that the primary motive that underlies the large bids is globalization and the urge to become a giant of industry, and that this is due to the fact that firms that are competing in a global industry are very much more aware of the benefits to be gleaned from economies of scale (Gray and McDermott, 1989, p. 5). As such, the acquisition of already successful companies is particularly attractive because the benefits become immediately apparent and, due to the nature of the competitive process, when a major acquisition takes place, other capitalists will imitate to maintain their competitive position, not necessarily out of choice, but owing to the competitive imperative. This process becomes international in its aspect as part of

Table 10.1   The world's leading multinational companies, 1995

Corporation	Country of origin	Sales ($ billion)	Total employment	Foreign employment as % of total
Itochu Corp.	Japan	186.6	9 994	27(24)*
General Motors	United States	163.9	745 000	34
Mitsui & Co.	Japan	163.3	11 378	32(41)*
Sumitomo Corp.	Japan	152.5	11 200	n.a.(38)*
Marubeni	Japan	144.9	9 533	24
Ford Motor Co.	United States	137.1	346 990	30
Mitsubishi Corp.	Japan	124.9	9 241	42(41)*
Exxon Corp.	United States	121.8	82 000	54
Toyota Motor Corp.	Japan	111.7	146 885	23
Shell, Royal	UK/Netherlands	109.9	104 000	78
Hitachi Ltd	Japan	94.7	331 673	24
Nisho Iwai Corp.	Japan	89.1	6 684	31(33)*
Mobil Corp.	United States	73.4	50 400	52
Daimler-Benz	Germany	72.1	310 993	22
IBM	United States	71.9	225 347	50
General Electric Co.	United States	70.0	222 000	32
Phillip Morris	United States	66.1	151 000	58
Matsushita Electric	Japan	64.1	265 538	40
Siemens AG	Germany	62.0	373 000	43
Volkswagen AG	Germany	61.5	257 000	44
British Petroleum	UK	57.0	58 150	71
Nissan Motor Co. Ltd	Japan	56.3	139 856	43
Chrysler Corp.	United States	53.2	126 000	20
AT&T Corp.	United States	51.4	300 000	18
Unilever	UK/Netherlands	46.7	307 000	90

*Employment figures for Japanese companies are misleading. The numbers in brackets relate to the share of foreign sales in total sales.
Source: Kozul-Wright and Rowthorn (1998), p. 79.

the same imperative and leads to the proposition that globalization is a continuation of the trend that arises out of the capitalist mode of production for markets to be continually extended.

The extent of merger and takeover activity is again reaching a peak at the end of the 1990s with both hostile and friendly bids being reported on a daily basis in the financial press. The activity is both intra- and international, involving industry, finance and commerce.

Therefore, during the twentieth century takeover activity has become more and more a global phenomenon, in the sense that the mergers are very much cross-border with the rise of the multinational company. Table 10.1 illustrates this in terms of the level of foreign employment involved in the operations of the world's leading multinational companies.

Globalization

The history of capitalism, therefore, is one characterized by the continual extension of the market for goods, services and labour power from the local to the national and on to the international level. This becomes true not only of goods and services which use money as the medium of exchange, but also of money itself which becomes a commodity and is traded on the money markets on a global scale. Many authors in this area have either overlooked, or ignored, this factor in their examinations of the phenomenon of globalization, particularly those authors who attempt to refute the existence of globalization (cf. Hurst and Thompson, 1996, and Kleinknecht and Wengel, 1998). Giddens argues that more than a trillion US dollars per day is traded in international currency transactions and that since 1970 'institutionally managed money has increased by 1100 per cent on a world scale' (Giddens, 1998, p. 30). Based on this tremendous increase in the commodity trading of money in the past 30 years, Giddens argues that globalization does exist and that it is a totally new phenomenon, peculiar to the final quarter of the twentieth century, not a continuation of past trends (ibid.). However, Giddens overemphasizes the singular role played by financial markets in the process of globalization and therefore tends to pay too little attention to the role of trade and of the transnational nature of the capitalist enterprise. That the extension of the market to a greater or lesser extent, in terms of the degree of extension that takes place at a particular point in time, is an outcome of the capitalist relations of production is not a particularly difficult proposition to prove. Indeed, it is one of the supposed advantages of the system, according to its advocates, that it is able to continuously enlarge its sphere of exchange to the benefit of all. This is supposed to occur through economies of scale leading to lower prices, and through specialization and comparative advantage in free trade leading to greater efficiency.

One could argue that the move towards globalization began in the nineteenth century with the overseas expansionism of the British and

European powers in terms both of the extension of trade and of the overseas investment undertaken in this period, as capital sought the highest rate of return. In the twentieth century this was extended to multinational expansionism as companies sought economies of scale and new markets and although this has been interspersed with periods where trading blocs have been the order of the day, the majority of the last century has been a period of multilateral trade and the international mobility of capital. The origins of this process can be traced back to the eighteenth century to the beginnings of the transition to the industrial age. Production for the domestic market rapidly expanded to encompass export production and as the international market grew, capitalist firms had to decide whether to continue to expand their domestic operations, or to extend production to where the market was situated. The competitive process ensured that a continuous pressure was exerted on the capitalist enterprise to increase in size and to expand production to remain in a leading competitive position.

The period 1870–1913 has been described as a 'golden age' of international integration and, indeed, as an exemplary episode of rapid economic progress (Kozul-Wright, in Michie and Grieve-Smith, 1995, p. 139). During this period of an open regulatory framework, capital was free to move unhindered to where the highest rate of return was thought to exist and profits could be transferred without restriction. Britain was able to play the leadership role by engaging in free trade and providing expertise in financial and commercial markets. Within this environment, exports grew at an unprecedented rate and foreign investment was greater than the combined totals of trade and output.[4] Structures of colonial governance reinforced the gains to be had from international integration which accrued to the capital exporting, and thus commodity importing, countries. The diffusion of technology is closely associated with mobility in terms not only of people and goods, but also of ideas. During the second half of the nineteenth century mobility was greatly improved through innovations in transport and communications and, in particular, through the extension of international finance which facilitated the movement of labour, goods and capital between economies, with European economies dominating world trade up to the First World War, as illustrated in Table 10.2. Hence, the resulting flows of economic resources became important channels for the spread of new industrial technology. The incentive to employ such techniques was the expansion of the market which itself was a product of foreign trade.

Table 10.2 The distribution of world trade 1876–1913 (%)

Region	1876–80			1913		
	Exports	Imports	Total trade	Exports	Imports	Total trade
Europe	64.2	69.6	66.9	58.9	65.1	62.0
N. America	11.7	7.4	9.5	14.8	11.5	13.2
L. America	6.2	4.6	5.4	8.3	7.0	7.6
Asia	12.4	13.4	12.9	11.8	10.4	11.1
Africa	2.2	1.5	1.9	3.7	3.6	3.7
Oceania	3.3	3.5	3.4	2.5	2.4	2.4
World	100.0	100.0	100.0	100.0	100.0	100.0

Source: Kenwood and Lougheed (1992), p. 81.

The growth of foreign investment has its beginnings at the end of the Napoleonic Wars with the establishment and growth of specialized financial institutions in both borrowing and lending economies. This included the commercial banks, who operated in foreign exchange, and the investment houses, both of whom made foreign investment less risky and easier to undertake. The funds for expansion of foreign lending were provided by the accumulation of savings of a middle class willing and able to invest these overseas. In addition, the City of London became more diversified and aided the expansion of foreign investment and international trade through the use of more advanced financial instruments such as bills of exchange and credit money. From the end of the Napoleonic Wars to the mid-1850s, £420 million was invested abroad by Britain alone, but by 1870 the total value of foreign investments had trebled. After 1870, a great era of international lending occurred and by 1900 foreign investment totalled £4750 million rising rapidly to reach £9500 million in 1914 (Kenwood and Lougheed, 1992, p. 26).

The interwar years saw a discontinuity in the expansion of international trade, and although there was continued growth in the volume of foreign trade, the rate of growth slowed considerably. This was due, in large degree, to the response of the United States to the recessionary phase which the advanced capitalist world had entered and the stance that the United States took was to drastically increase tariffs through the Smoot-Hawley Act of 1931, which, in a country running a trade surplus with the rest of the world caused an immediate downturn in world trade. Thus the world entered a period of protectionism, the intensity of which had not been experienced before in the industrialized world. The knock-on effects were far reaching as primary product

Table 10.3   The regional distribution of British foreign investment 1830–1914

	1830 %	1854 %	1870 %	1914 %
Europe	66	55	25	5
United States	9	25	27	21
Latin America	23	15	11	18
British Empire:				
India			22	9
Dominions	2	5	12	37
Other Regions			3	9
Total	*100*	*100*	*100*	*100*
Total £m	110	260	770	4107
Investment				
$m	536	1266	3750	20 000

Source: Kenwood and Lougheed (1992), p. 30.

prices collapsed, debtor nations defaulted and, in Britain, devaluation and tariff protection for the whole of the British Empire took place (Tylecote, 1993, pp. 240–1).

A touchstone of the modern era, for many commentators, is the Bretton Woods agreement of 1944, which, it is argued, ushered in a 'golden age of capitalism' characterized by rapid economic growth and high levels of employment in the advanced capitalist economies. The stability of the international monetary system aided the rapid growth in both trade and output through the mechanism of specialization and export-led growth. From 1950 to 1990, world output grew at a faster rate than in any previous period, growing at an average annual rate of 3.9 per cent. During the same period, world trade grew at an average annual rate of 5.8 per cent, also a rate that was unprecedented in earlier periods. The breakdown of the Bretton Woods system in 1973 initiated a period of instability, but alongside the continuation of the trend towards greater international specialization. This also coincided with the continuing ascendancy of the multinational companies in what Dunning has described as a transitory phase from the 'golden age' to a 'globalizing age' (Dunning, 1994).

Two views on this development of the late twentieth century have emerged. First, there is the argument that what is in the interests of the multinational companies is also in the interests of national economies, due to their efficient allocation of resources on a global scale, marginalizing the nation state in the world economy.[5] The other view is that capitalist firms attempt to extend their rivalry through the competitive dynamic into the international level in a search for market leadership.[6] Giddens argues that the idea that the nation state, and therefore governments, are becoming obsolete because of this globalization is incorrect, but that their 'shape is being altered' (Giddens, 1998, p. 31). Quite what he means by this is not at all clear, except that in the Marxian sense the state is adapting its role in the interests of capital which is now global in scope and therefore forces governments into international collaborations.[7] What one must be careful not to do is to analyse the state as a single entity, to suggest that the reaction to globalization will itself be global and homogeneous. The state will react in different ways depending upon the state of development of the economy and the history of the economy and, as such, over-exaggeration of the power of the state in the past leads one to conclude that the rise of the multinational has had a much greater impact than in fact is the case. The situation is much more complex in that all states operating within the structure of the capitalist relations of production must ensure a regulatory framework that is in the interests of capital accumulation; this may involve greater collaboration between states both in economic and political spheres and indeed while states engage in greater integration at these levels, multinational capitalism can flourish. Mann has suggested that the networks of global interaction are strengthening through three elements. First, technological and social relations of capitalism create a more global scale of transnational relations. Second, the differential position of nation states leads to segmentation of the global networks. Third, this segmentation tends to be moderated by global political and economic relationships (Mann, 1997, p. 495). An example of this is to be found in the policies adopted by the Bretton Woods institutions, the International Monetary Fund (IMF) and the World Bank, as well as the World Trade Organization (WTO). As the international relations of production have changed in the postwar era, so too have the policies of these institutions changed. Essentially moving from the position of enabling the reconstruction of the capitalist relations of production in a war ravaged Europe and Japan to providing the free-market, competitive environment within which capital accumulation can flourish.

Summary

The phase of development that is denoted as monopoly capitalism is the outcome of the dynamic of the capitalist relations of production and therefore, the transition from a local to a national and then international market is a movement that is inherent in the competitive imperative of the capitalist system. The globalization of the market in commercial and industrial terms is therefore best understood within such an analysis. The capitalist desire for accumulation not only produces technological innovation but also the need to extend exploitation to avoid a realization crisis in the narrow national market. However, it also ensures that fewer and fewer capitalists survive as competition forces mergers and takeover on an ever larger scale. 'The need of a constantly expanding market for its products chases the bourgeoisie over the whole surface of the globe. It must nestle everywhere, settle everywhere, establish connexions everywhere' (Marx and Engels, 1985, p. 83).

11
Unemployment

Introduction

In Marxian terms, unemployment represents the reserve army of labour in capitalism and this is fundamental to the workings of the capitalist system. Unemployment is created by and is a necessary coadjutor of the capitalist system itself. Marx explains this as follows:

> ...in all spheres, the increase of the variable part of the capital, and therefore the number of workers employed by it, is always connected with violent fluctuations and the temporary production of a surplus population. ... Owing to the magnitude of the already functioning social capital, and the degree of its increase, owing to the extension of the scale of production, and the great mass of workers set in motion, owing to the development of the productivity of their labour, and the great breadth and richness of the stream springing from all the sources of wealth, there is also an extension of the scale on which greater attraction of workers by capital is accompanied by their greater repulsion; an increase takes place in the rapidity of the change in the organic composition of capital and in its technical form, and an increasing number of spheres of production become involved in this change, sometimes simultaneously, and sometimes alternatively. The working population therefore produces both the accumulation of capital and the means by which it itself is made relatively superfluous; and it does this to an extent that is always increasing.
>
> (Marx, 1976, pp. 782–3)

Hence technological advance, itself a product of the dynamics of capitalism, not only ensures that the capitalist is less dependent on specific workers through the substitution of their strength and skills, but also adds to the reserve army of labour putting pressure on the remuneration of those who remain in employment, as their power in the bargaining process is reduced and their fear of losing their jobs is increased.

However, economists of different convictions emphasize different causes and consequences of unemployment. Therefore to understand fully the unique manner in which this phenomenon is viewed in the Marxian context, it is important that we explore some of the alternative explanations. The first distinction is that between the Keynesian and the classical theories of unemployment; the second is the theory of hysteresis, incorporating the concept of the Non-Accelerating Inflation Rate of Unemployment (NAIRU). These represent the most frequently discussed theories of unemployment and the intention here is to highlight the inadequacies of such approaches and then to focus upon the insights that are available, given the empirical evidence, from an analysis of the reserve army of labour as an integral part of the capitalist relations of production.

Classical unemployment

For the classical economists, general unemployment occurs when the actual real wage rate (w_1) exceeds the market clearing real wage rate(see Figure 11.1). At the real wage rate w_1 employers will only be willing and able to employ L_1 workers, but could, if the real wage rate were to

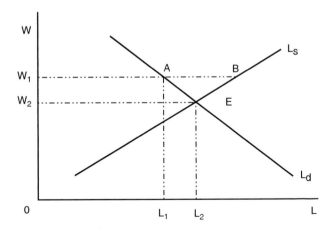

Figure 11.1 Labour market adjustment

be w_2, employ L_2 workers. Hence, the cause of unemployment here is the fact that the real wage is too high. Pigou argued that, in a competitive economy, those who were unemployed would compete with employed workers to gain employment, and the only option open to the unemployed would be to offer their labour at a rate of money wages lower than those already in employment. Therefore, a general decline in the level of money wages would result in reductions in real wages, which would cause employers to take on more workers (Trevithick, 1992, p. 183). Hence, unemployment in the classical sense was due to the inability of the market for labour to clear at point E. The cause of this disequilibrium (producing a real wage higher than the equilibrium) was said to be the monopolistic practices of the trades unions which did not allow for the downward adjustment of money, and therefore real, wages. Pigou argued that workers were more occupied with the money wage than they were the real wage and this led to the situation where they would oppose reductions in money wages, even in the situation where prices were falling and the real wage was actually rising. The policy prescription that follows is thus that the market for labour should be allowed to operate freely and without obstruction, and that real wages must be allowed to fall to the level of equilibrium. Hence, if unemployment exists it is due to the fact that those in employment are demanding, and receiving, wages which are too high for the market to clear.

This was the prevailing view of unemployment in the 1920s as most politicians and many economists believed that wage flexibility (that is wage reductions) would aid exports. The classical economists argued that the high cost of labour was the major factor in high prices and thus lost markets and that until wages were reduced unemployment would remain high. In July 1925, Prime Minister Baldwin reportedly stated that: 'All the workers of this country have got to take reductions in wages to help put industry on its feet' (Constantine, 1994, p. 63). As shown in Tables 11.1 and 11.2, recorded unemployment fluctuated around the 10 per cent level in Britain during the 1920s, which was higher than elsewhere in Europe (Floud and McCloskey, 1994, p. 304). This was also at a time when prices were falling, thus apparently justifying the case put forward by the classical economists. However, Keynes highlighted two major shortcomings in the argument of Pigou. First, Pigou had assumed that a reduction in money wages would increase the demand for goods. However, the fallacy of composition would suggest that a reduction in the wage bill of one firm, which allows it to sell more output, does not necessarily indicate that this would be the case

Table 11.1 Unemployment rates 1920–38

Year	Unemployment (%)
1920	3.9[a]
1921	16.9
1922	14.3
1923	11.7
1924	10.3
1925	11.3
1926	12.5
1927	7.4[b]
1928	8.2
1929	8.0
1930	12.3
1931	16.4
1932	17.0
1933	15.4
1934	12.9
1935	12.0
1936	10.2
1937	8.5
1938	10.1

(a) 1920–6 – unemployment as percentage of insured labourforce.
(b) 1927–38 – total unemployment as proportion of total employees.

Source: Garside (1990), Tables 1 and 2, pp. 4–5.

Table 11.2 Average unemployment in seven industrial countries 1874–1973 (% of civilian labour force)

	Pre-1914	1925–9	1930–7	1952–64	1965–73
UK	4.7	8.4	13.9	2.5	3.2
US	4.2	3.5	18.3	5.0	4.5
Sweden	n.a.	11.2	16.4	1.7	2.0
France	n.a.	n.a.	n.a.	1.7	2.4
Germany	3.6	11.1	24.1	2.7	0.8
Italy	n.a.	n.a.	n.a.	5.9	3.4
Japan	n.a.	n.a.	5	1.9	1.3

Source: Matthews, Feinstein and Odling-Smee (1982), Table 3.23, p. 94.

for the economy as a whole. In fact, Keynes suggested that it would have the effect of reducing consumer demand without stimulating the additional investment required to compensate for the reduction. The redistribution of income that would occur from workers to capitalists would also reduce effective demand, as capitalists tend to spend a smaller proportion of their income on consumption than do workers. These effects combined would produce an increase in unemployment, the opposite of the effect that the classical economists wished to achieve. Therefore, by cutting money wages this would lead to rising unemployment, as effective demand was reduced, leading to further cuts in money wages. Second, he suggested that even if an individual worker, or group of workers, wished to reduce their real wages, they could not do so. This is because even classical theory itself suggests that prices depend, at least in part, on wages and therefore, if all workers accepted a reduction in their wages then all prices would fall and real wages would not be reduced. Joan Robinson summarized the argument as follows:

> The Keynesian revolution began by refuting the then orthodox theory that cutting wages is the best way to reduce unemployment. Keynes argued that a general cut in wages would reduce the price level more or less proportionally, and so raise the burden of debt, discourage investment and increase unemployment.
>
> (Robinson, 1980, p. 34)

Keynesian unemployment

In the Keynesian explanation of the causes of unemployment, one must turn, not to the incorrect real wage level, but to a deficiency of aggregate demand as shown in Figure 11.2, and, as such, the culprit must be government, as the state has the power to raise aggregate demand through macroeconomic instruments. Hence, the argument here is that the state can manipulate the level of aggregate demand to ensure a high and stable level of employment in the economy. Thus, it would be possible to observe Keynesian unemployment when the real wage is at its market clearing level and this can be illustrated in a slightly different manner.

In Figure 11.3, the point Z represents the point where both the goods market and the labour market clear and, as such, is a position of Walrasian equilibrium. However, even though the real wage rate is at the market clearing level the economy can only attain point C, a temporary equilibrium, due to a sales constraint on output. That is, firms would be willing to produce Y* output and therefore employ L* labour,

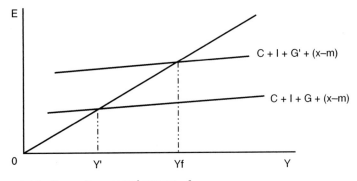

Figure 11.2 Keynesian unemployment – I

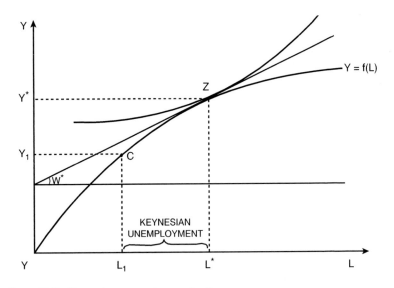

Figure 11.3 Keynesian unemployment – II

but only be able to sell Y_1 output and thus employ L_1 labour. This results in the amount of unemployment $L^*–L_1$, not because the real wage is too high but because at this wage aggregate demand is too low. Therefore, Keynes was able to insist that it is the conditions that underlie demand, and not supply, that are the fundamental cause of unemployment in a monetary economy (Davidson, 1994, p. 10). In doing so Keynes had overturned three essential classical axioms: the neutrality of money axiom, the substitution axiom and the prediction axiom. This allowed him to propose that unemployment, rather than full employment is the normal outcome of a *laissez-faire* economy.

As we have seen, the world depression of the 1920s and 1930s was a period of substantial and incessant unemployment with no obvious tendency for money wages to adjust speedily in order to clear the market for labour. The publication of Keynes's *General Theory* in 1936 therefore revolutionized the manner in which the economy was viewed and macroeconomic analysis focused on the categories of aggregate expenditure, consumption, investment, government expenditure and exports (where $E = C + I + G + (x - m)$). Total spending in the economy is seen as being determined by these combined expenditures and total spending determines the level of total national income. Hence, in a depression, because there would be unemployment, there would be an absence of a supply constraint and therefore the only limiting factor must be demand. The largest component of total expenditure in the Keynesian macroeconomic models was personal consumption, and this was assumed to be dependent upon the level of national income and would therefore increase with national income. Investment was a matter determined by the expectations held by individual entrepreneurs, and the level of exports was determined by the income of foreigners and hence, these latter two factors were exogenously determined. Finally, government expenditure offers the policymakers a control function to alter the level of total expenditure in the economy by use of fiscal stabilization policy, using taxes and government spending. Thus, Keynesian macroeconomics provided an intellectual defence of the active intervention by the state in the economy, including the setting of a budget deficit to increase aggregate demand. For over twenty years after the Second World War there was widespread belief that the problem of unemployment had been overcome as unemployment rates of less than 2 per cent were considered to be normal. Table 11.3 shows the estimates of unemployment rates for international comparison and illustrates that Britain enjoyed relatively low and stable rates of unemployment in the 1950s and 1960s. In Britain the Barber Boom of 1972 is an example of the attempt by the state to deliberately incur a deficit to stimulate the economy in order to raise national income and reduce unemployment and previously, during the period 1968 to 1970, the Labour Chancellor, Jenkins, attempted to engineer a budget surplus to slow down the economy that was seen to be overheating. Economics

Table 11.3   Unemployment rates 1950–70 (%)

	1950	1955	1960	1965	1970
USA	5.3	4.4	5.5	4.5	4.8
Japan	1.8	2.4	1.7	1.2	1.1
Belgium	7.1	4.6	4.3	1.9	2.1
Germany	10.2	4.3	1.0	0.5	0.8
Italy	12.2	10.5	5.5	5.3	5.3
Netherlands	2.0	1.3	1.2	0.8	1.4
Norway	2.7	2.5	2.5	1.8	1.6
Sweden	2.2	2.5	1.4	1.1	1.5
UK	2.9	1.9	2.9	2.5	3.1

Source: Broadberry, in Floud and McCloskey (1994), vol.3, Table 7.1, p. 201.

could in this light be viewed therefore as a technicist operation whereby it was known that the state could manipulate macroeconomic factors, the question was just one of how much by, when and for how long.[1] The efforts of economists therefore went into the conceiving of models that would address these questions and thereby improve the techniques of stabilization policy. In the 1950s and 1960s, it appeared as though these models had achieved some degree of success, but as we moved into the 1970s, the Keynesian models were increasingly incapable of explaining economic phenomena such as inflation.

What links these two seemingly opposing views is that full employment is seen as an equilibrium position which can exist within a neo-classical framework of perfect competition. It is therefore the task of both the classical and the Keynesian economists to explain the divergences from full employment in the economy involving analysis of trade unions, imperfect competition, asymmetric information, efficiency wages and flexible labour markets.

In 1958 Professor A. W. H. Phillips appeared to have found a determinate, stable, inverse relationship between the unemployment rate and the rate of change of money wages (see Figure 11.4) which had continued to hold good for almost a century. Thus lower levels of unemployment were associated with higher rates of inflation and vice versa. It now appeared as though governments could choose to use aggregate demand policies to reduce the level of unemployment only if they were prepared to accept the consequent rise in inflation. Indeed, they could simply choose between a menu of higher (or lower) unemployment with lower (or higher) inflation.

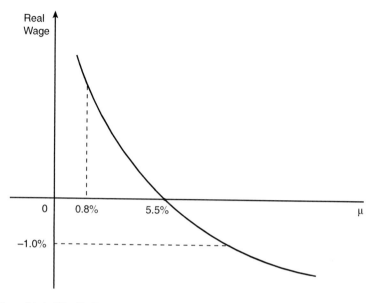

Figure 11.4 The Phillips curve

However, Friedman (1968) criticized the Phillips curve in that he argued that real, rather than money, wages respond to the pressure of labour markets. The result of this modification is that there exists not one Phillips curve but a different curve for each expected rate of inflation and if current inflation is higher than expected then expectations will be revised upwards. Friedman was then able to argue that only at the level of unemployment where expectations are fulfilled will the rate of inflation be stable. This level of unemployment is called the natural rate of unemployment. If unemployment is above this natural rate then inflation will be decelerating whereas if unemployment is below the natural rate inflation will be accelerating. Only when unemployment is at the natural rate will the rate of inflation be stable.

Hysteresis

The basis of the theory of hysteresis is the non-accelerating inflation rate of unemployment (NAIRU), which in turn is based upon three macroeconomic propositions. Firstly, there is the argument of the Phillips curve, that a fall in unemployment will tend to accelerate wage inflation. Secondly, autonomous factors such as trade unions, exist which will 'push' the system to higher levels of inflation. Thirdly, once inflation is present and rising it will tend to continue to increase as expectations adjust. Thus, if unemployment is low, then inflation will have a tendency to increase, due to the fact that employers will offer higher wages to labour in order to attract workers to take up unfilled vacancies. On the supply side, trade unions will be in a stronger position to bargain for wage settlements above those justified by productivity increases. Conversely, if unemployment is high then inflation will tend to fall as trade unions will be in a much weaker position and employers will not be attempting to attract labour to unfilled vacancies. Therefore, it is argued that there will be a critical level of unemployment at which inflation will neither be rising nor falling, it will be stable at NAIRU, Figure 11.5 (Layard, 1986, pp. 29–30).

The NAIRU is given by the intersection of the feasible real wage, derived from the fact that if workers obtain an increase in their money wages, firms will increase prices and the higher money wages do not represent an increase in real wages, and the target real wage, derived from the inverse relationship between the level of unemployment and trade union bargaining power. The intersection of the two is the position where the feasible real wage and the target real wage are consistent with each other and the result is that there is no tendency for inflation to accelerate.[2]

Hysteresis is a term used by economists to denote an influence of economic events that is persistent in character. For example, the dependence of NAIRU on the history of unemployment constitutes hysteresis as it is then dependent upon past events. The argument here is that the behaviour of NAIRU is path dependent and therefore a

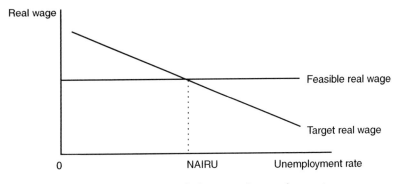

Figure 11.5   The non-accelerating inflation rate of unemployment

sustained rise in unemployment above NAIRU will result in a rise in NAIRU itself. Thus, an essentially static system is transformed into a dynamic model. Many Keynesian economists were able to accept the proposition that there existed a level of unemployment that corresponded to a rate of inflation that was neither rising nor falling, but, unlike the neoclassicals, they were unwilling to accept that this rate may be associated with overall full employment (Trevithick, 1992, p. 197). Screpanti has suggested that two types of hysteresis in unemployment can be observed. These he defines as 's-hysteresis' where inflation stabilizes when unemployment stabilizes, and 'm-hysteresis' where inflation stabilizes as the rate of unemployment continues to change.[3] He argues that m-hysteresis can be accounted for in 'persistence' models, which treat the existence of a particular level of unemployment in a Phillips curve relationship. However, persistence is not equivalent to hysteresis as a stable NAIRU can exist independent of past history (Screpanti, 1996, p. 94). In his article, Screpanti suggests that a 'wage conflict curve' exists in which the rate of inflation is dependent upon the rate of change of unemployment such that a unique NAIRU does not exist because the level of unemployment at which inflation is stabilized depends on past history both deterministically and stochastically. Essentially the concept of hysteresis as employed in these models of the unemployment–inflation trade-off focuses on the relation between the long-term unemployed and the bargaining power of the trade unions and suggests that an insider–outsider effect takes place whereby those on the inside of the labour market have pressure put upon their position as insiders by the outsiders who wish to join the employed labour force. When the number of outsiders is large, then the ability of the trade unions to successfully bargain on behalf of the insiders is diminished and vice versa when the number of outsiders is smaller. It is argued that the number of long-term unemployed as a proportion of the total unemployment will affect the bargaining relation in that the higher the proportion the lower will be its impact. In other words, the greater the number of long-term unemployed, the less they will affect the ability of the trade unions to successfully bargain on behalf of the insiders.[4]

It has been suggested that the construct of NAIRU itself has become outdated in terms of its usefulness to the policy-makers. Galbraith argues that although it remains valid as a purely mathematical construct, it would be much more productive for policy-makers to adopt the pursuit of a lower rate of unemployment than to trust to the predictions of an economic model which itself is the subject of uncertainty and disagreement (Galbraith, 1997, pp. 106–7). Hence, he advocates a return to policy designed to produce solutions to immediate problems, rather than policy based on economic models that suggest the manner in which certain economic instruments may affect certain economic variables. While there is nothing to be said against such an approach in general, it is flawed in a particular respect that takes us back to the understanding of the problem of unemployment. It is not the case that unemployment or any other economic problem can be examined in isolation from the system as a whole. Indeed as we have seen in Part I, it is necessary to examine the economic whole within which the problem occurs to be able to determine the cause and the possible solutions. In the case of unemployment, we can argue that the model of NAIRU inclusive of the underlying theory of hysteresis approaches the analysis in a Marxian sense because it attempts to discover the essential features of the relationships involved.[5]

For Marx, the reserve army of labour is a necessary feature of the capitalist mode of production and indeed must exist if capitalism is to continue. Hence, the economic system of the capitalist mode of production inherently requires unemployment to maintain the wage at the subsistence level in the long run. As with the insider–outsider, hysteresis view of unemployment, it is the bargaining power of labour that is affected by the level of unemployment and therefore it is fundamentally the power relations between capital and labour that determine the relative shares that accrue to each side of the relations of production.

This relationship is discernible in Figures 11.6 and 11.7, where, in the case of unemployment, there is a rising trend but in the case of the increase in hourly earnings the trend is downwards. Thus the power of labour to increase remuneration is diminished as the rate of unemployment rises in direct relation over time.

The postwar consensus

The social democratic view that emerged during the Second World War was presented as a modification of socialist views and employed the ideas associated with John Maynard Keynes, and suggested that there was a possible compromise with capitalism. This contained three related aspects. First, market capitalism is inherently unstable due to the booms and slumps, not necessarily caused by external shocks to the system, but as a consequence of the unregulated nature of capitalism. Second, it was recognized that 'democracy' was here to stay, which

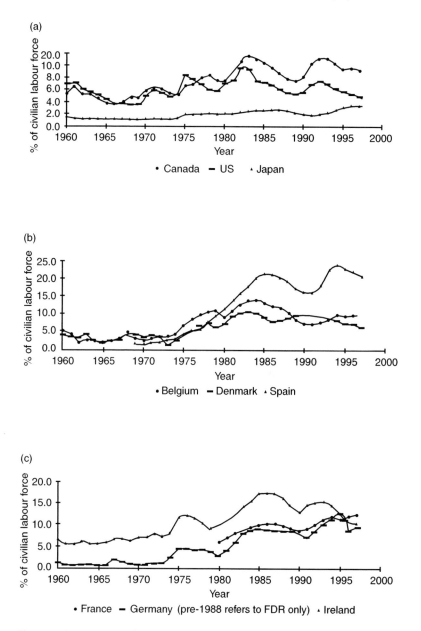

Figure 11.6(a–e) Unemployment (% of civilian labour force).
Source: OECD (1976) Main Economic Indicators 1960–1975, derived from Paris
DECI (1988).

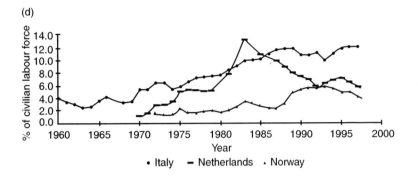

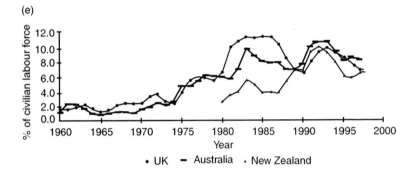

Figure 11.6   continued

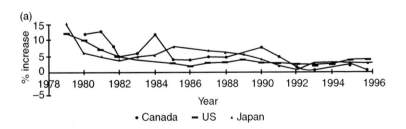

Figure 11.7(a–e)   Hourly earnings (manufacturing)
Source: OECD (1976) Main Economic Indicators 1960–1975, derived from OECD (1998).

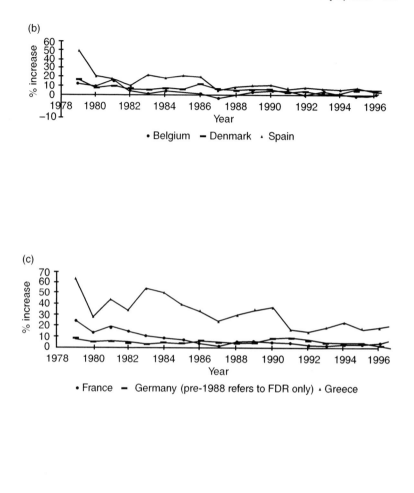

(b)

• Belgium — Denmark ᐧ Spain

(c)

• France — Germany (pre-1988 refers to FDR only) ᐧ Greece

(d)

• Ireland — Italy ᐧ Netherlands

Figure 11.7 continued

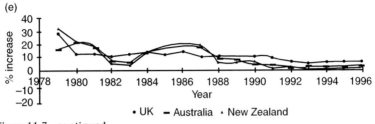

Figure 11.7   continued

led to pressures for high levels of employment and welfare as well as the experiences of the interwar period which had shown the possibility of social revolution resulting in both fascism and Soviet socialism. Third, the belief that state power could be used in a 'neutralizing' manner to foster economic growth and to form a consensus of views in society. Thus, it can be argued that Keynesianism was bound up with the universal franchise and the foundations of capitalism. Two very different views emerged. These we can describe as the weak and the strong versions of Keynesianism. In the weak version, the state should have only a limited role through the influencing of investment decisions and through the manipulation of fiscal measures to stimulate aggregate demand. In the stronger version there is a much wider role for the state as state expenditure replaces private investment decisions. From the Second World War to the early 1970s both of these views were employed, but mainly the weak version. The weak version became known as the neoclassical synthesis (Bastard Keynesianism) out of which emerged the Phillips curve trade-off. This limited role was seen by many to be insufficient and Michal Kalecki and Joan Robinson argued that it would be insufficient for long-term full employment and that the state should take over the role of private investment. However, the drawback to this latter view is that it requires a large measure of restructuring of the economy and there would be much resistance to these reforms. Kalecki in particular argued that the weaker version would not be sufficient to maintain full employment due to the problems that this would cause in terms of inflationary pressures and balance of payments problems. There would also be political barriers to restructuring of this nature and the governments in Western Europe in particular would find themselves in a difficult position. They would need to attempt to control the institutions of capitalism but balance of payments and inflationary problems would emerge. Hence, for Kalecki, a political business cycle would emerge in the absence of government control and in the face of these problems, the state would engineer high unemployment to discipline the working class, while promising full employment and economic growth. However, because they had not taken over the institutions, the need to discipline the working class meant also a dampening down of expectations. Thus the barriers to the introduction of the stronger version are political and institutional, hence the failure of Keynesianism was not just intellectual or theoretical, it involved a clash of social and economic factors which a Marxian critique can account for in the relations of production.

Indeed Keynes's ideas were introduced in the special circumstances of the Second World War and its aftermath. Keynes's ideas were introduced in the budget of 1941 as part of the whole idea of a planned economy to win the war. Cooperation between capital and labour was seen as being essential to prosecute a successful war, thus it was agreed that a workable policy could only be negotiated with the TUC and the wider labour movement. There developed the negotiated settlement which gave real material gain in exchange for rigid controls including a ban on strikes. The effect was to improve the condition of the working class despite the war and the measures appeared to work. Hence, towards the end of the hostilities, Ernest Bevin began to form the institutional framework for reconstruction of the economy after the war. The Joint Consultative Committee was established during the war as a forum for union leaders, employers and the Ministry of Labour in a form of tripartism and a forerunner to corporatism. The Reconstruction Survey was initiated to learn lessons from the wartime experience and included G. D. H. Cole, Joan Robinson and Roy Harrod. This was an attempt to discover how Keynes's ideas could be implemented on a permanent basis, the long-term application of Keynesianism. In addition, the Beveridge Report on Social Welfare was published in an attempt to bribe the working class who expected welfare after the war. Very few resisted these measures due to the circumstances of the war and they set the institutional base for consensus after the war. In the immediate postwar period the settlement with labour was continued by the Labour government with the welfare state legislation being passed and state economic planning and cooperation and negotiation in a tripartite manner.

However, in 1951 this came to an end with the election of the Conservative government which began to liberalize the economy by discontinuing the stronger version and moving quickly towards the weaker version. But, two changes had already occurred: first the change in the nature of working-class expectations in the form of full employment and increasing living standards, and second the changes as a consequence of the welfare state and the obligations that the state had undertaken in terms of social policy. This had particular significance . with respect to employment policy as claims became rights and were no longer a matter of whether or not they could be afforded by the state of the economy. The state's role became one of a guarantor of prosperity and employment. This created a mess because only continued economic growth could meet the demands, but at the same time as the state had taken these ideas on board it had begun to retreat from the strong version. This was precisely Kalecki's scenario and the state was faced with a choice: to move back to the strong version, or to revert to a periodic disciplining of the working class through high levels of unemployment to dampen down their expectations. Hence, the introduction of Keynesian policies was based on the attempt to construct an institutional framework for collective bargaining and to provide for a consensus in society through the introduction of the welfare state. Although the process continued, the attempt to return to free trade was encouraged and sterling was placed again as one of the main world currencies. This led to conflict between internal and external policies leading to a compromise on domestic policy, as balance of payments problems emerged.

Thus the abandonment of Keynesian demand management techniques coincided with the re-establishment of the capitalist relations of production, with the labour–capital relationship returned to its former identity, that of a power relationship. The reconstruction of the economy was complete and the private sector no longer required the aid of the state and, therefore, the postwar settlement was also no longer required. Hence, the policy of the maintenance of high levels of employment was abandoned in favour of a policy of low inflation, allowing unemployment to rise. High levels of unemployment ensured that the power was back with the capitalists, holding down the increase in the wage level through the disciplining of the working class and therefore producing the desired effect in terms of the level of increase in the price level and with it a reaffirmation of the Phillips curve and the NAIRU relationship.

Summary

Much of the analysis of unemployment in the Keynesian tradition has emphasized the power relation that exists in the labour market. However, it is modelled in isolation from the totality of the capitalist relations of production and, therefore, must be only a partial analysis. Therefore, attempts to engineer higher levels of employment in capitalism cannot succeed because of the crucial role that is played by the reserve army of labour. Michal Kalecki understood this in his analysis, and in this way one could argue that Kalecki's discussion of the role of unemployment lacks some of the naiveté of the social democratic view because it is rooted firmly in the Marxian tradition. Hence, the maintenance of full employment is not possible in the long term in a capitalist economy because this would undermine the very force which maintains capitalism, the accumulation of capital.

12
The Public Sector

Introduction

The role of the public sector has obviously changed considerably over the past century and the relationship between the state and private capital is one which can define the historical episodes in the development of capitalism to the present day. Marx had little to say in *Capital* about the role of the state and did not fully develop his theory of the state, dealing only with the state in terms of intervention through the Factory Acts and the role of the state in the process of primitive accumulation. However, the size of the public sector has grown inordinately during the twentieth century to match the ever changing requirements of the capitalist class and the economic environment. This has included not only the expansion in the size and scope of the public sector, but also concerted attempts at its reduction in both aspects, particularly since the mid-1970s. The dramatic increase in the level of state intervention after the Second World War has, in the past twenty years, undergone an equally dramatic revision in the form of deregulation. The emphasis has been in terms of the requirements of the capitalist class given the dynamics of the system as a whole such that, the size and function of the public sector is a reflection of the economic conditions that prevail.

The increasing size of the public sector

Wagner's Law suggests that there exists a tendency in all industrializing economies for the public sector to expand in both absolute and relative terms and predicts that this relationship will continue due to the need for the continuous expansion of administration and law and order services, the increasing concern over distributional issues and a need to regulate private monopolies. Empirically, many studies have shown the law to be an accurate reflection of the development of public sector growth in the now mature capitalist economies such that, as per capita income increases, the public sector grows in relative importance. Indeed, the increase in state activity during the twentieth century can be viewed as one of the most dramatic changes to have occurred in capitalist economies. In contrast, the nineteenth century can be characterized, particularly in Britain, as the high period of *laissez-faire* and, although there is much controversy among economic historians as to the degree and influence of government economic policy before 1914, in general most would agree that the goals of fiscal and monetary policy were to provide a stable environment within which capitalism could flourish and, at the same time, competition and efficiency were encouraged by allowing foreign goods to enter the country free of protective tariffs and where there were 'natural' monopolies, the state would regulate private enterprises by determining rates and standards of service. In industrial relations, Victorian and Edwardian governments were comparatively inactive, in contrast to the governments post-1914, given their belief that intervention would have a distorting effect on the labour market. Overall the period pre-1914 was one in which state legislation increased in the area of social welfare to accommodate changes in the social environment, but in the economy it retained a belief in the competitive free market through sound finance, free-trade and social harmony. Thus, the trend throughout the twentieth century has generally been to extend the role of the state from essentially the maintenance of internal and external security into an all-pervasive role including income transfer, the ownership of means of production, and the expansion of health and education. The extent of this extension of the role of the state in Britain can be seen in Table 12.1.

'Orthodox' views of the public sector

In contrast, what may be described as 'mainstream' economics suggests that there is a division between economic power and political power, with the latter being viewed as a possible counteractive force to economic power. However, such an analysis fails to grasp the essential feature of the system as a whole, which necessitates the intervention of the state. The really important question, therefore, is as to whether the state is proactive or reactive in its defence of, and promotion of, the

Table 12.1   General government expenditure (total) (£ million)

1948	4236
1952	5865
1957	7580
1962	10447
1967	16789
1972	26242
1977	61450
1982	128125
1987	166747
1992	257707
1997	316061

Source: Office of National Statistics (1998) *Economic Trends, Annual Supplement*, Table 5.4, p. 236.

interests of the capitalist system. One could suggest that the politician is, by nature, much more likely to be reactive than proactive and as an instrument of the system the state cannot be in a position to predict the requirements of the economy far in advance. Hence, government policies are a reflection of the current position, although changing in character through time, as the economic environment undergoes continuous transformation.

In 'orthodox' economics the role of the public sector has undergone transformations in the manner in which it is discussed due to the enormous changes that have occurred since the eighteenth century in terms of the legitimate areas of government intervention. In the classical tradition, Adam Smith argued that regulation by the state of economic activity was unacceptable due to the expression of privilege that it entailed and the interruption that it caused to the 'natural' course of the market. The exceptions to this for Smith were the defence of the realm and the maintenance of law and order, incorporating a judicial system to ensure the fulfilment of contracts in the market. Alfred Marshall, in the neoclassical tradition, commenting over a century later, argued that although the market was largely benevolent, certain circumstances exist whereby socially undesirable results would obtain from a totally unregulated market. These circumstances include where, mainly for technical reasons, the market would produce outcomes that were inefficient and wasteful of resources, such as the 'natural' monopolies of public services. Hence, government intervention in these areas was advocated by Marshall, as were the provision of public education and the reallocation by government of resources through taxation and subsidy. Hence, traditional economics had already recognized the need for greater state intervention in the economy well before the publication of Keynes's *General Theory,* as the structure of the economy had changed and the requirements of the private sector had been transformed through capitalist development.

Much of the neoclassical analysis of the role of the public sector concerns the concept of the optimal level of output of the public sector in a mixed economy. Here their analysis employs the assumptions of perfect competition with an infinitely elastic demand curve for each product and use of the equi-marginal principle to explain relative consumption among individual consumers. Thus the relative consumption of goods and services depends upon the marginal values placed upon them by individual consumers and these marginal valuations are proportional to their relative prices. In the optimal situation of the private sector, the marginal rate of substitution in consumption is equal to the marginal rate of substitution of purchase in the market, which is also equal to the marginal rate of substitution in production. By using the Pareto Criterion, where it is impossible to make one person better off if at least one person is made worse off, an optimal amount of output can be derived for the private sector. However, pure public goods, by their very nature, are consumed in equal amounts by all individuals, and differences occur only in the marginal valuations placed on the quantity of the goods by different individuals. Hence, private goods have the same price but differing levels of consumption, and pure public goods have different marginal valuations but the same consumption levels. In a neoclassical general equilibrium analysis, the combination of public and private goods is computed to maximize the utility of two consumers, and therefore to discover the Pareto efficient distribution. In this manner, it is argued, it is possible to discover the optimum level of output for the public sector in a two-sector economy. However, notwithstanding the unrealistic nature of the underlying assumptions that are employed in such a model, the major problem is that people tend to conceal their preferences in regard to their marginal valuations of the consumption of public goods and therefore, we can conclude that 'orthodox' economic theory cannot, in any objective sense, reveal the optimum allocation of output between the public and the private sector in a mixed economy (Atkinson, Livesey and Milward, 1998, pp. 324–7). As always, the neoclassical analysis represents a static approach to a dynamic problem and is an apolitical model addressing a highly political question.

The Marxian approach

The Marxian approach to the role of the state is generally that public sector activity is influenced by the needs of the capitalist class and therefore the state acts largely in the interests of capital. One important aspect of this is the legal framework that is set by the state within which the market operates and economic activity is organized. For example, the legal position of workers' organizations will have an impact upon their ability to bargain successfully in terms of the power that they have relative to that of the employers. By the same token, legislation passed in the area of monopolies and mergers may influence the structure of production in the short term. However, the point here is that the legislation that is passed will always endeavour to be favourable to the capitalists and to create the superstructure that is most appropriate to accumulation and, therefore, economic growth. Yet, as we shall see, this creates a paradox in the context of the dynamic of the capitalist relations of production. The individual capitalists wish there to be less intervention but collectively, the capitalist class requires ever greater levels of state expenditure and legislation. As development proceeds there arise certain requirements that can only be met by third party intervention. For example, as the market expands goods must be transported over greater distances and the provision of roads is not profitable for private enterprise. Hence, the state becomes an important provider and facilitator within the changing environment of a capitalist economy.

Although the virtues of the 'enterprise' economy are extolled by the neoliberals and the social democrats alike, there exist fundamental asymmetries in terms of structural, organizational and institutional power in a capitalist economy. Hence, democracy takes its form from the need to ensure that such asymmetries remain in place for the continuation of the functioning of the capitalist economy in the interests of corporate and commercial power, to ensure the continuation of the opportunities for the accumulation of capital and therefore to protect and promote the perpetuation of the capitalist relations of production. Hence, changes in the structure of the economy will induce changes to the institutional structure, or superstructure, including the legal and political systems. This explains the different legal and political institutional frameworks that now exist in mature, capitalist economies. Varying historical experiences in science, technology, culture and other fundamental social systems give rise to a variety of institutional forms within the same relations of production. Jessop argues that in this sense 'all social relations are polyvalent [and] can be articulated into different institutional orders, and have varying centrality to economic performance' (Jessop, 1997, p. 565). Screpanti holds that different property rights regimes and governance structures which produce different institutional arrangements within the capitalist mode of production, '...all have a basic property in common: the ability to regulate surplus uses so as to serve capital accumulation' (Screpanti, 1999, p. 23).

The expanding role of the state is therefore set by historical development of the economic relations and is conditioned by the economic environment required to ensure that capital accumulation is possible and to guarantee that there exists a harmonious society in the face of class conflict. Therefore, the state must maintain its legitimacy by disguising its use of power in the sole interests of the capitalist class using ideology to convince the working class that, for example, capital accumulation is in the interests of all in society.[1] The ruling class is able to dominate government decision-making because of its economic power given the prevailing economic environment and the relations of production. Hence, its political and legal objectives are to ensure that they retain ownership of the surplus and that the accumulation of capital is facilitated through appropriate policy regarding the position of the working class. The ruling class also have power over the *ideas* of the state, including those of the political parties that may form a government.[2] This is not to suggest that *all* aspects of state policy *only* furthers the interests of the capitalist class, rather it is the capitalist *system* that is the beneficiary of government action. Hence, gains accrue also to the working class, but tempered by the costs that they incur in the provision of state-sponsored welfare.[3]

In the Marxian tradition, Kalecki argued that because a high level of unemployment is a necessary element in *laissez-faire* capitalism, the attainment of full employment would necessitate considerable state intervention of a particular form. First, it would require the adoption of fiscal and monetary policies involving a persistent budget deficit to provide the appropriate level of demand and second, the development of an appropriate institutional structure to reflect the changing relations of production as labour increases its power, relative to the capitalists. However, such institutional reform would involve the loss of an important economic control, that of unemployment. Hence, the period of high employment in the 1950s and 1960s was brought to a halt by the pressures of rising inflation and balance of payments crises. Thus, in Kalecki's view, the state is not neutral in its approach to policy, rather it is subject to the pressures of big business and the policies adopted will reflect those pressures. This is a similar approach to that of Gramsci who argues that:

> ...the dominant group is coordinated concretely with the general interests of the subordinate groups and the life of the State is conceived of as a continuous process of formation and superseding of unstable equilibria (on the juridical plane) between the interests of the fundamental group and those of the subordinate groups – equilibria in which the interests of the dominant group prevail, but only up to a certain point, i.e. stopping short of narrowly corporate economic interest.
>
> (Gramsci, 1971, p. 182)

Elsewhere, Gramsci employs the idea of the 'historical bloc' to show the relationship between the economic foundation and the political superstructure, whereby values and norms have a major role in the regulation of the relations of production. Hence, the historical bloc is a historically created and socially reproduced conformity between the economic foundation and the political superstructure of social formation.

(ibid., pp. 366–7)

Social democracy and the public sector

The social democratic view that emerged during the interwar years was essentially an attempt at a modification of socialist thought in that it fundamentally believed that there could be a socially acceptable compromise with capitalism. It involved three related aspects. First was a belief that market capitalism is inherently unstable, as evidenced by the periodic booms and slumps, not caused by external factors, but as a consequence of the unregulated nature of capitalism itself. Second, it was recognized that 'democracy' was a permanent feature and that pressures from the electorate for high levels of employment and welfare could not be ignored. Third, there was a belief that state power could be used in a neutralizing manner to provide economic growth and form a consensus of views in society. The role of the state, therefore, was seen as an overarching mechanism for growth, stability and social harmony. The manner in which this was attempted involved the increasing role of the state to overcome the failings of *laissez-faire* capitalism, that had been so evident in the interwar years, in a regulatory framework, designed to be in the interest of the general public. In addition, certain activities were directly undertaken by the state through the nationalization of strategic industries and government provision of public goods out of taxation, in the overarching framework of Keynesian demand management techniques. This period of state regulated capitalism, associated with the 'golden age', was introduced in the special circumstances of the aftermath of the Second World War and the need to reconstruct economies across Europe and the Far East. The collapse of this social democratic approach can be viewed as the reassertion of the capitalist relations of production, overcoming the more corporatist, state regulatory model. This involved a return to the use of the disciplinary tool of unemployment and deregulation of the economy. The relative harmony of the postwar years was essentially attributable to the severe dislocation of the western economies due to the Second World War and in Britain, as elsewhere, the intercession of the war rescheduled the capitalist crisis and accommodations between capital and labour, which would otherwise not have been possible, became a reality. However, as Kalecki argued, this uneasy peace resting on the weak version of Keynesianism could not last as capital inevitably had its need for domination over labour traduced. The fissures in the western world's economic structures, which became evident in the 1970s were inevitable as the postwar reconstruction was built on a flimsy compromise. The foundations of this compromise were stronger in countries such as Western Germany, Sweden and Japan, but nonetheless, the architect of these structures remained social democracy and the fundamental contradictions of capital and labour remained unresolved.

An attempt to revive the social democratic view has been underway for several years, exemplified by the approach of Hutton who has suggested that '...the great challenge of the 20th century after the experience of both state socialism and of unfettered free markets, is to create a new financial architecture in which private decisions produce a less degenerate capitalism' (Hutton, 1996, p. 298). He concludes that what is required is the democratization of civil society, the republicanization of financial systems and a recognition that the market economy must be regulated and managed at home and abroad through the construction of a stable international financial order (ibid., p. 319).

However, such an analysis fails to grasp the totality of the capitalist relations of production and their role in the determination of the superstructures of society. Hence, as we have seen, the crucial question is, how is production organized to create the surplus and how is this surplus distributed. In feudalism the control of the means of production is not coincident with the legal relations, the lord owns the land and the serf works the land. Therefore, the lord owns the labour power of the serfs directly, but the serfs are in *de facto* possession of the means of production. The product is for the serfs' own consumption and a surplus. Hence, the surplus must be extracted politically, physically taken away, and the class struggle is over the relative shares of the product. This relationship gives feudalism politically forced labourers. However, in capitalism, non-labour both owns and possesses the product, while the labourer owns and possesses labour power. The surplus appears to be a result of free exchange between equals as it is extracted economically. Thus, in capitalism individual freedoms are legally necessary for free labour and capital to coexist and, therefore, formal legal equality makes substantive class struggle inevitable. The separation of political and economic status is the central institutional feature of capitalism and allows exploitation to be expedient as it serves as a mask to conceal the real rule by the owners of the means of production. With representative democracy the working class appears not to be dominated politically. On this point Lenin argued that when exploitation appears as a free exchange, dictatorship takes the guise of democracy, the democratic republic is but the political shell for capitalism and thus, once in possession of this shell no institution or change can shake it (Lenin, 1976). Three propositions then present themselves out of such an analysis. First, the nature of the bourgeoisie state is such that real power does not reside in parliament and, if this is the case, the parliamentary road to socialism will succeed only in subverting the proletariat and lead the working class into more exploitation because parliament contains the agents of the capitalist class. Secondly, capitalism is structured so that the working class can only defend itself by creating trade unions, and trade unions are themselves bourgeoisie working class politics which will lead to further enslavement. Thirdly, capitalism's economic collapse is inevitable as markets will always ultimately fail and thus, the party needs to explain where the real power lies as parliamentary democracy is but a sham and a representation of the separation of the politic from the economic. Hence, social democracy is doomed as it can only possibly contribute to the further enslavement of the working class as parliamentary systems distort rather than represent within a framework of 'free' individuals while the system is based on class conflict and class-based communities. The existence of the capitalist mode of production sets limits to political forms and policies and because the state is not simply a neutral instrument, the state cannot but act in ways that are favourable to the interests of capital. There are two possible interpretations of why the state should act in this manner, the instrumental view and the structural view.

The instrumental view

This is derived from Marx's writings in that the state is in the hands of the capitalist class because of its vast economic power and this puts constraints on state power. The bourgeoisie dominate all institutions of the state and all form a tightly knit framework. Hence, the major aspects of economic policy are always formulated in the interests of the ruling class. It follows that parliament as a representative body is unimportant, it is there to ensure the persistence of the capitalist system. The problems associated with this view are mainly that it tends to assume that the ruling class form a coherent entity that can implement policy in its favour. In fact one could argue that in capitalism the ruling class must be disunited because of the very nature of the competitive forces at work. In Britain for example not only are individual capitalists in competition but there is historically a separation to be made between industrial and financial capital which has been at odds for well over a century. In addition, many policies that have been generated from the parliamentary system of government are in the interests of capital, and capital has to be persuaded that they are in its best interests.[4] However, we could argue that it is axiomatic that the political system must reflect the economic system.

The structural view

This is an attempt to demonstrate how the capitalist state acts in favour of the capitalists no matter what the underlying conditions. Hence, the role of the state is to create and recreate the function of the capitalist class. In a *laissez faire* capitalist economy, the state permits competition to take place but automatically the state changes policies when the structure of the economy changes as monopoly takes over because in capitalism the larger firms can ride the slumps and booms. In wartime the cooperation of the working class becomes necessary and their bargaining power increases. Thus, the actions of the state are determined by this and the role of the state is determined by the structure of the economy and not by the people in power. As we have seen there is a basic contradiction within capitalism because of the ever increasing social character of production and the intensification of private appropriation. Hence, the state plays the decisive role in the introduction of policies which will disunite the working class and unite capital. But the state can only do this if it is seen to be relatively autonomous from the capitalist class. As capitalism develops, its requirements become more complex, particularly in terms of the provision of skills and education, whose costs cannot be borne by the individual capitalist, as labour power is owned by labour, and there can be no guarantee that labour, educated and trained at the expense of the capitalist, will remain in employment with that particular employer. This is particularly true where the skills obtained are not specific to an individual employer and it would therefore be rational for an employer not to fund education and training but rather to attract labour with pay that is slightly higher, using the funds saved by not investing in skills.

Globalization and the state

Giddens had suggested that individual nations will retain governmental, economic and cultural power in some considerable degree into the foreseeable future, but that government is becoming less identified with the nation state as their powers become more dependent upon their active collaboration with other nations and regions (Giddens, 1998, p. 32). In this respect Giddens may well be correct, but the important question in this context is why this is the case and to what extent this is a trend that is sustainable within the present analysis of the state. As capitalism itself becomes global, not through the imperialism of individual conquering nations as in the nineteenth century, but through multinational imperialism as transnational corporations compete in terms of foreign direct investment and the exploitation of cheap labour in less developed regions and as a logical outcome of the growth of monopoly capitalism, the economic structure is changing nationally and globally and as such the state must change to accommodate this shift. The global nature of capitalist relations of production, in both the industrial and the financial spheres, requires the nation state to collaborate and to coordinate policy to sustain the multinational nature of capital in a global market that has made capital footloose and intensely internationally competitive. However, Giddens's optimism concerning what he calls 'cultural pluralism' may appear to be somewhat misplaced given the role of labour in this new order. While capital is free to move to where the greatest rate of return is offered, labour is not. Immigration controls put in place by the advanced capitalist countries against the underdeveloped world ensure that wage levels do not equalize in an upward fashion and that exploitation can take place globally, putting downward pressure on the rate of increase in the subsistence wage, offsetting the tendency for the rate of profit to fall by opening new markets and hence increasing the rate of exploitation. In addition, it could be argued that the working class are kept in a state of division through the use of conflict as the newly collaborating states exercise their power through a succession of conflicts, for example in Iraq and the Balkans. They also attempt to form economic and political blocs to reflect the new economic environment. Thus, the role of the state within the capitalist relations of production continues to change as the needs of capital change due to the dynamism of the system. However, it is this very dynamism that will ensure its demise as the market becomes global and the impact of a financial collapse in one area has an immediate effect in another. Also the problems of the firms become multiplied, as with capital having ultimate mobility investors are always attempting to maximize their return, intensifying the move to monopoly and ensuring that the social return continues to fall. Low wages and a rising reserve army of labour lead to a realization crisis on a national and international scale with which even collaborative states could not cope.

Summary

As the capitalist system approaches the impasse of increasing concentration requiring greater power for capital over labour, which in turn requires higher levels of unemployment, the options for the ruling class become gradually and inexorably closed. For example, to reduce the budget deficit, which is seen to be bad for 'sound money', the state must either raise taxation or reduce public spending (or a combination of the two). To raise taxation, particularly in terms of direct taxation, is for the neoclassicals, a counterproductive policy, because higher taxation on those who accumulate will reduce motivation and therefore reduce investment. There is, however, apparently little motivational problem for labour and indirect tax increases become the favoured policy option. This reduces the level of consumption, and hence investment, leading to higher unemployment, lower corporate profits and, therefore, no reduction in the deficit. The second option, to reduce public spending, also increases unemployment and leads to the same outcome. There does exist a third option of a much more sinister character, and one which is already in evidence in the advanced capitalist economies – the rise of fascism. The reaction of the ruling class to the threat of economic collapse is to turn the working class in on itself, by appealing to reactionary elements, beginning with attacks upon collective working-class groups, such as the trade unions. Kalecki put this clearly when he wrote that

> ...the ruling class as a whole, even though it does not cherish the idea of fascist groups seizing power, does not make any effort to suppress them and confines itself to over zealousness...The fascism of our time is a dog on a leash, it can be unleashed at any time to achieve definite aims and even when on the leash, serves to intimidate the potential opposition.
>
> (Kalecki, 1972, p. 100)

13
The Crisis of the Welfare State

Introduction

The welfare state can be viewed as a large confidence trick perpetrated by the capitalist class, in collaboration with the state, to appease the growing demands of the working class, against the background of the rise in Fascism and Socialism in Europe during the interwar years, and the promises made to labour during the Second World War as part of the settlement with labour designed to produce a successful prosecution of the war. The confidence trick is that the state provides certain basic necessities for the working class that the capitalists either cannot provide, or are unwilling to undertake. These include a minimum payment for those whom the system is not able to employ and, therefore, form the reserve army of labour so essential to the workings of the capitalist system, and those who are no longer required for exploitation due to their age or incapacity. In addition, capital requires a fit and healthy workforce who are also well educated, thereby assisting in the production of social capital by maintaining a productive and malleable workforce. Therefore, rather than the individual capitalist providing these for those employed, the working class are taxed both on their income and their consumption and the state provides unemployment benefit, income support, state pensions, a national health service and state education. Yet, while the capitalist class gains the most from their provision, it is the working class that actually pays for such services. One could argue further, that actually the capitalist class pays nothing towards the collective provision of the welfare state as any taxation levied on them is passed onto the working class in the form of higher prices for the goods and services produced.[1] Hence, capitalists pay no taxes and do not have to take responsibility for their failure as a class to provide full employment, health and education.

The history of welfarism

It can be argued that the history of welfarism in Britain goes back to the introduction of the Poor Law which provided a statutory framework for the relief of poverty from 1598. It gave relief on a strict test of need and, at best, recipients received cash, clothing, housing and/or medical care. There was an overhaul in the system with the Poor Law Amendment Act of 1834 which was caused by an increase in population and economic structural change in the late eighteenth century. The Amendment Act established new principles in England and Wales whereby parishes were grouped together into unions, and property owners elected a board of guardians to administer poor relief. Each union was required to establish a workhouse grim enough to deter all but the severely destitute from applying for relief and outdoor relief was available only to those whose poverty was not of their own making. By 1870 at least 70 per cent of the 647 Poor Law unions in England and Wales had built workhouses. The poor law was supervised by central government through the Poor Law Board (1847) until 1871 when local government boards were established to supervise the growing functions of local government. In 1871 there was the enforcement of a clause making close relatives of the aged poor liable to support them on liability of prosecution and, in addition, it was aimed that charities should be used and to persuade them to offer relief only to those who could be helped to become independent. In 1871 there were 166 407 female outdoor paupers in England and Wales (Thane, 1996, p. 34). The unemployment of the 1880s made the policy unsustainable as the workhouses were not large enough to contain all of the unemployed. Hence, outdoor relief for males was extended, but it included stonebreaking in the workhouse yard as a daily test of their intent to find work.

In other areas, there were infirmaries in many towns which were initially voluntary institutions alongside the Poor Law hospitals which offered free health care and the Medical Relief (Disqualification Removal) Act of 1885 went a long way towards removal of the stigma of pauperism and led to vast improvements in both medical techniques and the successful treatment of a wider range of illness (Thane, 1996, p. 35). By the turn of the century free education existed in principle for all children to the age of at least eleven in England and Wales. The Housing Acts of 1885 and 1890 facilitated greater local authority borrowing for housebuilding and between 1890 and 1904, £4.5 million was borrowed, the majority of which was undertaken by the London County Council (Thane, 1996, p. 41). At the end of the nineteenth century pressure was mounting for central government to provide Old Age Pensions and subsidized housing for the working class, but the expenditure associated with the Boer War (1899–1902) held back legislation in these areas. However, public debate on the question of the physical fitness of volunteers for the war, coupled with concerns for the state of the economy, brought to the forefront demands for state sponsored measures to address the problem of national efficiency. The pressure for welfare reform thus came from the belief, mainly among the politicians, that economic growth was dependent upon there being a healthy and reasonably well educated workforce. In addition the social surveys of Rowntree in 1901 and Booth in 1902 pointed to the extent of the problem of poverty and the lack of effectiveness of the system of charitable relief. Together these developments made it politically much more acceptable to contemplate intervention by central government in the area of social welfare.

The Liberal reforms of 1906–14 have been presented as representing a fundamental break with previous economic and political axioms both in terms of the interventionist philosophy that the reforms introduced and the relative rapidity of their introduction (Barr, 1998, p. 23).

Summary of the main Acts and their effects

1905	Unemployed Workmens Act	Established distress committees to distribute voluntary funding.
1906	Workmen's Compensation Act	Extended the Act of 1897 whereby employers became liable for accidents in the workplace and were obliged to insure against such an event and to compensate the worker.
1906	Trade Disputes Act	Gave trade unions immunity from prosecution for non-violent acts in furtherance of an industrial dispute.
1906	Education (Provision of Meals) Act	Permitted local authorities to provide school meals for needy children (but were not compelled to do so).

1907	Education (Administrative Provisions)Act	Set up medical inspections of schoolchildren.
1907	Probation Act	Established the probationary service.
1907	Matrimonial Causes Act	Provided maintenance payments to divorced and separated women; consolidated the previous legislation with payment enforced through the courts.
1908	Old Age Pensions Act	Payment from national funds without a test for destitution; a non-contributory pension of 5s. (25p) per week for those over 70 on an income below £31 per year.
1908	Childrens Act	Made it a punishable offence for parents to neglect children, established separate juvenile courts, set up remand homes for children and stopped children from betting, entering brothels and smoking in the street.
1908	Smallholdings and Allotments Act	An attempt to reduce rural poverty by increasing job opportunities.
1909	Trade Boards Act	To fix minimum wages in 'sweated' industries covering 200 000 workers.
1909	Housing and Town Planning Act	Removed the obligation on local authorities to sell houses to the private sector and gave them the power to build new houses and to close unfit dwellings. Also encouraged urban planning.
1911	National Insurance Act	Provided sickness benefit of 10s. (50p) per week for men (7s.6d. for women) for the first 26 weeks of sickness,

provided disability pension of 5s. (25p) per week, maternity benefit of 30s. (£1.50) and enabled full treatment by a doctor and free treatment in a TB sanatorium. Contribution was 9d. ($3\frac{3}{4}$p), of which 4d. paid by the worker, 3d. paid by the employer and 2d. paid by the state.

1914   Education (Provision of Meals) Act   Made the provision of school meals for needy children compulsory for all local authorities.

Although the reforms may appear to be quite comprehensive and radical in terms of what had gone before, closer inspection would suggest that actually they only reflect a requirement of capital for an increase in labour efficiency. Unemployment and sickness insurance was based on a regressive tax system and only applied to a limited number of workers. Health care benefit only applied to the breadwinner and, as Barr has shown, similar reforms had been introduced in other European states as well as New Zealand (Barr, 1998, p. 23). Thane has argued that '[f]or all their imperfections, these new provisions represented a quite remarkable shift in social action by the British state in the period between 1906 and 1914' (Thane, 1996, p. 90).

The interwar period

At the end of hostilities Britain faced two major problems: how to demobilize over 5 million servicemen and reabsorb them into civilian life, and the problem of what would happen to approximately 5 million workers currently employed on government war work, half a million of whom were employed directly by the state in national factories. Plans for demobilization and the restoration of 'normal' economic conditions had begun to be developed by the government in early 1917 and the strategy was to be one of the rapid 'decontrol' of industry, with the winding up of war production as quickly as possible, even if that meant an increase in short-term unemployment. However, military demobilization was planned to proceed more slowly in order to stop a 'flood' of the domestic labour market. There existed a broad consensus around the need to free the economy from state regulation and even the trade unions expressed only limited objections, as most were anxious to remove state intervention in industrial relations. Resistance was only serious in those areas where there had historically been pressure for greater intervention, such as the call for the nationalization of the railways and of the coal industry. The government, mindful of events in Europe, were in some degree fearful of Britain being on the verge of social revolution due to increased industrial unrest and sporadic urban disturbances. In reaction to this, the government introduced the 'Out of Work Donation' in November 1918. This covered all workers laid off during the transition to peace and the benefit scales were, for the first time, varied according to a claimant's dependants and was universal in scope. Against the backdrop of the fear of social revolution, the government was expected to introduce policies for 'social reconstruction'. This expectation came from the fact that government committees had been active throughout the latter stages of the war devising schemes for social reform. At the General Election of November 1918, the pledge to 'build a land fit for heroes' had been embraced by all of the political parties. However, there also existed powerful forces ranged against the prospect of sweeping social and economic reform, not least of whom were the Treasury. The Treasury had been strengthened politically by the importance of war finance and, after the war, was determined that the reorganization of the nation's massive war debt should not be jeopardized by new expenditure commitments and obligations. The Treasury orthodoxy of balanced budgets and the restoration of the Gold Standard was, nevertheless, enshrined soon after the armistice in government policy. Throughout the interwar years, orthodox theory ruled out any possibility of stimulating a recovery through government expenditure and, indeed, the Treasury policy was to ensure that government departments should restrict their levels of spending. Initially, the influence of the Treasury view was felt mainly in the scaling down of what they saw as the more ambitious wartime schemes for social and economic reform. This included the evaporation of wartime plans for universal secondary education and a drastic scaling down of plans for a comprehensive system of public health provision. The Addison Housing Act of 1919 did come closer to realizing the aims of reconstruction and, in theory at least, it committed the Treasury to reimburse Local Authorities for all building costs above a penny (1d.) rate. However, the Act proved to be a failure, partly because no attempt was made to limit the escalating costs of building or to redirect the activities of private builders towards public housing schemes, and partly because it appeared to offer a blank cheque to the local authorities. It has often been argued that in the period 1918 to 1920, many noble plans for postwar reconstruction were betrayed by a government portrayed as 'hard-faced men who look as if they had done well out of the war' (Stanley Baldwin describing the MPs returned to Parliament in 1918). It may be that this comes close to a true assessment, but it would tend to overlook the fact that many on the left were also deeply sceptical at that time about state-centred welfare schemes. Indeed, the voluntary hospitals had as many allies among the trade unionists and local Labour politicians as among the professional health workers and, in addition, local Labour Party campaigns to transform the Poor Law administration can be viewed as part of a postwar emphasis by the left on local, rather than national, issues. There is also a tendency, within the traditional view, to underestimate the extent to which the government intervened, particularly in attempts to offset the adverse effects of rapid decontrol and demobilization. For example, the regulations restricting Out of Work Donation benefits were relaxed during 1919 as workers threatened to exhaust their entitlement, while the Rent Restrictions Acts in 1919 and 1920 extended the scope of rent control greatly, increasing the redistribution of income from landlord to tenant put in train by emergency wartime legislation. Possibly the most important of all was the state's decision to unpeg the sterling–dollar exchange rate and come off the Gold Standard in March 1919. The effect of coming off the Gold Standard was that the government was pledging itself to maintain a loose monetary policy, despite the rapid acceleration of inflation during the postwar boom. It may be fair to argue that inflation was tolerated, being viewed as a price worth paying to stall social unrest and to secure a smooth transition of millions of displaced service personnel and munitions workers back into the growing labour force.

The period 1914 to 1921 saw a wholesale transformation of the state societal relations in Britain. This is perhaps best illustrated by the contrasting government responses to the prospect of mass unemployment as between 1914 and 1918. At the beginning of the war, the government appeared content to rely on private charity (such as the Prince of Wales Relief Fund) to relieve distress, but by the end of the war few doubted that the government would have to provide a guaranteed minimum payment to all unemployed workers and ex-servicemen and their dependants. It was this which subsequently became the blueprint for interwar social payments as opposed to either the charity of the relief fund or the limited flat-rate insurance scheme introduced by Lloyd George in 1911. Once this commitment to the principle of 'work or maintenance' had been made, it was extremely difficult if not impossible for it to be rescinded. As a result, the absolute destitution which had been a hallmark of the Edwardian era in Britain was much reduced (some would even argue that it was banished), although deprivation continued to exist in urban Britain throughout the interwar period.

The mass unemployment of the 1920s effectively destroyed the basis of the unemployment insurance scheme and the government effectively deserted the principle of insurance as the insurance fund went into a continuous deficit. The Unemployment Insurance Act of 1922 contained a clause whereby only those 'genuinely seeking whole time employment but unable to obtain such employment' could receive extended benefit, which effectively excluded married women from the benefit (Thane, 1996, p. 164). Attempts to reduce the costs of the insurance scheme continued with the introduction of the means test in 1922 and, although the Labour government removed it in 1924, it was reinstated by the Conservatives in 1925. The National Government of 1931 imposed budget cuts as part of its belief in the Treasury orthodoxy which led to rising unemployment, and with it a rapid enlargement of benefit payments. The reaction of the government was to cut benefits by 10 per cent with the eligibility criteria being tightened, along with the continued application of the means test. The health care system fared little better during this period with cuts in the government contribution to the health insurance scheme by Churchill and the National Government instituted a wide range of cuts in 1932.

We can argue that in the immediate aftermath of the First World War the economic environment was such that the state was required to foster a degree of welfare to return to the normalcy of the capitalist relations of production through the 'guiding hand' of government and to avert the imminent social and economic upheaval that threatened. Once the threat had diminished a return to 'orthodoxy' meant that many of the reforms could be reversed or, at the extreme, halted. The important thing to note here is the manner in which the working class were disciplined through high levels of unemployment, while at the same time having their expectations reduced in terms of the levels of welfare that should be expected.

The post-Second World War experience

The Second World War caused major dislocation to the world economy and led to significant economic developments in the postwar period.

The influence of Keynes was keenly felt in the establishment of postwar regulatory mechanisms, including the Bretton Woods system, and at the close of the Second World War a set of social, economic and political factors combined to create an environment favourable to the adoption of Keynesian policies in the advanced capitalist economies. In Britain, as elsewhere, it was felt that the economy could be con-trolled by the government, and governments were seen to have their hand firmly on the economic tiller and could, therefore, alter direction when neces-sary to maintain high levels of output and employment in the econ-omy. Keynes's ideas were introduced in the Budget of 1941 as part of the entire conception of a planned economy to win the war, and thus it was seen as essential to obtain cooperation between capital and labour for a successful outcome to the war. Hence, it was argued in the early years of the war by numerous economic and political commenta-tors and government advisers, that a workable policy for a wartime economy had to be negotiated with the TUC and the wider labour movement, to ensure a lack of conflict between capital and labour in the domestic economy. What developed was the 'negotiated settle-ment', with labour gaining real material rewards in exchange for rigid controls, including a ban on strike action. As for capital, the introduc-tion of an excess profits tax gave a degree of control over inflation through price controls rather than through an incomes policy. The effect was to improve the conditions of the working class, despite the war. In the immediate postwar period, the settlement with labour was continued by the Labour Government, mainly due to the needs of reconstruction. This included the cooperation and negotiation between state and industry, the continuation of state planning and the introduc-tion of the welfare state.

The Beveridge Report of 1942 was based on several assumptions as to the social policies that would be adopted after the war. These included the provision of a comprehensive system of health care, the creation of a scheme of family allowances and the maintenance of full employ-ment. The report foresaw a system of social insurance that would be universal in scope, with all contributing at a flat rate to a compulsory, national insurance scheme through weekly contributions from the employee, the employer and the Exchequer. The majority of the recom-mendations in the 1942 Report were adopted in the 1944 White Paper on Social Insurance which became the 1946 National Insurance Act and the 1948 National Assistance Act. The National Health Service Act of 1946 was also based on the 1944 White Paper and established a system of comprehensive health care, free at the point of delivery, financed

Table 13.1   Welfare spending 1900–95

	% GDP	£ billion[a]
1900	2.60	3.60
1910	4.16	5.60
1921	6.36	8.80
1926	8.08	10.90
1931	10.79	15.30
1936	9.16	17.00
1941	5.57	12.70
1946	8.00	16.20
1951	11.19	28.00
1956	11.52	33.50
1961	13.17	43.70
1966	15.22	58.10
1971	17.27	75.10
1976	21.28	102.70
1981	22.28	112.00
1986	21.85	130.50
1991	22.61	147.00
1995	23.96	169.80

[a] At 1995/96 prices.
Source: Glennerster and Hills (1998), Tables 2A. 1 and 2A. 2.

mainly from general taxation. Thus, on 5 July 1948, the provisions of the Acts came into effect, and ushered in the era of the welfare state.[2]

Table 13.1 illustrates the rapid rise in welfare spending in the second half of the century with a particularly large increase in the trend in the past twenty years. This is in contrast to the policies that were adopted during the period, where in fact a recurrent theme in the last thirty years has been the desire to reduce the size of the welfare bill. This has created a paradox. The requirement of the capitalist mode of production is for the existence of a reserve army of labour, but under the provisions of the welfare state, working-class expectations are such that those who constitute the reserve army are provided for out of the taxation of those in employment. Expectations also operate in the National Health Service in terms of what services can and should be provided. Here technological advance serves to continuously increase the services available, while extending the life expectancy and increasing the expectations of what the service should provide. Also, in education, the introduction of more complex technologies requires a more highly trained workforce and therefore a more highly educated workforce, raising the expectations of the education system such that a much

Table 13.2 Expenditure of general government in real terms by function (£ billion at 1997 prices)

	1987	*1991*	*1995*	*1996*	*1997*
Social protection	96	109	113	132	131
Health	33	37	43	44	44
Education	12	15	17	16	16

Source: Office of National Statistics (1999), *Social Trends*, Table 6.22, p. 116.

greater number expect to receive a university education. The rise in expenditure in these areas is shown in Table 13.2.

Working-class expectations

In the immediate postwar period, the settlement with labour, initiated in the war, was continued by the Labour government, mainly due to the requirements of reconstruction. This included the cooperation and negotiation between state and industry, the continuation of state planning and the introduction of the welfare state. The profits for larger companies were generally much higher than ever before, but middle-sized and smaller companies did not do as well, due to the power given to the larger companies. This close cooperation with the state led to an increase in the bureaucracy devoted to industry. However, this came to an abrupt end in 1951 with the election of the Conservative government which began to liberalize the economy, that is, they discontinued the strong version of Keynesianism and moved quickly towards the weaker version. However, two important changes had already occurred: first, there had been a radical change in the nature of working-class expectations with the adoption of the policy of the maintenance of full employment and the consequent increase in living standards; and second, changes as a consequence of the introduction of the welfare state. This change could be described as the development of the institutionalizing of citizenship which gives importance to social rights, that is the right to economic welfare and security, including a right to share in the highest material standards in society at any given time. This has particular significance with respect to employment, whereby claims become rights and the question then becomes not one of whether they can be afforded. However, what are the consequences when workers continue to demand employment as a right, even if market conditions do not allow for full employment as 'normal' relations of production are reinstituted? Hence, the state's legislative role becomes one of the guarantor of prosperity, and rights to employment and welfare become social rights.[3] This creates a dilemma because only continued economic growth can meet rising demand and, at the same time as the state had adopted these ideas, the Conservative government had begun to retreat from the strong version of Keynesianism, precisely Kalecki's scenario of a choice between moving to the strong version, or a periodic disciplining of the working class through a high level of unemployment to dampen down working-class expectations. The attempt to return to free trade was encouraged and sterling was placed again as one of the main world currencies, but the pursuit of domestic policies which included a welfare state and the use of sterling in this manner in external policy was contradictory and led to a compromise on domestic policy. Therefore, with the changes in the state's legislative role as a guarantor of social welfare, this weak version of Keynesianism could not provide the goods that had been promised.

It became clear by the 1960s that the apparent economic success predicated on Keynesian policies was not inevitably going to continue into the future. Throughout the period of postwar reconstruction the USA has performed a crucial hegemonic role with the US dollar operating as the world currency. This position was undermined in the 1960s as the USA funded the Vietnam War through the expansion of the world supply of dollars, thus placing serious strains on other currencies, notably the deutschmark. The Bretton Woods system, which had provided relatively stable exchange rates and was a major symbol of postwar economic stability and regulation, had collapsed in the early 1970s, and the floating exchange rates of the 1930s returned. Instability created by the oil price rises of 1973–4 and the growing strength of the Pacific Rim countries, combined to pose threats to the established world economic order. It became increasingly evident that the weak version of Keynesianism was not working and a theoretical vacuum developed. As western economies found themselves grappling with problems such as high unemployment and stagnant output, governments turned to creeds such as monetarism, which was a thinly veiled return to the policies of the 1930s, or the Treasury View. This is particularly evident in Britain, which saw the development of monetarily constrained Keynesianism under a Labour government from 1976 and full-blown monetarism under Thatcher's Conservative government from 1979 to 1982, and Treasury orthodoxy to the present day.

This change in policy was a reflection of the reassertion of the capitalist relations of production and the need to liberalize the economy.

One immediate outcome of this was the abandonment of the state's commitment to the maintenance of full employment in order to return power to the capitalist class. However, the existence of the welfare state required continued economic growth to deliver rising standards of living and full employment, and to generate the tax revenue required to fulfil expectations in social protection, health and education. In addition, the liberalization of the economy produced a rise in the inequality of income distribution, putting a further strain on the welfare state in terms of the social safety net. The increase in income inequality that has occurred since 1979 is unprecedented in the postwar period in Britain, with the share of the poorest tenth falling from 3.7 per cent in 1961–3 to 2.9 per cent in 1991–3, while the share of the richest tenth rose from 21 per cent to 26 per cent during the same period (Goodman et al., 1997, p. 112). The return to mass unemployment during the past twenty years has greatly contributed to this rise in inequality, but the repercussions for the economy are now evident in terms of the paradox that has appeared: the existence of the welfare state requires full employment and economic growth, but the capitalist relations of production cannot provide economic growth without the existence of a large reserve army of labour. Hence, either the economy must return to the strong version of the immediate postwar years, which is an unrealistic prospect given the different conditions of the national and international economy, or the expectations of the working class must be much reduced through a 'moral re-education'. This latter scenario is the process that was set in train by the successive Conservative governments since 1979, and is continuing under the present Labour government. In terms of the welfare state, this requires that individuals make much more provision for themselves in terms of private pension plans, private health insurance, redundancy protection insurance and the payment of tuition fees in higher education. The argument is that individuals should be responsible for their own welfare by postponing consumption in the present to make provision for the uncertainties of the future, reducing the burden on the state – that is, the collective responsibility discharged by the state. This strategy presents further problems in the fact that, with a large reserve army required who cannot postpone their consumption to provide private insurance, the safety net of the welfare state is still necessary, which in turn requires that those in employment must contribute through taxation. However, the precise nature of the welfare state becomes more transparent as taxpayers begin to question as to why they contribute to welfare and must make insurance provision for themselves at the same

Table 13.3 Public sector net
cash requirement (£ million)

1964	982
1967	1 846
1970	−219
1973	4 069
1976	8 911
1979	12 750
1982	5 347
1985	7 625
1988	−11 460
1991	7 006
1994	39 342
1997	11 846

Source: Office of National Statistics
(1998) *Economic Trends, Annual
Supplement*, Table 5.3, p. 229.

time. The pressure on government finances shows itself in the gap between income and expenditure shown in the public sector net cash requirement as shown in Table 13.3.[4]

Hence, the rise in inequality as the capitalist relations of production are reasserted and the rising reserve army of labour have an immediate impact upon the welfare state that is a historical legacy from the period of reconstruction. The problem faced by the state is therefore one that an institution that was vital to secure the support of the working class in an earlier period becomes a millstone around the neck of the free market, adding transparency to the system of exploitation. Only a continued dismantling of the welfare state will have the effect of returning the economic superstructure to one in which unfettered capitalism can survive, at least in the short term, but that will require a rapid transformation of the expectations of the working class.

The inadequacy of the 'third way'

Advocates of the so-called 'third way' argue that the welfare state requires a set of clear boundaries to the operation of the market and promotes some form of social cohesion, regulated in terms of its social outcomes and funded through some form of tiered contributions such that some individuals could pay above the minimum to guarantee themselves higher than the minimum benefit level (Hutton, 1996, pp. 309–10). They argue that although unemployment benefit should continue to be paid, it is with the proviso that the individual must be obliged to actively seek work and that the state should provide 'meaningful' work after a period of unemployment. Reform of the welfare state for these commentators involves collaboration between the state and the capitalists in terms of the generation and distribution of welfare, in what is termed 'the social investment state' and 'positive welfare' (Giddens, 1998). Although a definitive explanation of what is meant by the 'third way' is elusive to say the least, one definition could be '...a model with a more European emphasis on social cohesion, citizenship, the mixed economy and high investment' (Hutton, 1996, p. 337). However, the aims of the policy are incompatible in that capitalist relations of production require the environment that provides for the exploitation of labour and the accumulation of capital and, as such, a compromise between the state and the capitalists is not possible in the longer term. They advocate a return to the corporatist model that has failed in the past and would fail in the future, not through any lack of will on the part of the individuals involved, but due to the dynamics of the capitalist system itself. Full employment, for example, as we have seen, is only to be tolerated while it is in the interests of the capitalist class. Similarly, the welfare state cannot become some kind of capitalist charitable organization in which they invest alongside the state, because that would not be compatible with the need for inequality as an incentive to the working class to raise productivity and because of the global nature of monopoly capitalism where individual capitalists must compete with those for whom investment in social welfare is not a precondition. In many ways the policies that are promoted are reminiscent of the attitude of the late nineteenth century, described above.

Hence the 'third way' is a phrase that suggests it is neither capitalism nor socialism; it is a hybrid that attempts to overcome the social problems of a capitalist market economy, while internalizing the economic problems of the social market. The reality is that capitalist relations of production cannot be reformed in this manner and indeed the state does not have the capacity, in such a 'democratic' structure , to carry out the necessary reforms. Hence, the advocates of the 'third way', are attempting to revive a model that appeared to be successful in terms of the reconstruction of a capitalist economy following the devastation of the Second World War, but cannot be replicated half a century later in totally different national and international circumstances. The model neglects the fact that the economy is not a blank sheet that can have imprinted a blueprint for success. We do not live in a Rawlsian original state where social contracts can be negotiated as if we were all in the womb. In reality, late twentieth-century capitalism is on the brink of yet another crisis, a crisis that has been heightened by the legacy of the welfare state and if the 'third way' is the social democrats' reaction to the impending crisis, it is, at best, intellectually inferior to the last social democratic reaction to a crisis and, at worst, looking in entirely the wrong direction for its solutions.

Summary

The crisis of the welfare state is itself a product of the crisis of capitalism in that its existence is due to the need for a settlement with labour for post-war reconstruction. However, as capitalist relations of production have come back to the fore it presents itself as an anathema to the capitalist class. At its inception it was a clever piece of duplicity, ensuring that the welfare that was offered was paid for in full by the working class themselves, in return for a commitment to full employment. As the need for the support of the working class receded, the policy priorities were overturned to return to the environment demanded by the capitalists, that of unemployment, as the disciplinary tool. However, the legacy of the welfare state remains and is proving difficult to remove due to the entrenchment of working-class expectations. This leaves the state with the unworkable task of either raising the taxes of those in employment, which will also reduce consumption, causing a problem of realization, or cutting the level of welfare in terms of social protection, health and education, which is not feasible, at least into the foreseeable future, due again to the historically generated expectations of the working class. Thus, one could argue that the problems that were faced in the interwar period have resurfaced, but with the added complication of the welfare state and the intensification of monopoly capitalism.

14
Conclusions

During the discussions that have formed the central elements of this book, we have been endeavouring to discover whether the approach of Marxian political economy is still relevant to contemporary society, given the enormous changes that have occurred since Karl Marx put pen to paper in the second half of the nineteenth century. The answer lies on several spheres of economic, philosophical and political thought, in the understanding of Marx's method and one's perception of the validity of the framework within which the theory is set. However, the alternative explanations can be seen to be at best a partial analysis, and at worst a misrepresentation of the realities involved in a capitalist economy. Thus, as a critique of this system, we have seen that Marxian political economy represents a logically consistent and coherent examination of the whole, and the role of factors within that whole, in a realistic and practical manner. The neoclassicals employ a set of assumptions that do not conform to the observed facts, such as perfect competition, asymmetric knowledge and constant returns to scale. In addition, they employ measures of utility that cannot be applied to individuals let alone whole communities and ignore the factor of time and then base theory and policy on these improbable constructs. Others attempt to model an economy based on free markets, but tempered by state intervention to overcome the antisocial outcomes of an unfettered market system, without incorporating the contradictions that exist within the system itself. What they lack is a framework of analysis that takes into account the whole system, its contradictions and its interactive, dynamic nature. Therefore, they can truly be described as partial analyses and it follows that their policy prescriptions must also be no more than partial in their application. Therefore, we have reason to suggest that the method employed by

Marx was superior in its use of the dialectic which permits the incorpo-ration of the essential dynamic of the capitalist mode of production, and the theory of history, historical materialism.

Thus, to understand a society, one must comprehend the economic structure of that society, in the manner in which the relations of pro-duction have developed and the development of the class relations. On this basis the political superstructure arises with a definite form of social consciousness, to ensure that the ruling ideas originate from the ruling class, the ideology. It follows that as the relations of production change over time, then so too does the superstructure, and rather than modelling the individual and then relating the outcome to society as a whole, as in the neoclassical paradigm, an understanding of the indi-vidual aspects of society comes from comprehension of the totality of the structure. In this manner, the framework is dynamic in the sense that it can be applied through time and space and therefore what we have is a method that is not specific to the late nineteenth century, but one which remains applicable. Logically this must be the case because the driving force is history and one cannot know history in advance. Therefore, in this aspect we can argue that Marxian political economy remains relevant in its mode of analysis.

The Marxian approach to the theory of value places it as an essential tool in the explanation of economic and social conditions, and empha-sizes the historical relativity of economic categories. Hence, value rela-tionships are particular to a capitalist society and value itself is a social relationship. The exchange of products by commodity producers cre-ates a quantitative relation between those commodities and this exchange value expresses the social character of commodity produc-tion. Because commodities are reducible to the common property of having been the products of labour, the value of a commodity can be measured by labour-time, that is the socially necessary labour-time. With this construct it is possible to show how surplus value originates in production as the use-value of labour to the capitalist is greater than its exchange value, and that through the process of exploitation, the capitalist can appropriate the surplus from the labourer. Again it is only possible to arrive at this result if one has a full comprehension of the totality of the system through the primacy of the economic structure. In isolation, looking at a single firm, this would not be logical, but then the economy is not represented by a single firm.

A major criticism of the Marxian schema concerns the so-called 'transformation problem', but as we have seen, the whole debate can be interpreted in terms of a 'complicating detour' on the part of those who wish to find 'complete' solutions, and also those who wish to prove that a solution does not exist at all. The essential point to make is that Marx was not engaged in a mathematical exercise to show that each value and each surplus value could be transformed into a price and an amount of profit, or that when all are added together then value is equal to price and surplus value is equal to profit. Rather, it is a mechanism which enabled Marx to illustrate, specific to the capitalist mode of production, how the value of labour power is 'transformed into the wage' and surplus value is 'transformed into profit'. It would follow, therefore, that far from there being a fundamental flaw in the Marxian schema, Marx himself provided a 'complete' solution showing that price is but the outward form of value, as a counterpart of value in circulation. Again, much confusion arises because of a supposed level of inconsistency that has been perceived out of the different levels of abstraction that Marx employs during the volumes of *Capital*, but there are two things that require reiteration here. First, Marx uses these different abstractions as part of his overall method that we have labelled as Marx's realism and they differ according to what he wishes to illustrate. Second, many of the supposed inconsistencies between the three volumes are more to do with the difficulties that Engels encountered when editing the notes that Marx had left. Therefore, it is the contention here that there is no transformation problem in the sense that the transformation of values into prices of production and of surplus value into profit logically follows from the nature of the capitalist relations of production and shows that values are logically prior to prices and surplus value is logically prior to profit because values and surplus values are created in production and prices and profits arise out of the circulation process. It is therefore irrelevant as to whether the procedure can be carried out mathematically using a small number of sectors, or indeed by attempting to model the economy as a whole. The point is not to prove whether it can be done, but to show the mechanism by which it occurs as part of the whole perspicacity of the dynamics of the capitalist mode of production.

This dynamism of capitalism also has to be understood as a historical process, developing itself through a succession of stages which can be distinguished by their particular forms of property relations. Hence the formation of capitalism arises as a consequence of the collapse of earlier forms, due to the contradictions that cannot be overcome in those stages. This relates to the thesis–antithesis–synthesis nature of the dialectic and each transformation of the property relations produces a new structure of social relations. Hence, the economic structure of capitalism emanates from the inadequacy of the feudal mode of production, given the historical development of productive forces. It is important, therefore, to recognize the manner in which ownership of the means of production came to be held by the capitalists and Marx points to theft, piracy and slavery as important aspects in this primitive accumulation. Within this there is much debate as to how contrived was the enclosure of the open fields in Britain in order to progress this primitive accumulation and to provide industry with plentiful and cheap labour. It would appear that again Marx has been misinterpreted as suggesting that the state was acting as an accommodating institution by *consciously* providing the legislation which would pave the way for the capitalist agriculturalists to take command of the means of production, and to provide an urban proletariat to be exploited by capitalist industry. In fact, it is not the conscious decision-making process that Marx is alluding to, but the process of historical development that makes such decisions inescapable; not all land was enclosed by Act of Parliament – it was done as and when necessity decreed with or without parliamentary sanction. The arguments of proto-industrialization tend to put this into context, illustrating how the process of change from feudalism to capitalism occurred on several different planes, but at varying degrees of pace depending upon the sector and the region. Thus, the proto-industrialization thesis, although not a sufficient argument to vindicate totally the Marxian model, does add significantly to the understanding of the process that occurred in the transition from one mode of production to another out of the contradictions inherent in the system. In the same manner, therefore, the dynamics of capitalism are explained by Marx in the models of simple and extended reproduction, and it must be reiterated here that Marx was not examining the growth process in capitalism but demonstrating that, even using the constructs of bourgeois economics, it can be shown that value is logically prior to price and surplus value is created in production and is logically prior to profit. The relevance of this for contemporary capitalism may at first sight seem to be obscure, but if the contradictions that are evident in capitalism are to lead to its collapse, then out of the ashes there will rise a different set of property relations that are appropriate for the circumstances and this need not be a product of armed conflict.[1]

The contradictions that are inherent in the capitalist mode of production concern the ever increasing social nature of production and the concomitant increase in the concentration of the appropriation of the surplus. This is caused by the necessity to replace labour power with new technology, not by every individual capitalist, but on the whole and in general, by the systemic totality.[2] Given the fact that unemployment is a key factor in the long-term maintenance of the subsistence wage, this process ensures that the size of the reserve army of labour is a reflection of the necessary power required by the capitalists to maintain the level of surplus value. However, because value is produced by labour, the fewer workers that are employed the lower the value of the commodities produced. In addition, the realization problem becomes more acute as the reserve army of labour increases through technological unemployment, which is an outcome of the competitive process because individual capitalists must imitate the innovator to survive. Hence, as individuals the capitalists are attempting to increase their surplus value, but the capitalist class, because of the competition inherent in the system, experience the opposite over time. This is a logical consequence of the capitalist mode of production as the contradictions of its success in increasing productivity through the introduction of labour-saving technology produces the crisis of capitalism. The crisis emerges as the tendency for the rate of profit to fall over time, a tendency that is an important factor in the cyclical nature of capitalism.

The requirement for a reserve army of labour to exist in order to maintain the subsistence wage has evidently been the case in the twentieth century, and the so-called 'golden-age' of the 1950s of high levels of employment is an episode that in fact reinforces this claim. The period of full employment occurred at the time when the reconstruction of the economy was essential after the Second World War and a settlement with labour was necessary for this to be successfully completed. It was a task that the capitalists as a class could not undertake without state intervention, but once completed the 'normal' relations of production were reinstituted, and the reserve army of labour was again a necessity. Kalecki analysed this in terms of the need to discipline the working class, because at high levels of employment, the sack becomes no longer a sufficient threat and disciplinary tool, and there is a relative shift in power to the workers who can more successfully bargain for increases in wages and improvements in working conditions. Hence, the level of industrial unrest was at its highest in periods of high employment when those in work were less threatened by the existence of a reserve army, ready and willing to take their place.[3] Several theories of unemployment have begun to approach this analysis and even some neoclassical theories have an implicit understanding of the power relationship that is involved, but they tend to view this in isolation from the system as a whole. It is at this level that Marxian political economy appears to have, not only a lucid theory of unemployment, but a theory that can explain why it is necessary to maintain a reserve army of labour for the needs of the capitalist class, and also why this must lead to a crisis in the system. It is therefore of great contemporary significance, given that unemployment, in all of its many guises, continues to be a large and increasing problem in all of the advanced industrial nations.[4] It is a heightened problem due to the increasingly global nature of capitalist production as we witness the increasing level of concentration and centralization of capital in the phase of monopoly capitalism. This is not a new phenomenon, but has come to be known as globalization in recent years with some commentators suggesting that it represents a new regulatory paradigm in capitalism to follow Fordism, post-Fordism and Japanization, among others. However, we can see that it logically follows from the capitalist imperative and the competitive nature of the system that regional markets expand to become national markets, and subsequently expansionism ensures the move to international markets. Within this, competitive forces ensure that the imperialism of an earlier stage of development becomes the monopoly capitalism of the multinational companies. Again the Marxian analysis would appear to have contemporary relevance in the fact that it is much more able to explain the way in which this globalization has emerged and its impact on the role of the state. For example, Giddens (1998) has argued that it is now the role of the state to collaborate and to coordinate policy and in many respects this may be true, given that the state must ensure that there exists an environment within which capitalism can flourish, and if this capitalism is global then a single state cannot guarantee that such a situation would arise. However, at the same time, individual states are in conflict as they attempt both to retain existing multinationals sited in their nation and also to attract new companies. This is because the decisions by multinational companies as to where they will site their operations have a large impact on the host countries' economy. Similarly, the decision to move operations could have serious implications for the economy that is deserted. The notion of nationality and loyalty to that nation has disappeared for these large, often conglomerate, multinational companies, in competition with others of the same persuasion in a global economy. Thus, while the state is required to collaborate, it also has to attempt to secure the continued presence of these large companies in its own economy, a target which becomes increasingly difficult to attain.

The state also has to contend with the increasing domestic problem of how to fund rising welfare provision, while the needs of capitalism continue to involve not only a large element of unemployment, but also a highly educated and healthy workforce. Hence, the legacy of the postwar settlement with labour has given added impetus to the contradictions that Marx highlighted and caused a crisis within the welfare state to which solutions are politically unpalatable: either, to increase taxation (which in turn reduces consumption), or to change the way in which welfare is provided. Neither would prove to be politically acceptable, at least in the short term, and a moral re-education of the working class would take far too long, given the state of working-class expectations of what the state should provide as a right. Thus, the policies that were adopted in the face of the need to reconstruct the economy are now adding to the crisis of capitalism through, on the one hand, the increasing unemployment and the concomitant rise in inequality in society that is a necessary outcome of the capitalist relations of production, and on the other hand, the commitment of the state to provide accepted levels of welfare through taxation which falls primarily on those who are employed and on all the working class in the form of indirect taxation. The question also has to be raised as to whether a welfare state can still be afforded in a global economy, with nations in competition for multinational company participation in their economies and it could be that those economies at earlier stages of development have a competitive advantage in terms of lower wages, lower taxation and governments without the increasing budgetary pressures involved in the delivery of complex welfare services.

The distinctive approach of Marxian political economy would therefore appear to offer much greater clarity of analysis and greater logic of argument both in terms of the explanations for past events in the history of capitalism and the interpretation of contemporary trends. The contention here is that the Marxian critique of capitalism has greater resonance than either the neoclassical defence of the system or the social democratic attempt at appeasement. Hence, Marx still has much to offer the economist, the philosopher, the sociologist and the politician, both as a framework for the analysis of contemporary capitalism and as a way of raising social consciousness as to the exploitative nature of the capitalist mode of production.

Notes

1 Introduction

1 In 1994 1514 million people were living below the poverty threshold of per annum income of $370, defined by the World Bank as the total poor, and 428 million were existing on a per capita income of less than $275 per annum (Atkinson et al., 1998, p. 156). In addition, approximately 60 per cent of the total global population, who live in the low income economies, receive only 6 per cent of world income, but the 25 per cent who live in the rich industrialized economies receive 77 per cent of the world's income (Thirlwall, 1994, p.13).

2 The concept of economic democracy in a capitalist system should not be confused with political democracy. If the latter suggests that each person is entitled to the same vote as all others, the same is not true for economic democracy, where the votes (i.e. units of money) are distributed unequally and, therefore, the demands of the rich have a higher priority for production that those of the poor. For example, people who live on the streets have a demand for housing; large numbers of workers in the building industry are unemployed; capital, in the form of unsold bricks, is available; land is unused, subsidized by taxpayers as 'set-aside' where nothing can be grown as part of the Common Agricultural Policy of the European Union. Hence, a demand exists, scarce resources lie idle, but the 'market' cannot function due to the lack of economic votes of the homeless who are therefore disenfranchised from the economic system.

3 Much of this confusion actually arose because of the fact that, although the first volume of *Capital* was published in 1867, when Marx died in 1883, Friedrich Engels was left to assemble the almost illegible manuscripts into volume two which was published in 1885. The third volume was far from finished by Marx, but again Engels edited and published this in 1894. In addition, what Marx had envisaged as a fourth volume on the history of economic ideas, was published under the title of *Theories of Surplus Value*, itself in three volumes.

2 Marx's Method

1 The term 'contradictions' does not refer here to logical error, but to internal conflicting forces which transform the entity of which they are a part. This has caused much misconception of Marx's writing as he uses the term in its Hegelian form.

2 For a useful summary of the debates and an alternative interpretation see Rosenthal, J. (1998) *The Myth of Dialectics. Reinterpreting the Marx–Hegel Relation*, London, Macmillan.

3   In this context, Marx discusses the concept of prehistory, where prehistory is that state in which human beings are moving towards the understanding of the true nature of the relations of production that prevail in the capitalist mode of production.

3   The Theory of Value

1   On this point, Joan Robinson suggests that 'latter-day economists are careful to avoid this naiveté. They treat utility as an ordinal, not a cardinal quantity (and many refine it still further), that is to say, they regard the consumer as putting commodities through a competitive examination, and choosing those that score the best marks' (Robinson, 1969, p. 389).

Sawyer explains that 'the ordinal utility approach which has become the neo-classical orthodoxy, indicates that utility as such is not measurable, but that the price ratio of two products will be equated with the marginal rate of substitution between the two products' (Sawyer, 1989, p. 227).

2   Brewer (1984) suggests that a self-sufficient commune could exist without market exchange, while at the same time having a division of labour and Robinson Crusoe, without the presence of Man Friday, would constitute useful labour in the absence of a division of labour.

3   Marx does not suggest that commodities will actually exchange in ratios that are proportional to their relative values. In general, in Volumes I and II of *Capital*, he assumes that prices are proportional to values as a simplification. In Volume III, he relaxes this assumption to explain how prices are related to values.

4   This suggests that the level of subsistence will change over time given the level of capitalist development. What is really meant by a subsistence wage, therefore, is the wage that keeps the labourer's household in an acceptable, customary norm for contemporary society. It is not a fixed level of income to provide a fixed standard of living.

5   Although the term 'commodity' in modern economics is used in the context as being synonymous with a product or a good, for Marx products and goods are use-values and a product acquires the form 'commodity' only when it embodies a social relation, that is the social relation of value. Hence, for Marx, a product, which is a material thing, acquires the form of commodity, which is an abstraction, as in the capitalist mode of production the social relation of capital is embodied in a material thing. This concept of social relations taking on the form of things is referred to by Marx as 'commodity fetishism'.

6   There has been much debate on the distinction between productive and unproductive labour over many years, and its relevance to a labour theory of value, without resolution. (Cf. Gough, 1979; Laibman, 1992, 1993; Moseley, 1986; Houston, 1997; Mohun, 1996).

4   Marx's Critique of Classical Political Economy

1   As we saw in Chapter 2, in the capitalist mode of production the process can be described in the terms M–C–C'–M', but in simple commodity production it is, C–M–C.

2 Circulating capital alludes to those inputs that are fully utilized in a single production period, whereas fixed capital refers to those inputs whose depreciation takes place over several production periods.

3 What Say's Law suggests in terms of the circulation process of M–C–C'–M', is that under all circumstances $M' = C'$.

5 The Transformation Problem – Some Complicating Detours

1 Ladislaus von Bortkiewicz wrote two articles in 1906–7 on the transformation problem originally published in *Archiv für Socialwissenscaft und Sozialpolitik*, vols.XXII and XXIII, and in *Jahrbuche Nationalokonomic und Statistik*. They were translated into English and appeared as an appendix in Sweezy, P. M. (ed) (1949), *Karl Marx and the Close of his System*, New York, Augustus Kelly.

2 Desai (1979) suggests that this theorem was suggested by Okishio (1974), Morishima (1974) and Wolfsetter (1973); Howard and King (1992) suggest that the originator of the theorem was in fact Georg von Charasoff in 1909–10, and anticipated Seton (1957).

3 Cf. Hodgson (1982).

4 In fact, Morishima (1974) sees a connection between Marx and Walras as being general equilibrium theorists. 'Indeed, Marx's theory of reproduction and Walras' theory of capital accumulation should be honoured together as the parents of the modern dynamic theory of general economic equilibrium' (Morishima, 1974, p. 2).

6 The Dynamics of Capitalism

1 The similarities between this episode in British history and the fate of the Samurai in Japan after the Meiji restoration in 1868 are quite obvious. However, the disbanding of this class of feudal retainers in Japan was to prove beneficial to the economy in many more ways than just as an increase in the numbers of propertyless labourers. It is argued that it formed the basis of the tripartite state with the same cultural and ethical concerns in the three main branches of the economy: government, finance and industry. This allowed the Japanese economy to develop capitalist relations of production which subjugated the working class within a corporatist state (the developmental state) using the Samurai moral code of the Confucian hierarchy and a state religion (Shintoism).

2 Probably the most influential of the works at that time was that by J. L. Hammond and B. Hammond published in 1911, *The Village Labourer*. Other notable publications in the same vein were Gilbert Slater's *The English Peasantry and the Enclosure of Common Fields* (1907) and R.H. Tawney's *The Agrarian Problem in the Sixteenth Century*. (For a more in depth analysis of the literature on enclosures up to 1920 see Mingay, 1997.)

3 This is not to say that this was the only manner in which the capitalist class emerged. The transformation of agriculture into capitalist agriculture with

the emergence of a much more national market meant that some artisans became capitalists as did some of the sons of the landed gentry.

4 Much could be written on this point alone, but the fact that Russia at the time of the revolution was only an emerging capitalist nation was a fact that Lenin recognized and attempted to cater for by rewriting Marx for such a situation. He decided that the economy should be 'guided' through capitalism until it was ready for socialism and therefore sought the reintroduction of market exchange, private property and entrepreneurship. Unfortunately this New Economic Policy was only in its early stages when Lenin died in 1924, and the history of the Soviet Union changed direction with the move to heavy industrialization and the big push for economic growth under Stalin.

7   Capital Accumulation and Technical Change

1 It is quite important to note here that this essentially assumes that there is no technical change in the system.
2 The managerial theories that have come to be associated with Baumol are very similar in this context in terms of the sociological nature of the motivations and objectives of the individual capitalist.
3 Neoclassical economics also has as an essential assumption, the profit maximization motive of the capitalist
4 This must also be true of the price domain, because if one capitalist innovates and produces at a lower cost, then the capitalist can still sell the commodity at its price of production and hence receive 'excess' profits.

8   The Tendency for the Rate of Profit to Fall and the Realization Crisis

1 This lack of appreciation of the importance of the three concepts of the composition of capital is alluded to in Saad-Filo (1993) and also Fine and Harris (1979).
2 Moseley (1997) disagrees with Glyn on this point, suggesting that the fall in the profit level in the 1970s was associated with an increase in the employment of unproductive labour and the recovery of profit levels in the last decade coincides with a slowdown in the relative increase in unproductive labour. This is a debate that has continued over the past three decades and some of the important earlier references are Glyn and Sutcliffe (1972), Weisskopf (1979), Wolff (1986), Laibman (1993) and Moseley (1992).
3 Clarke (1994) notes that Marx corresponded with Engels to ascertain his view as an industrialist as to the periodicity of the replacement cycle of fixed capital and has this in mind when commenting on the historical relevance of the cycle.

9   Michal Kalecki and Piero Sraffa

1 For example, Mongiovi suggests that '[t]he theoretical project to which Sraffa devoted his life, from 1925 onwards, was concerned with the development

of an apparatus that could explain the laws which govern capitalist reality' (Mongiovi, 1996, p. 222). Kerr sees Kalecki's work as an application of Marx's ideas in the contemporary situation attempting to explain the contradictions of capitalism in 'their historically specific form' (Kerr, 1997, p. 45). See also in this context, Robinson (1980, ch. 5), Harcourt (1996, ch. 15) and Harcourt (1982, Part IV).

2 This phrase is very often attributed to Kalecki, but Joan Robinson, in discussing the determination of gross real profits states that, 'this was summed up in Kalecki's saying (which I have not found in print in English): the workers spend what they get and the capitalists get what they spend' (Robinson, 1973, p. 89). However, Sawyer discussing the same point suggests that 'this...led to the famous dictum that capitalists earn what they spend, whilst workers spend what they earn' (Sawyer, 1985, p. 73).

3 Harcourt writes that 'it was a typical Sraffa gesture, original and helpful, that he opened an unlimited credit account for Gramsci at a Milan bookshop when Mussolini imprisoned Gramsci' (Harcourt, 1982, p. 199).

4 Ibid.

5 Constant returns to scale would be apparent if output were to vary, but Sraffa does not consider this possibility.

6 This represents one of the more complicated of the systems that is employed by Sraffa, but not the most complex.

10   Monopoly Capitalism

1 These take the form either of vertical, horizontal or conglomerate concerns, with greater emphasis on a particular form depending upon the level of capitalist development. For example, as products become obsolete, those firms that were producing them search for other areas of production and diversify through conglomerate takeover. Hence, in the later stages of the capitalist relations of production this form of takeover tends to become more prevalent than either the vertical or the horizontal.

2 The discussion of rentiers leads Lenin to describe this class as parasites of the capitalist system, living on the productive activity of others, while they themselves do nothing but clip their coupons, a reference to the cashing in of dividends from shareholding. Lenin does not elaborate further in any theoretical sense, but we can suggest that he is alluding to the enormous increase in stockholding that occurred from the turn of the century and therefore to the growing number who were attached to this parasitic class.

3 For example, Aaronovitch and Sawyer (1975), Hannah and Kay (1977), Chandler (1990), Supple (1991), Walshe, in Crafts and Woodward (1991) and Mercer, in Jones and Kirby (1991).

4 It has been estimated that, by 1914, the total stock of long-term overseas investment had reached $44 billion, with a third being in the form of direct investment (Michie and Grieve-Smith, 1995, p. 141).

5 Cf. O'Brien (1992) and Ohmae (1990).

6 Cf. Panic (1988), Auerbach (1988) and Kozul-Wright, in Michie and Grieve-Smith (1993).

7 This is not to suggest that Giddens engages in a Marxian analysis at any stage in his exposition. He certainly does not, but a much more coherent argument would include at its heart the idea that governments change because of change in the economic environment, rather than the social democratic ideal that governments are a force for change.

11 Unemployment

1 This point is well exemplified by the hydraulic machine built by A. W. H. Phillips at the London School of Economics in the 1950s. The machine was representative of the circular flow model of a Keynesian economy. It consisted of a tank of water at the bottom of the machine, which personified the level of national income, and the water flowed around the machine experiencing leakages and injections before returning to the tank. The leakages and injections could be varied by use of levers, to show how variations would affect the level of national income in terms of taxes, saving, government spending, investment and imports and exports. It therefore represented the technicist vision whereby all that was required to provide rising national income was for the government to pull the correct levers.

2 It should be noted that although the concept of the NAIRU is alarmingly similar to the Friedman-Phelps notion of a natural rate of unemployment, the important difference lies in the fact that, unlike the NRU, the NAIRU is not determined by the operation of competitive forces in the market for labour. In addition it has been argued that Friedman's definition of the NRU appears to possess characteristics consistent with an economy at full employment (Trevithick, 1992, p. 197).

3 Screpanti denotes 's-hysteresis' as hysteresis with stationary inflation and 'm-hysteresis' as hysteresis with moving NAIRU.

4 For a full discussion on the 'insider–outsider' model see Lindbeck and Snower (1986), Corruth and Oswald (1987), and Lindbeck and Snower (1989).

5 Lavoie (1996a and 1996b) examines this aspect in the context of a Kaleckian model.

12 The Public Sector

1 J. K. Galbraith discussing the state of democracy introduces the idea of a 'contented majority' that the policies of the mainstream political parties are aimed at, because these are the voters that will ensure their election to government. The votes of those who do not benefit from the economic system are therefore rendered ineffectual and this section of society is in effect disenfranchised. The government that is elected has an obligation through its manifesto to provide low taxes, law and order and the furtherance of the position of the contented (Galbraith, 1992).

2 Indeed, the electability of the Labour Party in Britain rested on their appeal to big business who control the greater part of the media and to a large extent, therefore, public opinion and the prevailing ideas.

3   Gough has criticized many who overlook the gains for workers that have arisen from working-class pressure and the reactions of government in order to defend the capitalist system in the face of such pressure, citing the extension of the welfare state as representing a real gain for workers (Gough, 1979, pp. 13–14).

4   For example, Marx analyses the Factory Acts and shows that intervention in the interests of the capitalist class as a whole is a necessary undertaking of the state in the situation where the process of competition prevents the capitalist class from adopting measures that would be in its interests both as a class and individually. In the case of the Factory Acts, the reduction in working hours introduced by one capitalist would result in a loss of competitive position and others would not follow suit, but a reduction in working hours introduced collectively may well be in the interests of all capitalists.

13   The Crisis of the Welfare State

1   In addition, in 1976 British Petroleum paid no tax on profits of £1784 million, Rio Tinto Zinc paid no tax on profits of £279 million, Imperial Group paid £9 million in tax on profits of £130 million, while Guest, Keen and Nettlefolds paid no tax on profits of £98 million (Alford, 1996, p. 328).

2   The term 'welfare state' became commonly used after the publication of the report, although it had been coined previously, but Beveridge disliked the phrase preferring to refer to the 'social service state' (Thane, 1996, p. 237).

3   Lindbeck (1997) has suggested that, over a protracted period, the existence of social benefits will change social norms, such that the stigma of reliance on benefits gradually disappears as they become regarded as an entitlement.

4   The net cash requirement of the public sector was formerly the Public Sector Borrowing Requirement.

14   Conclusions

1   This is not the appropriate vehicle for a discussion of the definition of the proletarian revolution, and the debate between the democratic socialists and the socialist revolutionaries is one that has been unresolved since the beginning of the twentieth century. However, given the dialectic and the materialist concept of history, the manner of such a transition cannot be predicted and if the debate rests upon a definition of the word 'revolution', then we must remember that a Keynesian revolution took place throughout the advanced capitalist world, followed by a monetarist revolution. In this light, revolution represents a change in orthodoxy, one which occurs due to a change in the economic environment, caused by the dynamic of capitalism.

2   Some technology that is introduced will be of the labour-using variety in the first instance. For example, an individual firm that produces computers will initially employ workers as an addition to the employed population. However, the application of the computers will represent a replacement for workers in, for example, the banking sector. Thus the overall effect will be a reduction in employment.

3 In recent time there have been several instances where workers in dispute with an employer have been replaced *en masse* by unemployed workers. The highest profile episodes of this kind are probably the print workers of News International at Wapping and the Timex workers in Dundee.

4 It should be borne in mind that the official figures for unemployment in Britain have been subject to enormous change both in terms of the definition of unemployment and the manner in which the figures are collected, the overwhelming majority of which have had the effect of reducing the number of people who are officially classed as being unemployed. Therefore, one can argue that there is a large discrepancy between the level of unemployment and the size of the reserve army of labour.

Glossary

Abstract labour
The set of qualities that are common to labour power and the value which labour produces.

Accelerator model
This is the hypothesis that the level of investment will vary directly with the rate of change of output. Thus, it suggests that at all levels of output investment will be proportional to the rate of change of output.

Aggregate demand
The total demand in an economy for goods and services.

Aggregate supply
The total supply of goods and services in an economy.

Balanced growth
The possible, but highly unlikely, situation in an economy where all of the major economic aggregates are growing at the same percentage rate over time.

Bourgeoisie
In the Marxian schema the bourgeoisie are the class in capitalism who own the means of production.

Bretton Woods
The site of the meetings in July 1944 among the allied powers of the Second World War which created the World Bank and the International Monetary Fund and instigated a system of fixed exchange rates in an attempt to stabilize the world trading system in the immediate postwar era.

Capital
Essentially, capital refers to the stock of goods that are utilized in production and have themselves been produced. It should be noted that in Marxian political economy the term is also employed to denote the owners of physical capital.

Circulating capital
More normally referred to as working capital, it is that part of capital that is embodied in stocks and production in progress. Essentially the stocks of raw materials and components that are being used in production.

Commodity
A commodity is a good or service that is bought through market exchange and therefore, under capitalism labour power and money, although not objects of capitalist production, are commodities.

Comparative advantage
The theory of comparative advantage holds that economies should export those goods and services that it can produce with greater relative efficiency than other economies and import goods and services that other economies can produce at a greater relative efficiency. Hence, nations should specialize in those goods and services in which they have a comparative advantage.

Constant capital
That portion of the value of materials and machinery that is used up in production and added to the value of the product.

Constant returns to scale
This refers to a constancy in the cost of a good as its production enlarges.

Corporatism
The involvement in the decision-making process of the state of industrial capitalists and workers' representatives in an attempt to form a consensus of opinion.

Depreciation
The reduction in value of an asset through wear and tear.

Division of labour
The specialization of workers whereby their function relates to a specific aspect of the production process rather than to the process as a whole.

Economies of scale
The reduction of costs that is caused by an increase in output as a result of total production costs increasing less than proportionally with output.

Exchange value
In commodity markets it is the set of ratios in which use-values are exchanged for one another.

Fixed capital
Durable goods such as plant and machinery that are employed in the production of goods.

Free trade
Refers to the situation where there is an absence of barriers to international trade such as tariffs and quotas.

Hegemony
This refers to the domination of the state (or other body of leadership) over its citizens particularly in terms of the prevailing ideas and principles.

Innovation
The introduction of new production processes or new products and represents the culmination of research and development.

International Monetary Fund
An organization devoted to the stabilization of the international monetary system through the use of loans to member states who are experiencing serious balance of payments difficulties. Set up as part of the Bretton Woods agreement.

Labour power
Labour power is the commodity in the capitalist mode of production that the labourer has to sell and, in more general terms, is the capacity to perform labour.

Malthusian population principle
Thomas Robert Malthus suggested that as population increases at a geometric rate and food availability only rises at an arithmetic rate, the tendency is for population to increase at a faster rate than its subsistence. The outcome for the human race would be famine, disease, war and death.

Marginalist
The school of thought generally concerned with the analysis of optimizing behaviour through the search for optimum values for specific variables such as the maximization of utility by individual consumers, the maximization of profit by firms and the maximization of social welfare by the policy-maker.

Oligopoly
A market structure in which there is a high level of concentration such that a small number of firms account for a large proportion of output and employment.

Organic composition of capital
The ratio of constant to variable capital.

Perfect competition
A theoretical market structure that assumes a large number of buyers and sellers, all with perfect information, a homogeneous product and no barriers to entry. The outcome is that no one producer can set the price of the product, all producers are price takers and must set the level of their output to maximize their profit.

Primitive accumulation
The historical process whereby the capitalists gained ownership of the means of production.

Protectionism
The use of artificial barriers to trade such as tariffs and quotas to reduce the level of imports into the economy and to protect domestic production from overseas competition.

Rate of exploitation
The ratio between the value of the surplus product and the value of the real wage.

Say's Law
Simply put this states that 'supply creates its own demand'. In other words, the sum of the values of all commodities produced is always equal to the sum of the values of all commodities bought. Hence, resources cannot be under-utilized in the sense that if excess demand or excess supply were evident, the market mechanism would ensure that they were eradicated. For example, in the long run, unemployment or overproduction could not exist according to Say's Law.

Simple commodity production
A form of commodity production that is distinguished from capitalism by the fact that labour is not a commodity in the sense that each worker has ownership of her/his means of production and therefore, commodities exchange in terms of the quantities of labour required to produce them.

Socially necessary labour-time
The time that is required for production of a commodity, assuming the use of modern machinery, with an average degree of skill and under normal conditions.

Surplus product
That product which remains after the deduction from total product of the real wage, depreciation costs of machinery and the replacement cost of raw materials.

Surplus value
The value of the surplus product. It is the value that is appropriated by the capitalist, but created by the labourer.

Use-value
The property of a commodity which makes it useful in terms of the satisfaction of human wants and which is bestowed by its physical properties.

Utility

In neoclassical theory it is the individual satisfaction or fulfilment that is obtained from the consumption of some quantity of a good. It is a psychological concept which cannot be measured in absolute units although neo-classical theory is constructed with the assumption that it could be measured. The consumer is assumed to be able to rank quantities of goods on the basis of preference or indifference, and then to conclude that one combination of goods has 'greater utility' than another combination of goods.

Variable capital

Refers to the part of capital that is represented by labour power.

World Bank

The World Bank was created at the Bretton Woods agreement and was originally charged with the task of aiding the reconstruction of economies in Europe in the aftermath of the Second World War.

World Trade Organization

Formerly the General Agreement on Tariffs and Trade, the body that negotiates reductions in trade barriers and enforces the agreements.

Bibliography

Aaronovitch, S. and Sawyer, M. C. (1975) *Big Business; Theoretical and Empirical Aspects of Concentration and Mergers in the UK*, London, Macmillan.

Alford, B. W. E. (1996) *Britain in the World Economy since 1880*, Harlow, Longman.

Allen, R. C. (1992) *Enclosure and the Yeoman: The Agricultural Development of the South Midlands 1450–1850*, Oxford, Oxford University Press.

Alt, J. E. and Chrystal, K. A. (1983) *Political Economics*, Brighton, Wheatsheaf.

Altvater, E. and Mahnkopf, B. (1997) 'The world market unbound', *Review of International Political Economy* vol. 4, no. 3 Autumn, pp. 448–71.

Anderson, J. L. (1995) *Explaining Long-term Economic Change*, Cambridge, Cambridge University Press.

Arestis, P. and Sawyer, M. (eds) (1994) *Radical Political Economy*, Aldershot, Edward Elgar.

Atkinson, B., Livesey, F. and Milward, B. (eds) (1998) *Applied Economics*, London, Macmillan.

Auerbach, P. (1988) *Competition: The Economics of Industrial Change*, Oxford, Blackwell.

Baran, P. and Sweezy, P. M. (1966) *Monopoly Capital: An Essay on the American Social and Economic Order*, New York, Monthly Review Press.

Barr, N. (1998) *The Economics of the Welfare State*, 3rd edn, Oxford, Oxford University Press.

Basile, L. and Salvatori, N. (1994) 'On the existence of a solution to Kalecki's pricing equations', *Journal of Post-Keynesian Economics*, vol. 16, no. 3, Spring, pp. 435–8.

Beckett, J. V. (1977) 'English landownership in the later seventeenth and eighteenth centuries: the debate and the problems', *Economic History Review*, vol. 30, pp. 567–81.

Berg, M. (ed.) (1990) *Political Economy in the 20th Century*, Hemel Hempstead, Philip Allen.

Blaug, M. (1997) *Economic Theory in Retrospect*, 5th edn, Cambridge, Cambridge University Press.

Bohm-Bawerk, E. (1896) '*Karl Marx and the Close of his System*', in Sweezy, P. (ed.) (1949).

Bradley, I. and Howard, M. (eds) (1982) *Classical and Marxian Political Economy*, London, Macmillan.

Brewer, A. (1984) *A Guide to Marx's Capital,* Cambridge, Cambridge University Press.

Brewer, A. (1980) *Marxist Theories of Imperialism: A Critical Survey*, London, Routledge & Kegan Paul.

Byrne, D. (1977) 'Social exclusion and capitalism: the reserve army across time and space', *Critical Social Policy*, vol. 17, pp. 27–51.

Carson, J. (1994) 'Existence and uniqueness of solutions to Kalecki's pricing equations', *Journal of Post-Keynesian Economics,* vol. 16, no. 3, Spring, pp. 411–34.

Chambers, J. D. (1953) 'Enclosure and labour supply in the industrial revolution', *Economic History Review*, vol. 3, pp. 319–43.

Chandler, A. D. (1990) *Scale and Scope; The Dynamics of Industrial Capitalism*, Cambridge, Mass., MIT Press.

Chang, H. J. (1997) 'The economics and politics of regulation', *Cambridge Journal of Economics*, vol. 21, pp. 703–28.

Chapple, S. (1995) 'The Kaleckian origins of the Keynesian model', *Oxford Economic Papers*, 47, pp. 525–38.

Chitty, A. (1997) 'Introduction: the direction of contemporary capitalism and the practical relevance of theory', *Review of International Political Economy*, vol. 4, no. 3, Autumn, pp. 435–47.

Clarke, S. (1994) *Marx's Theory of Crisis*, London, Macmillan.

Colletti, L. (ed.) (1975) *Karl Marx: Early Writings*, Harmondsworth, Penguin.

Constantine, S. (1994) *Unemployment Between the Wars*, Harlow, Longman.

Corruth, A. A. and Oswald, A. J. (1987) 'On union preferences and labour market models: insiders and outsiders', *Economic Journal*, no. 79, pp. 431–45.

Cowling, K. (1982) *Monopoly Capitalism*, London, Macmillan.

Crafts, N. F. R. and Woodward, N. (eds) (1991) *The British Economy Since 1945*, Oxford, Oxford University Press.

Davidson, P. (1994) *Post Keynesian Macroeconomic Theory*, Aldershot, Edward Elgar.

Desai, M. (1979) *Marxian Economics*, Oxford, Basil Blackwell.

Dobb, M. (1973) *Theories of Value and Distribution Since Adam Smith: Ideology and Economic Theory*, Cambridge, Cambridge University Press.

Dumenil, G. (1980) *De La Valeur Aux Prix De Production*, Paris, Economica.

Dunning, J. (1994) *Globalisation, Economic Restructuring and Development*, Geneva, UNCTAD.

Eatwell, J., Milgate, M. and Newman, P. (eds) (1990) *Marxian Economics*, London, Macmillan.

Fazzari, S. M. and Variato, A. M. (1994) 'Asymmetric information and Keynesian theories of investment', *Journal of Post Keynesian Economics*, vol. 16, no. 3, Spring, pp. 351–69.

Fine, B. (1982) *Theories of the Capitalist Economy*, London, Edward Arnold.

Fine, B. and Harris, L. (1979) *Re-reading Capital*, London, Macmillan.

Fine, B. and Murfin, A. (1984) *Macroeconomics and Monopoly Capitalism*, Brighton, Wheatsheaf.

Floud, R. and McCloskey, D. (1994a) *The Economic History of Britain Since 1700, Vol. 2, 1860–1939*, 2nd edn, Cambridge, Cambridge University Press.

Floud, R. and McCloskey, D. (1994b) *The Economic History of Britain Since 1700, Vol. 3, 1939–1992*, 2nd edn, Cambridge, Cambridge University Press.

Foley, D. (1982) 'The value of money, the value of labour power and the marxian transformation problem', *Review of Radical Political Economics*, no. 14, pp. 37–47.

Foley, D. (1986) *Understanding Capital: Marx's Economic Theory*, Cambridge, Mass., Harvard University Press.

Freeman, R. (ed.) (1962) *Marx on Economics*, Harmondsworth, Penguin.

Friedman, M. (1968) 'The role of monetary policy', *American Economic Review*, no. 58, pp. 1–17.

Galbraith, J. K. (1997) 'Time to ditch the NAIRU', *Journal of Economic Perspectives*, vol. 11, no. 1, Winter, pp. 93–108.

Galbraith, J. K. (1992) *The Culture of Contentment*, New York, Sinclair-Stevenson.

Garside, W. R. (1990) *British Unemployment 1919–1939: A Study in Public Policy*, Cambridge, Cambridge University Press.

Gaughan, P. (ed.) (1994) *Readings in Mergers and Acquisitions*, Oxford, Basil Blackwell.

Giddens, A. (1998) *The Third Way: The Renewal of Social Democracy*, Cambridge, Polity Press.

Giovannini, A. (1997) 'Government debt management', *Oxford Review of Economic Policy*, vol. 13, no. 4, pp. 43–52.

Glennerster, H. and Hills, J. (eds) (1998) *The State of Welfare: The Economics of Social Spending*, 2nd edn, Oxford, Oxford University Press.

Glick, M. and Ehrbar, H. (1987) 'The transformation problem: an obituary', *Australian Economic Papers*, no. 26, pp. 294–317.

Glyn, A. (1997) 'Does aggregate profitability really matter?', *Cambridge Journal of Economics*, vol. 21, pp. 593–619.

Glyn, A. and Sutcliffe, B. (1972) *British Capitalism, Workers and the Profits Squeeze*, Harmondsworth, Penguin.

Goodman, A., Johnson, P. and Webb, S. (1997) *Inequality in the UK*, Oxford, Oxford University Press.

Gough, I. (1979) *The Political Economy of the Welfare State*, London, Macmillan.

Gouverneur, J. (1983) *Contemporary Capitalism and Marxist Economics*, Oxford, Martin Robertson.

Gramsci, A. (1971) *Selections From the Prison Notebooks*, London, Lawrence & Wishart.

Gray, S. J. and McDermott, P. (1989) *Mega-Merger Mayhem: Takeover Strategies, Battles and Controls*, London, Paul Chapman.

Grout, P. (1997) 'The economics of the private finance initiative', *Oxford Review of Economic Policy*, vol. 13, no. 4, pp. 53–66.

Gulap, H. (1989) 'The stages and long-cycles of capitalist development', *Review of Radical Political Economics*, vol. 21, no. 4, pp. 83–92.

Hannah, L. and Kay, J. A. (1977) *Concentration in Modern Industry*, London, Macmillan.

Harcourt, G. C. (1996) 'Critiques and alternatives: reflections on some recent (and not so recent) controversies', *Journal of Post Keynesian Economics*, vol. 19, no. 2, Winter, pp. 171–80.

Harcourt, G. C. (1982) *The Social Science Imperialists*, ed. Prue Kerr, London, Routledge & Kegan Paul.

Harman, C. (1996) 'The crisis in bourgeois economics', *International Socialism*, no. 71, Summer, pp. 3–56.

Hodgson, G. (1982) *Capitalism, Value and Exploitation: A Radical Theory*, Oxford, Martin Robertson.

Houston, D. (1997) 'Productive–unproductive labor: rest in peace', *Review of Radical Political Economics*, vol. 29, no. 1, pp. 131–47.

Howard, M. C. and King, J. E. (1992) *A History of Marxian Economics, Vol. II, 1929–1990*, London, Macmillan.

Howard, M. C. and King, J. E. (1989) *A History of Marxian Economics, Vol. I, 1883–1929*, London, Macmillan.

Howard, M. C. and King, J. E. (1985) *The Political Economy of Marx*, 2nd edn, London, Longman.

Marx, K. (1979) *The Class Struggle in France 1848 to 1850*, Moscow, Progress Publishing.

Marx, K. (1981) *Capital, Vol.3*, trans. David Fernbach, Harmondsworth, Penguin.

Marx, K. and Engels, F. (1987) *The Communist Manifesto*, New York, Pathfinder.

Marx, K. and Engels, F. (1985) *The Communist Manifesto*, Harmondsworth, Penguin.

Marx, K. and Engels, F. (1978) *Feuerbach. Opposition of the Materialist and Idealist Outlooks*, Moscow, Progress Press.

Marx, K. and Engels, F. (1970) *The German Ideology*, London, Lawrence & Wishart.

Matthews, R. C. O., Feinstein, C. H. and Odling-Smee, J. C. (1982) *British Economic Growth, 1856–1973*, Oxford, Oxford University Press.

Meiksins Wood, E. (1997) 'Modernity, post modernity or capitalism', *Review of International Political Economy*, vol. 4, no. 3, Autumn, pp. 539–60.

Mendels, F. F. (1982) *Proto-industrialization: theory and reality. General Report*, Eighth International Economic History Congress, 'A' Themes (Budapest), pp. 69–107.

Mendels, F. F. (1972) 'Proto-industrialization: the first phase of the industrialization process', *Journal of Economic History*, vol. 32, pp. 241–61.

Michie, J. and Grieve-Smith, J. (eds) (1995) *Managing the Global Economy*, Oxford, University Press.

Mingay, G. E. (1997) *Parliamentary Enclosure in England: An Introduction to Its Causes, Incidence and Impact 1750–1850*, Harlow, Addison Wesley Longman.

Mingay, G. E. (1968) *Enclosure and the Small Farmer in the Age of the Industrial Revolution*, Basingstoke, Longman.

Mohun, S. (1996) 'Productive and unproductive labor in the labor theory of value', *Review of Radical Political Economics*, vol. 28, no. 4, pp. 30–54.

Mokyr, J. (1976) *Industrialization in the Low Countries, 1795–1850*, New Haven, Yale University Press.

Mongiovi, G. (1996) 'Sraffa's critique of Marshall: a reassessment', *Cambridge Journal of Economics*, vol. 20, pp. 207–24.

Morishima, M. (1973) *Marx's Economics: A Dual Theory of Value and Growth*, Cambridge, Cambridge University Press.

Moseley, F. (1997) 'The rate of profit and the future of capitalism', *Review of Radical Political Economics*, vol. 29, no. 4, pp. 23–41.

Moseley, F. (1992) *The Falling Rate of Profit in the Postwar United States Economy*, New York, St. Martin's Press.

Moseley, F. (1986) 'Estimates of the rate of surplus value in the postwar United States economy', *Review of Radical Political Economics*, vol. 18, no. 1, pp. 168–89.

Mott, T. and Slattery, E. (1994) 'Tax incidence and macroeconomic effects in a Kaleckian model when profits finance affects investment and prices may respond to taxes', *Journal of Post Keynesian Economics*, vol. 16, no. 3, Spring, pp. 391–409.

Naples, M. I. (1989) 'A radical economic revision of the transformation problem', *Review of Radical Political Economics*, vol. 21, pp. 137–58.

Neeson, J. M. (1993) *Commoners: Common Right, Enclosure and Social Change in England 1900–1820*, Cambridge, Cambridge University Press.

O'Brien, R. (1992) *Global Financial Integration: The End of Geography*, New York, Council on Foreign Relations.

Office of National Statistics (1999) *Social Trends*, no. 29, London, Stationery Office.

Office of National Statistics (1998) *Economic Trends, Annual Supplement*, London, Stationery Office.

Ohmae, K. (1990) *The Borderless World: Power and Strategy in the Interlinked Economy*, London, Collins.

Okishio, N. (1974) 'Value and production price', Kobe University Review, no. 20.

Ormerod, P. (1994) *The Death of Economics*, London, Faber and Faber.

Osiatynski, J. (ed.) (1991) *Collected Works of Michal Kalecki, Volume II, Capitalism: Economic Dynamics*, Oxford, Clarendon Press.

Osiatynski, J. (ed.) (1990) *Collected Works of Michal Kalecki, Volume I, Capitalism: Business Cycles and Full Employment*, Oxford, Clarendon Press.

Panic, M. (1988) *The National Management of the International Economy*, London, Macmillan.

Parsons, S. D. (1996) 'Post Keynesian realism and Keynes' general theory', *Journal of Post Keynesian Economics*, vol. 18, no. 3, Spring, pp. 419–41.

Pheby, J. (1988) *Methodology and Economics: A Critical Introduction*, London, Macmillan.

Philip, B. (1996) 'Inequality, exploitation and socialism: perspectives from analytical Marxism', *Review of Political Economy*, vol. 9, no. 3, pp. 335–50.

Pitelis, C. (1994) 'On the nature of the capitalist state', *Review of Political Economy*, vol. 16, no. 1, pp. 72–105.

Popper, K. R. (1972) *Conjectures and Refutations: The Growth of Scientific Knowledge*, 4th edn, London, Routledge & Kegan Paul.

Robinson, J. (1966) *An Essay on Marxian Economics*, 2nd edn, London, Macmillan.

Robinson, J. (1969) *The Accumulation of Capital*, 3rd edn, London, Macmillan.

Robinson, J. (1973) *Collected Economic Papers, Vol. IV*, Oxford, Blackwell.

Robinson, J. (1975) *Collected Economic Papers, Vol. III*, 2nd edn, Oxford, Blackwell.

Robinson, J. (1980) *Further Contributions to Modern Economics*, Oxford, Blackwell.

Rosenthal, J. (1998) *The Myth of Dialectics: Reinterpreting the Marx Hegel Relation*, London, Macmillan.

Rosenthal, J. (1993) 'Value and consumption: prolegomena to the theory of crisis', *Capital and Class*, no. 51, Autumn, pp. 53–80.

Rowthorn, Bob (1980) *Capitalism, Conflict and Inflation*, London, Lawrence & Wishart.

Rubery, J. (1994) 'The British production regime: a societal-specific system?', *Economy and Society*, vol. 23, no. 3, pp. 335–4.

Saad-Filo, A. (1997) 'An alternative reading of the transformation of values into prices of production', *Capital and Class*, no. 63, Autumn, pp. 115–36.

Saad-Filo, A. (1993) 'A note on Marx's analysis of the composition of capital', *Capital and Class*, no. 50, Summer, pp. 127–46.

Samualson, P. A. (1974) Insight and detour in the theory of exploitation: a reply to Baumol, *Journal of Economic Literature*, vol. 12, pp. 62–70.

Samualson, P. A. (1971) Understanding the Marxian notion of exploitation: a summary of the so-called transformation problem between Marxian values and competitive prices, *Journal of Economic Literature*, vol. 9, pp. 399–431.

Sardoni, C. (ed.) (1992) *On Political Economists and Modern Political Economy: Selected Essays of G.C.Harcourt,* London, Routledge.

Sawyer, M. (1990) 'The economics of Michal Kalecki', in Berg, M. (ed.), *Political Economy in the 20th Century,* Hemel Hempstead, Philip Allan.

Sawyer, M. C. (1989) *The Challenge of Radical Political Economy,* Hemel Hempstead, Harvester-Wheatsheaf.

Sawyer, M. (1985) *The Economics of Michal Kalecki,* London, Macmillan.

Sayer, A. (1995) 'Liberalism, Marxism and urban and regional studies', *International Journal of Urban and Regional Research,* vol. 19, no. 1, pp. 79–95.

Schwartz, J. (ed.) (1977) *The Subtle Anatomy of Capitalism,* Santa Monica, Calif., Goodyear.

Screpanti, E. (1999) 'Capitalist forms and the essence of capitalism', *Review of International Political Economy,* vol. 6, no. 1, pp. 1–26.

Screpanti, E. (1996) 'A pure insider theory of hysteresis in employment and unemployment', *Review of Radical Political Economics,* vol. 28, no. 4, December, pp. 93–112.

Seton, F. (1957) 'The "transformation problem"', *Review of Economic Studies,* vol. 24, pp. 149–60.

Shaikh, A. (1977) 'Marx's theory of value and the "transformation problem"', in Schwartz, J. (ed.).

Shaw, M. (1997) 'The state of globalization: towards a theory of state transformation', *Review of International Political Economy,* vol. 4, no. 3, Autumn, pp. 497–513.

Sinha, A. (1997) 'The transformation problem: a critique of the "new solution"', *Review of Radical Political Economics,* vol. 29, no. 3, pp. 51–8.

Sraffa, P. (ed.) (1981) *The Works and Correspondence of David Ricardo, Vol.I, On the Principles of Political Economy and Taxation,* Cambridge, Cambridge University Press.

Sraffa, P. (1960) *Production of Commodities by Means of Commodities: Prelude to a Critique of Economic Theory,* Cambridge, Cambridge University Press.

Steedman, I. (1975) 'Positive profits with negative surplus value', *Economic Journal,* vol. 85, pp. 114–23

Steedman, I. (1977) *Marx and After,* London, New Left Books.

Steedman, I. et. al. (1981) *The Value Controversy,* London, Verso.

Steindl, J. (1952) *Maturity and Stagnation in American Capitalism,* New York, Monthly Review Press [1976].

Supple, B (1991) 'Scale and scope: Alfred Chandler and the dynamics of industrial capitalism', *Economic History Review,* vol. 44, pp. 500–14.

Sweezy, P. (1990) Monopoly capitalism in Eatwell, et al. (eds), *Marxian Economics,* London, Macmillan.

Sweezy, P. M. (ed.) (1949) *Karl Marx and the Close of his System,* New York, Augustus Kelly.

Thane, P. (1996) *Foundations of the Welfare State,* Harlow, Addison Wesley Longman.

Thirlwall, A. P. (1994) *Growth and Development,* 5th edn, London, Macmillan.

Trevithick, J. A. (1992) *Involuntary Unemployment: Macroeconomics from a Keynesian Perspective,* Hemel Hempstead, Harvester-Wheatsheaf.

Turner, M. (1998) 'Enclosures re-opened', *Refresh,* no. 26, Spring.

Turner, M. E. (1980) *English Parliamentary Enclosure,* Folkestone, Dawson.

Tylecote, A. (1993) *The Long Wave in the World Economy: The Current Crisis in Historical Perspective*, London, Routledge.

UNCTAD (1993) *Concentration of Market Power and Its Effects on International Markets*, New York, United Nations.

Weisskopf, T. E. (1979) 'Marxian crisis theory and the rate of profit in the post-war U.S. economy', *Cambridge Journal of Economics*, vol. 3, pp. 341–78.

White, G. (1998) 'Disequilibrium pricing and the Sraffa–Keynes synthesis', *Review of Political Economy*, vol. 10, no. 4, pp. 459–75.

Williams, M. (1998) 'Money and labour power: Marx after Hegel, or Smith plus Sraffa?', *Cambridge Journal of Economics*, vol. 22, pp. 187–98.

Wolff, E. N. (1986) 'The productivity slowdown and the fall in the rate of profit, 1947–76', *Review of Radical Political Economics*, vol. 18, pp. 87–109.

Wolfsetter, E. (1973) 'Surplus labour, synchronised labour costs and Marx's labour theory of value', *Economic Journal*, vol. 83, pp. 787–809.

Yaffe, D. S. (1973) 'The Marxian theory of crisis, capital and the state', *Economy and Society*, no. 2, pp. 186–232.

Index